BOOKS
IN GENERAL

V. S. PRITCHETT

1953
CHATTO & WINDUS
LONDON

Published by
CHATTO AND WINDUS
LONDON
*
CLARKE, IRWIN AND CO. LTD.
TORONTO

PRINTED IN GREAT BRITAIN
BY BUTLER AND TANNER LTD.
FROME & LONDON
ALL RIGHTS RESERVED

To Dorothy

NOTE

The title of this book is taken from the heading given to the opening literary page of *The New Statesman and Nation*, where all except one of the following essays have appeared more or less in their present form. The exception is the essay on Arthur Koestler, which appeared in Mr. Cyril Connolly's *Horizon*, and to the editors of both papers I make my grateful acknowledgments.

CONTENTS

The Poet of Tourism	*Page* 1
Cellini	7
An Italian Classic	13
Verga	19
The Early Svevo	25
Galdós	31
A Portrait of T. E. Lawrence	37
The Notebooks of Henry James	43
Butler's Notebooks	50
A Victorian Child	56
The Carlyles	62
Boswell's London	75
Swift to Stella	81
The Unhappy Traveller	88
Maupassant	94
A Love Affair	104
Zola	110
A Political Novel	123
André Gide	130

CONTENTS

The Early Dostoevsky	*Page* 141
Tolstoy	148
The Art of Koestler	155
Tristram Shandy	173
The Roots of Detection	179
The Poe Centenary	185
Oliver Twist	191
Meredith	197
Poor Gissing	209
An Emigré	216
The Octopus	223
Firbank	229
W. W. Jacobs	235
The Hill-Billies	242
The Eye-Man	248

I

The Poet of Tourism

THE Holy Door in St. Peter's is closed; the Holy Year is over. What impressions of Rome have the pilgrims taken back with them, those labelled train-loads, those families of peasants, the pious socialites and those big, bruising American priests? I turn back to what has always seemed to me the best evocation of the tourist's Rome, indeed of the tourist himself—the *Amours de Voyage* of Arthur Hugh Clough written a hundred years ago:

Is it illusion or not that attracteth the pilgrim transalpine
Brings him a dullard and dunce hither to pry and to stare?
Is it illusion or not that allures the barbarian stranger,
Brings him with gold to the shrine, brings him in arms to the
  gate?

Like Bagehot, Clough is one of the few Victorians who seem to belong to our time rather than their own. The lack of the histrionic air, the lack of that invoked and obligatory sense of greatness, so characteristic of the chief and, no doubt, excelling writers of the age, makes these two writers at once accessible to us. Clough, for example, makes no bones about calling himself a tourist in Italy; and although all the English writers who went to Italy from the time of the Romantic movement were tourists, part of that great check and tartan exodus which was one of the strange sights of the time to continental observers, Clough is the only one to confess and expound the role. It was he who perceived the tourist as a subject and suggested him as a symbolical figure. Uncommitted, detached, languid, Clough does not strain, as Browning does, to pass himself off as an Italian; there is no effort to "get to know the people" or to be "off the beaten track." As so often happens, the sceptic who is unable to make up his mind about ultimate things, drifts doggedly into the conventional and it has been said that Clough's weakness as a poet comes from shortness of imagination, from the logician's determination not to see beyond his subject. But if in isolating a theme, we drain the overflowing spirit from it, there are the advantages of freshness, truthfulness and exactitude. And to these qualities Clough added one of his own: a naturalness which is a relief, almost a revelation, after the usual manner of the Victorian stage. Not until the novels of E. M. Forster do we meet anything like Clough; and not until Forster, either, do we meet with the distinguishing portrait of the English tourist in our literature.

What is a tourist? A comic character, of course, for he is a fish out of his proper waters. A watered-down Hamlet, perhaps: will-less, unadapted and consumed by that self-consciousness which is the cruel psychological price exacted by regulated travel. There is a three-cornered relation: between one's countrymen, the foreigner and the base, disconnected self, haunted more than ever when it is abroad, by the vague, ghostly specification of what it might have been. The loneliness of the evenings! Stendhal exclaimed in Rome. The mild, doubting face of every tourist is haunted by the murder he ought, sometime in his life, to have committed. If only I could have brought myself to do it, the face seems to be murmuring, I should not be here alone, when the lights come up, with my dreadful dilemma.

Clough, as we know, from his life and his poetry, was the poet of dilemma. In an age of professional trumpets, he engaged the dubious, the personal, the inquiring, the definite but conversational flute:

Rome disappoints me much: I hardly as yet understand, but Rubbishy *seems the word that most exactly would suit it.*

It is the voice of the Common Room:

THE POET OF TOURISM

However, one can live in Rome as also in London.
It is a blessing, no doubt, to be rid of, at least for a time, of
All's one's friends and relations—yourself (forgive me!) included—
All the assujettisement of having been what one has been,
What one thinks one is, or thinks what others suppose one;
Yet, in spite of all, we turn like fools to the English.

The lines open *Amours de Voyage* and Hamlet, with his guide book, stands worried in the Eternal City which he had imagined to be marble and had found "instead brickwork." This is the opening despair of the tourist as he turns from the comfort of the lovely, grave, blank-minded domesticity of the Italians to the grim, cultural work that waits him. Not a street in the golden, rusted city but will ask him to take sides in the struggles of a dozen civilisations; not a building without murder, art, religion in its doors. There are the Greeks to deal with, the Romans, the endless underpinning of Western civilisation. There are the Goths and the decadence. There are the Christian question and the question of the unlikeableness of the early Christians. The Renaissance blocks the way, not as an idea only, but in solid instances of stone and acres of painted canvas. There are the beguiling and ambiguous corridors of the Vatican and St. Peter's, the tremendous railway terminal from which we set out on our ornate journeys to death. There are centuries of the Christian Party Line. There is Truth, but then there is also Beauty. There is Beauty, but there is also Art. And then—but that is enough for today. The tired don gives up as the domestic crowds watch the crimson Roman sunset from the Pincio, and comes back to his Victorian hotel to talk to the English to whom "like fools" we always turn when Art has become too much.

The English: *Amours de Voyage* is an epistolary novel in hexameters. Claude, the intellectual, writes to Eustace his friend. It is 1849. The English are the Trevellyns "with the seven and seventy boxes, Courier, Papa and Mamma, the children, and Mary and Susan." George is there too with moustachios, as grossly bent on marriage, as Claude is refined in evading it. But Claude is vulnerable. Alas, for the effect of days passed in the contemplation of statuary and in considering the highest questions—"the Coliseum is large; but is this an idea?"—one is inclined to sink into self-indulgence. One is likely to sink to the Trevellyns, who, like all the English met by the tourist abroad, are not out of the top drawer. Socially speaking they are prone to a sort of indecent exposure, and indeed this inability to conceal that they are not "quite quite" is a kind of secondary sexual characteristic of the English race. Claude is not quite unspeakable; tourism has simply encouraged afflicting introspection. He hangs round Mary Trevellyn—the chattering Georgina is too spry: no dons for her—snubs her, charms her, coolly relies on a mixture of *laissez faire* and *laissez aller*, or on not having his cake and not eating it, and at last, lets her go. Then, of course, he wakes up to what he has lost and chases her all the way to Como in vain and returns wretchedly to "the great massy strengths of abstraction" once more in Pisa, in time for the awful Italian rains. One more love affair without a bang in it has ended without a whimper.

That is not all there is to say about the tourist in Clough's light opera. While Claude is denouncing Ignatius and re-peopling the niches of the Pantheon with forms of "an older, austerer worship", while he is writing

Death may
Sometimes be noble; but life at the best will appear an illusion
While the great pain is upon us, it is great; when it is over,
Why, it is over. The smoke of the sacrifice rises to heaven,
Of a sweet savour, no doubt, to Somebody; but on the altar,
Lo, there is nothing remaining but ashes and dust and ill odour—

while he thinks and philanders, the still landscape starts to rumble and to move. From the Pincio one can see distant smoke. There is rifle fire. There are riots in the street. The French have broken their truce with Mazzini and their

THE POET OF TOURISM

troops are storming in from Civita Vecchia. The tourist takes on a torture familiar to our generation. Is he going to escape to the Embassy, become a reporter or even commit himself to the incitement of a patriotic war for liberty? Claude becomes a figure of the Nineteen-Thirties; the doubts and impulses of our wars become his. Clough had been in Paris in 1848, and now Claude, begging Eustace "not to whisper it in thy courts, Oh Christ Church!" dreams of great angers and a sword. But not to defend the ladies:

Now supposing the French or the Neapolitain soldier
Should by some evil chance come exploring the Maison Serny
(Where the family English are all to assemble for safety)
Am I prepared to lay down my life for the British female?
Really, who knows? One has bowed and talked, till, little by little,
All the natural heat has escaped of the chivalrous spirit.
Oh, one conformed, of course; but one doesn't die for good manners,
Stab or shoot, or be shot, by way of graceful attention.
No, if it should be at all, it should be on the barricades there;
Should I encarnadine ever this inky pacifical finger,
Sooner far should it be for this vapour of Italy's freedom,
Sooner far by the side of the d . . . d and dirty plebeians,
Ah, for a child, in the street I could strike; for the full-blown lady—
Somehow, Eustace, alas! I have not felt the vocation.

Claude does not fight, of course. But he is excitedly out for the news. Brilliantly Clough's eye for reality—the gift of a mind so fatally adroit at changing its position—captures the absurd, tragic, confused scene in the streets; the comic flicker of the tourists, the reactionary cries of the dear, bourgeois girls who spread wild tales about Garibaldi's Negro. And the episode has the perfect tourist ending; he has not killed, he has not been killed but he has *seen* someone killed:

. . . the swords are
Many and bare in the air. In the air? They descend; they are smiting,

*Hewing, chopping—At what? In the air once more upstretched?—
   And
Is it blood that's on them . . .
Passing away from the place with Murray under my arm, and
Stooping, I saw through the legs of the people the legs of a body.*

The critics of Clough used to be severe. He was not a great poet but (more serious for his reputation in Victorian times), he had not "the vocation", as he might have said, for importing greatness into his subjects. Lytton Strachey made fun of his continual doubts and his weak ankles. In fact, Clough was a champion athlete and his doubts suggest not vacillation but modesty, hardness of mind, the strength of integrity and candour, the point of naturalness. It will be noticed in the portrait of Claude (which is not, however, a self-portrait) how the moments of weakness are the admissions of an honest character and immediately lead to strength. The famous "Say not the struggle nought availeth" is the work of a courageous man. Clough was really in advance of his time; his unofficial manner, his truthfulness about personal feeling, his nonchalance, his curiosity, even his bitterness and his use of anti-climax, are closer to the poets of the Thirties than they were to his contemporaries. His line is clean. His lack of pretence is austere. The account of Rome is a wonderful evocation of the Rome that is in our minds, mixed up with our private life and business, our incapacity to answer the numberless questions that come from the city that has more of human fate in each of its stones than any city on earth.

2
Cellini

FOR 180 years the autobiography of Benvenuto Cellini has diverted a large number of English readers in every generation. Indeed, the English, perhaps because of their taste for eccentrics and for ripe and unabashed human portraiture in the 18th century, were the first to translate him from the Italian; and when the French and Germans followed, the fame of the book caught the Romantic movement at the flow. That is to say when, with faith in nature, love of energy and the sense of human beings as pieces of autonomous, emotional tumult, the long Romantic rule began. A second Renaissance looked back upon the first, and Cellini (as Mr. John Pope-Hennessy says in a thoughtful and instructive introduction to the Phaidon Press edition) is seen fermenting to the life in the historical novels of Scott and Dumas as if he were still clattering, with temper alert for affront, over the changeless cobbles of Rome.

It is easy to see what the Romantics got out of Cellini, but what about ourselves? Romanticism is discredited; the 16th century is far away and the Renaissance is frowned upon by those of religious and political mind who like to point out how individualism has come to no good in the end. Is the autobiography to become for us one of those classics whose vitality and vividness make them irresistible but of no moment? Shall we regard Cellini as part of the forgotten childhood of modern Europe, stamping, yelling, biting till the blood comes, and uncontrollable? Will he suggest to us the natural bombast of dubious genius in a gangster state? Or shall we continue (if we are humanists) to find some lasting human substance in his refractory figure, to toughen and feed our abused faith? If the arts are to survive in a society grown hostile to them, the portrait of Cellini ought to be read, for it is one of the elementary statements of one kind of artist's mind, above all of the power, range and detail of its sustained hallucinations. Cellini was a pestilentially dedicated figure.

Mr. John Pope-Hennessy's introduction does one important service to his subject. I am not qualified to criticise his view, but he does rehabilitate Cellini as an artist and especially as a sculptor; and he does seem to dispose of the general notion that he was a second-rate artist who happened to write a book of genius in order to inflate the value of his own works. No one would deny Cellini's capacity to go in for something as shameless and cunning as this; but his exorbitant self-praise is in itself so natural to him, that it amounts, by a paradox, to modesty. And he defers always to his masters.

> In common with other artists [Mr. Pope-Hennessy writes] who were brought up like himself under the shadow of the Battle of Cascina of Michelangelo and who gravitated to the Rome of the Sistine ceiling and Raphael's *Galatea*, Cellini reacted against the classicism of the Renaissance. But the sophisticated and eclectic forms which he and his contemporaries evolved were not, as Symonds and the 19th century supposed, an aberration from an aesthetic norm, but an autonomous independent style.

It was fostered by the climate of autocratic Courts. For the ordinary reader that judgment has the importance of taking Cellini out of the class of entrancing but ill-founded liars, who are covered, in Mr. Pope-Hennessy's words, by the ambiguous term "artistic personality." Behind him is the single conviction of his kind of truth.

In the Renaissance, the individual broke bonds and silence and in his own right came alive. If Montaigne gives birth to the self, that stoic and questioning invalid, with the first sad, luminous and broken eyes; if before him Rabelais has discharged upon us the chaotic imagination of the creature

CELLINI

and the sensualities it feeds upon, a figure like Cellini's is of the same exemplary kind. He parades for the first time—and, remember, he is contemporary with Rabelais and not with Montaigne—a nature, a libido which has never known the censor unless it is there in the mask of that surprising melancholy of temperament to which he lays claim. It is, no doubt, the melancholy of the serious artist and the face in the portrait certainly suggests the naïve and morbid sadness of some miracle-working friar. Despite the worm, or because of it, Cellini jumps from art to homicide, from the complacencies of intrigue and the ironies of persecution mania to the animal transfigurations of *le rage*. He can be held by no inner constraints, only by the unrestricted libidos of the other animals who gang up against him. His life is a vendetta. But even then, when his crimes have put him into the power of his enemies and he is left to waste his body in the squalor of a medieval dungeon, his pride is unconquered. For he strikes out into that famous vision in which, longing to see the light in his dungeon, he prays to see the sun and is at once led within sight of heaven. Led by his dream-guide "a young man whose beard is just growing, with a face of indescribable beauty, but austere, not wanton" he ascends by huge stairs until there is the sun before him:

> Albeit your rays may blind me, I do not wish to look on anything again but this. So I stayed with my eyes fixed steadily on him; and after a brief space I beheld in one moment the whole might of those great burning rays fling themselves upon the left side of the sun; so that the orb remained quite clear without its rays, and I was able to contemplate it with vast delight.

As always with Cellini, who understands the laws of narrative, he goes from strength to strength, from one important success to the next. Out of the sun bulges the figure of the Christ; another bulge and out comes the Madonna; and then, with his back turned, who should be there but St. Peter "pleading my cause, for the shame he felt that such foul wrongs should be done to Christians in his own house." And to cap that, as if God could never do enough, he finds that his forehead had been "meddled with." A halo has been affixed. He thoroughly understands lying as a fine art:

> This is visible to every sort of men to whom I have chosen to point it out, but those have been very few. This halo can be observed above my shadow in the morning from the rising of the sun for about two hours, and far better when the grass is drenched with dew.

It could also be seen at sunset and better in France than in Italy where the mists annulled the effect.

To this absolute pride which is carried away, so sympathetically, into condescending mania, there is only one response: his death or our deafness. The Popes, the Medici, can do nothing with an animal of such resources; and, as surely as when, turning his corners wide, he walked up the street that leads to the Palazzo Farnese and found the Corsican murderer waiting for him in the middle of it, it is our life or his. The autobiography might be said to commemorate the discovery of that part of the human self which declares there is no room for two.

Always the most "honest" man in any collection; always quarrelling, wounding and occasionally killing in the heat of the blood, but never (as witnesses can be brought to prove) in an unrighteous cause; always persecuted by the jealous, always getting the better of his enemies and avenging himself of real or imagined wrongs on every page of his book, Cellini is the libido at its most naïve. He alone saves Rome. It is *he* who shoots the Constable of Bourbon from that crenellated beer barrel, the fortress of San Angelo. We have laughed at his boasts but they are not empty stories, like the tales of Münchausen or the American frontier. They are (and this is their fascination) packed with people, the life of the palaces and streets, closely and vividly reasoned. They are, in the true sense, creative, for they spring out of

CELLINI

the interminable activity of Cellini's extraordinary egotism. He shoots fatter pigeons than anyone else, but then excellence is his aim; and he goes shooting to relax so that he may return to his fanatical and single concern in life: his art. If he kills a man, takes a girl or conspires with friends, his art is at the bottom of it. He is not merely a boaster; he is a maniac of consuming ingenuity. And this ingenuity convinces us that we have to deal not with an extravagant but a total man. He portrays, without knowing it, a complete character, for the lie on one page is shamelessly given away a page or two later.

Goethe said that a whole century comes to life in the autobiography of Cellini and that one learns more from him than from the historians. Stendhal said that he contained the Italian character. Violence goes with an unresting curiosity, cunning with a capacity for naïve surprise: one remembers his astonishment when his model (whom he had beaten up) came back for more, became his mistress and was the best of models as long as he had the energy to beat her once a day. Vanity and indignation led him to go, with tremendous zest, into the charges of homosexuality that were brought against him; he does not notice that it is perfectly clear he is homosexual. He cannot resist being the centre of any story: the heroic or the squalid. If he gets "the French disease" it leads to astonishing anecdote. When an attempt is made to kill him with powdered diamonds, he discovers in a few lines a plot which could come straight from Boccaccio; for the man who had been given the diamond to crush, had cheated his employer:

> poverty induced him to keep this for himself, and to pound for me a greenish beryl of the value of two carlines thinking, perhaps, because it was also a stone, that it would work the same effect as the diamond.

When there is a row at the inn it is Cellini who stays behind at the inn to avenge himself on the landlord by ripping the bedding to ribbons; when a lover seduces one of his mistresses he forces the man to marry her; and then takes her on as a mistress, in order to make her commit the greater sin of adultery. Never was a man more determined to extract the extra drop from the art of success. It may not be "life" that he is recounting, but it unquestionably makes a book.

We see before us, indeed, a many-sided man, released, fulfilled in all his powers to the full length of Freudian expectation. First, the one continuously the artist, utterly wedded to the point of pettifogging frenzy with his work, blind to the existence of anything else, humble only before his master, Michelangelo. Then the natural man, incited by the awakened scientific curiosity of his time—for what is the dream of looking full into the sun but a scientific experiment, inspired by the same spirit which moved him to the great labour of the casting of the famous horse—and finally the story-teller trained in all the fine points of the art. Ourselves, like the fourteen-year-old boy to whom, in middle age, he dictated his life in the Florentine dialect, must be agog as we listen to the pouring, exterminating voice which creates an age only for the purpose of portraying a man.

3
An Italian Classic

I PROMESSI SPOSI (in English, *The Betrothed*) is often said to be the only Italian novel. It is certainly the only Italian novel that can be compared with the great European novels of the 19th century. It was begun in 1821 when Scott dominated European taste and when Balzac had not emerged from the writing of shockers, and it was revised many times before the final edition of 1840. The last rewriting is said to have taken twelve years and the result is that we have a compendious Romantic work in a state of real digestibility which neither Balzac nor Scott troubled to attain. *The Betrothed* was Manzoni's only novel. It contained the fullness of his mind, his sensibility and creative power and (as Mr. Colquhoun, a new translator, says in a very informative preface to a new edition) seems to represent the culmination of an experience to which life could add no more. In Italy this novel is a kind of Bible; long passages are known by heart; its reflections are quoted in the political debates that have taken place in Italy since the war. But in England, possibly because the chief translation was done over a hundred years ago—and not very well, by a clergyman who disapproved of its theology—the book has been but mildly regarded. The English had already the novels of Scott, with their energetic romance, their bourgeois valuation of life, their alternating choice of the highly coloured and the domestic. Scott was a Tory and, though a generous man, he drew in his horns before the outcome of the Enlightenment, whereas Manzoni had exposed his mind to it in his youth. Our critical ancestors preferred a safer, unreal Italy and, later on, the libertarian, anti-clerical Italy of the Risorgimento. Among the mass of Victorian readers we must remember those who were drawn towards Manzoni by the Oxford movement; but in matters of piety the critics seem to have preferred their own Protestant vigour and sentiment to Manzoni's obedient, passive, Catholic gravity, and it is a good indication of Victorian feeling that the clergyman who translated Manzoni said that he wished the name of Christ could be substituted for that of the Virgin throughout.

Manzoni's reformed Catholicism—that old desire to do without the Jesuits and the temporal power—is a greater obstacle to Protestants, one seems to notice, than the ultramontane. Manzoni's religion is, in tendency, liberal and democratic, but it is also melancholy and pessimistic. In *The Betrothed* our ancestors would miss what they so much admired in the English novel—the high-minded woodenness of the exemplary characters. The chief victims of tyranny and evil in the story—the two peasant lovers who are forcibly separated by the lawless Don Rodrigo—are passive sufferers who do little to help themselves and are, in fact, finally rescued not by their own efforts but through the aid of a remarkable priest and the sudden conversion of the chief villain. There is no Protestant suggestion of an aggressive worth or a self-reliance that depends on direct access to God; on the contrary there is an ironical recognition of the mysterious drama of Fate and of the painful need for selfless love. It is true that the wicked are destroyed by the plague which comes to Milan at the end of the book—this is a magnificent episode—and that the good lovers are quietly rewarded; but the lasting impressions are not of righteous success but of moral good fortune, and of luck in catching the mysterious eye of the Almighty. One is reading a benign, spacious and melancholy fable of the most tender moral sensibility, an epic of understatement; whereas the English novelist of the 19th century—and the 18th century, too—commonly provided his readers with a number of obvious statues to socially estimable Virtue and the reader admired them because he hoped, if only in his own eyes, to become a statue himself.

AN ITALIAN CLASSIC

Changed times and a translation which is closer to our idiom make *The Betrothed* immediately sympathetic to the contemporary reader, once he allows for old-fashioned methods of narration and apostrophe. We turn with recognition to other times of chaos, as Manzoni himself transposed the upheaval of the French revolution into the material of the religious wars of the 17th century. Manzoni is the novelist of those who expose themselves but cannot take sides. They belong, where humanity abides, to the spiritual third force. His personal history was of the kind that makes the psychologist, the man whose thought and feeling are finely meshed; an aristocrat, a Voltarian and militant anti-Catholic, he married a Protestant woman and was reconverted by the Capucines to a profound if ambiguous faith. He writes with the gentleness, the irony, the anxiety and love of one who has passed through a deep personal crisis. His texture is rich, his variety is great; we enter a world of innumerable meanings and contrasts. Beside the account of the plague, which recalls the curious realistic precision of Defoe, must be put very different things, like an abduction to a brigand's castle or a flight to a convent. In contrast again with these, there are comic scenes like the famous one where the peasant lovers try to trick the timid priest into marrying them, which is at the height of Italian buffoonery; the portraits of politicians have the flowering malice of Proust; the historical reflections are wise, subtle and dyed with experience, and in every episode there are psychological perceptions that have the fineness of the French novelists without their often wounding vanity in their own effects. Manzoni was devoid of the intellectual's self-admiration. His grave manner removes the sickliness from piety and restores to it the refinement of nature.

I will quote two examples of Manzoni's kind of perception to which the reader of Proust will at once respond.

One is taken from the colloquy between the neurotic and tragic nun and the peasant girl who has found sanctuary with her.

BOOKS IN GENERAL

[The peasant] also tried to avoid replying to Gertrude's inquisitive questions about her story before her engagement. But here the reason was not prudence. It was because to the poor innocent girl this story seemed a thornier and more difficult one to describe than anything which she had heard or thought she was likely to hear from the Signora. Those dealt with tyranny, treachery and suffering—ugly, painful things, yet things which could be expressed but hers was pervaded by a feeling, a word, which she felt she could not possibly pronounce, and for which she would never be able to find a substitute that would not seem shameless—the word love.

Put this beside a very different situation, an innkeeper putting his drunken guest to bed. He covers the snoring drunk and

> Then, drawn by the kind of attraction that sometimes makes us regard an object of our dislike as attentively as an object of our love, and which is only the desire to know what it is that affects our sensibility so strongly, he paused a moment to gaze at this irksome guest, raising the lamp over his face, and shading it with his hand so that the light fell on him, almost in the attitude in which Psyche was painted as she gazed stealthily at the features of her unknown spouse.

In all the meetings of his characters, in the strong situations and in the neutral, there is this watchful, instinctive, animal awareness of the other person, a seeking of the meaning of their relationship. To compare the innkeeper to a spouse is not grotesque: the drunk man has already involved the innkeeper with the secret police, there is the marriage of two fears. Fear and love are, in fact, Manzoni's subjects.

The story of *The Betrothed* is a strong one. The hired bravoes hold up the cowardly priest. There is murder on the road. There are bread riots in Milan—Manzoni is an excellent narrative writer unencumbered by picturesque baggage —there are flights and pursuits, tremendous confrontations

AN ITALIAN CLASSIC

of the tyrannous and the good. The immunity of the priests gives them boldness. There are political intrigue, invasion and looting by foreign armies, the plague. Manzoni is as brilliant as a diplomat in recomplicating the moral issues; the brigand's sudden conversion, for example, frees the girl from her dangers and seems to guarantee her happiness but, perversely and in her terror, she now vows herself to the Virgin! To the obstacle of wickedness is added the obstacle of faith. That delicate tangle of faith and desire and pride has to be undone. The characters are not thrown on in crude, romantic strokes but are put together precisely by a writer who has understood their pattern and the point at which they will behave unexpectedly or feel the insinuations of time, fate and mood. There is not a stock character anywhere; nor can a too gifted author be seen bursting through these figures. The skill in the change of mood or in anticlimax is wonderful.

When Manzoni described how the notion of writing *The Betrothed* came to him—I quote from Mr. Colquhoun—he said:

> The memoirs of that period [the Counter Reformation] show a very extraordinary state of society; the most arbitrary government combined with feudal and popular anarchy; legislation that is amazing in the way it exposes a profound, ferocious, pretentious ignorance; classes with opposed interests and maxims; some little-known anecdotes, preserved in trustworthy documents; finally a plague which gives full rein to the most consummate and shameful excesses, to the most absurd prejudices, and to the most touching virtues.

With this stuff he did fill his book. The contemporary reader must reflect that this is exactly the kind of material which has, in our time, become degenerate in the novel. The great, even the extensive subjects, have fallen into inferior hands. They have become the fodder of the middle-brow novelist. Is it really true that this kind of material can no longer attract the best minds in the novel? Has it exhausted itself? Clearly Manzoni, like Scott and Balzac, had the excitement of doing something new and they had the tremendous intellectual and emotional force of the Romantic movement behind them. But they were more than capable inventors, copyists, historians or story-tellers who comfortably relied on a commonly accepted language and values. Indeed, although it is generally said that our lack of these common symbols is the central difficulty for contemporary artists, I wonder whether Manzoni's situation was as different from ours as it seems to be. He is a singular example of the artist, who, finding no common basis for himself and a disjointed society, sets laboriously to make one. His religion was uncharacteristic for a man of advanced ideas; as far as its elusive quality can be discerned, it seems to have connected the ideas of Pascal with those of liberalism and this profound change of spirit led him to seek an equally important change of language. He wished to find a language in which all men communicate with one another and to abandon literary language. Problems of belief raise at once problems of style: in both Manzoni was revolutionary. His case somewhat resembles Tolstoy's though, with Manzoni, conversion was not a mutilation of the artist but his fulfilment. He succeeded (where the English Protestant novelists on the whole failed) in creating characters who were positively good yet his "message" that love above all, self-sacrifice, courage, long-suffering and charity are the only, and not necessarily successful answers to tyranny and injustice, is not introduced as a sort of pious starch into the narrative, but is native to it. One is undermined rather than incited by this teaching, as in one or two of the Russian writers; and the very pessimism of Manzoni, by which he continually moves the rewards of the righteous just a little beyond their finger-tips with a gentle scepticism, is like that of Cervantes.

4
Verga

ITALIAN critics tell us that Verga is one of the greatest Italian novelists and, until recent years, the undisputed second to Manzoni; even so he is a neglected writer in Italy, though I have heard Victorini speak well of him. When D. H. Lawrence made his excellent translation of *Mastro Don Gesualdo*, Verga was known to us only by the stories in *Cavalleria Rusticana*; an earlier American translation of *I Malavoglia*, his greatest novel, was out of print. This translation was good, although it inclined to be mild and smooth, where Verga was evidently elliptical, hard and pungent. Eric Mosbacher's new version is harder; it retains the old title of *The House by the Medlar Tree*: Malavoglia is a surname meaning the Ill-willed. Destiny shows ill-will to this family and they were to have been part of a trilogy grimly called *The Defeated*. It was to be divided into a study of the very poor, the non-manual workers or Dons of Sicilian life and the upper classes. The last book was never finished.

These novels came from a revelation which, Verga says, he had in the Eighties. He had left Catania where he was born, and had become an adept writer of novels about "elegance and adultery" in Milan and Florence in the current Italian style. I quote Verga's words from D. H. Lawrence's biographical note on his translation of *Don Gesualdo*:

> One day, I don't know how, there came into my hand a sort of broadside, a halfpenny sheet sufficiently ungrammatical and disconnected, in which a sea Captain succinctly related all the vicissitudes through which his sailing ship passed. Seaman's language, short, without any unnecessary phrase. It struck me, and I read it again; it

was what I was looking for, without definitely knowing it. Sometimes, you know, just a sign, an indication is enough.

Verga set out on one of those returns to original and despised sources which have often been fruitful to novelists.

His first step from sophistication was effected by the naturalism of Zola. In *Cavalleria Rusticana* Verga became stark. Here he is a kind of Merimée without the velvet glove. We notice that the pride and violence of the Sicilians is hyperbolical, sublime and close upon us; whereas Merimée sees his Corsicans and Spaniards at one remove. They are the exotic if excellent anecdotes of a civilised connoisseur of primitive manners and passions. Corsican honour, too, is calculating; the Spanish, tragic. The wound in Merimée's nature gave him the aesthete's curious admiration of power and turned him outward to the primitive. Verga has the advantage of turning inward, of going home and is filled with instinctive knowledge. He is not a mystic, either, about "the people."

I Malavoglia indicates the second phase, the rapid arrival at the source. He is no longer the teller of frightening dramatic episodes which isolate the passions of people from the conditions of their life. The high passions, the murderous traditions of honour, have survived (we suspect) not only because of natural inheritance, but because old habits of feeling are preserved longest by the downtrodden and wretched. The upper classes evolve more rapidly and are more sensitive to change than the poor whose humane virtues emerge only every so often when civilisation cracks. Verga found himself inside the thoughts, words and interests of the poor Sicilian fishermen. He did not stand with one foot safely in the picturesque, as most of us do; but went into their life, found it complete, and took it, almost, at its own valuation. From the moment we open *I Malavoglia* we are pitched into the squabble of village life, straight among the talk of the misers, the spies, the honourable, the wasters, the modest, the hypocrites, the officials, the skirling village shrews. Their voices deafen us, their quarrels confuse our ears, their calamities catch us, and we are subject also to those strange truces in the rancour of a community when, for a day, a disaster will quieten it with a common emotion. Verga's aim was to write as closely as he could in the language of the people, for talk is the interminable litany of the poor. Especially he makes wonderful use of their metaphors and their vivid proverbs, and although the polished reader may wince at memories of books written by only too knowing outsiders in this manner, he will find that Verga has invented a style which carries these images and sayings naturally, and without the effect of tuition, on the one hand, or artificial colouring on the other:

> During the squall all the big fish, even the stupid ones, stayed under water without showing themselves, leaving Silkworm, the mayor, gazing skywards as though he were looking for a leaf to nibble.

or

> I bet he was going to wander about in the lava field behind St. Agatha's garden. You cannot ask more than to love the girl next door, for courting by the fence saves both trouble and expense.

or

> Piedipapera found Uncle Crocifisso only too ready to talk about that little matter which was dragging on and on, with no end in sight. Long things turn into snakes, as the saying is.

The matter of *I Malavoglia* is less a story than a stream of rabid country talk, built around the changes of fortune in an honourable family losing the boat on which they depend, getting into the hands of a moneylender, recovering the boat and after heart-breaking work, losing their house and the unity of the family altogether. 'Ntoni, the grandfather, is the dominant character, a figure of patriarchal passion, energy and rugged wisdom, a wonderful, powerful portrait of an honest man. His son, corrupted by military service, half showy, half good, is excellent too, on the downward path. In ten years one sees a family and a village change before the eyes in their fixed frame. There are three or four good set scenes; a funeral, a betrothal, an escape from shipwreck, a smugglers' affray and these—so hackneyed a part of picturesque literature—have a very different aspect in Verga. To begin with they are more raw; then, they are economically dealt with, not with a novelist's colour print in view, but to catch human beings in the act of living.

That is Verga's great virtue. He is closer to contemporary writers than to the writers of the 19th century, with their landscape, their explanations, their expatiations and their theories. One small incident which is at first incomprehensible to the sophisticated reader, shows how thoroughly Verga knew the minds of his people. Mena's pretty sister Lia has become the mistress of the gendarme; and Mena, because of this shame, refuses the lover she hoped to marry. The family honour has been injured; she must pay the price of the injury. She points out to her lover that the village tongues will never let a Malavoglia woman alone after this, and that her husband would live surrounded by scandal and backbiting. The lover recognises the truth of this and agrees that her argument is unsurmountable. Their deep love for each other is thus thrown away on a point of honour, which is communal virtue in disguise. The basic thing in the lives, in the culture of these people, is the role. Each one has a role in the community which he acts every day, elaborates and lives by. In a fixed community it is the reason for life. The cheat must cheat, the hypocrite must practise hypocrisy, the scold must scold, the humble man and the good must preserve their characters; everything is simple and public. Change will bring inner conflict and self-inflicted evils. The tongue rules the Mediterranean like a lash and its aim is to prevent change, to preserve the unity of the group which is greater in value than the life of any individual.

I have probably conveyed that *I Malavoglia* is a book of about the darker side of anchovy fishing. That is not the impression. Though it is generally described as a tragedy, it is rather a pungent, spluttering, vivid picture of life, often comic and sometimes lyrical; it is a rich description of circumstance. There are one or two long passages of rest in the middle of the book describing days on the sea, "green as grass" under the doubtful clouds, or those hard times when the Malavoglia, always anxious to pay off their debt, risked their damaged boat for the sake of a few fish:

> But when the weather was bad, and a nor' wester blew and the corks bobbed up and down on the water all day long as though someone were playing the fiddle for them to dance, and the sea was as white as milk or seethed as though it were boiling, and the rain poured down on their backs all day long and they got soaked to the skin, because no coat could possibly keep it out, and the waves leapt all round them like fish in a frying pan, then it was different ... and 'Ntoni with his coat collar buttoned up to his nose, had no desire to sing, and he had to keep bailing the *Provvidenza* the whole time, and his grandfather kept saying that a "white sea means a sirocco" or "a choppy sea means fresh wind", as though they were here to learn proverbs.
>
> And at dark, when the *Provvidenza* came in with her belly full of the grace of God and her sail billowing like Donna Rosolina's skirt and with the lights in the houses winking to one another behind the black Fariglioni rocks as though they were signalling, Master 'Ntoni would point out to the beautiful fire blazing in La Longa's kitchen ... "What did I tell you?" the old man would exclaim with delight. "Just look at the fire that La Longa has made for us."

In *Mastro Don Gesualdo* the scene was more violent. In the class above the very poor, there was a larger field for pride and for private war; there was the possibility of the great bourgeois madness, megalomania; Don Gesualdo had all the superb force of a rising man. He was a Lear tortured by the daughter who had married into the aristocracy. He was hoodwinked into violent political schemes. *I Malavoglia* is a quieter book. Its metaphors are less electric, its feeling is more pitiful. I do not find novels about foreign peasants of a hundred years ago tolerable unless they are done with economy. Verga, like Merimée, though in a very different mode, stripped his narrative to the bone. He is one of the few novelists still readable in his genre and very close to the tone of our own day.

5
The Early Svevo

THE last thirty years have been one of the great ages of the English translators. Scott Moncrieff's Proust, Arthur Waley's Chinese Poems, the Powys Mather's version of Mardrus's *Arabian Nights*, Madame Bussy's work on Gide, the work of Constance Garnett on the Russians, and many other translations of high talent or genius have transformed our knowledge of foreign authors. One has only to look at the muddy translations of two generations back, or to compare them with the mass of unfelt American work, to see how English translators have reached an extraordinary supremacy; and if we turn to a precise example like Miss Beryl de Zoete's admirable rendering of Italo Svevo, a most difficult author, we realise how fatally easy it would have been to ruin a delicate writer for us and to have shut him off for years. Italo Svevo's *As a Man Grows Older* (in Italian, *Senilità*) first appeared fifty years ago and, after its complete failure with the critics and the public, Svevo turned to his business in Trieste, became a rich man, and was persuaded to write again twenty-three years later only by the interest of James Joyce. To that persuasion we owe Svevo's comic masterpiece *The Confessions of Zeno*, which has been compared to the work of Joyce and Proust, and has called up the ghosts of Freud and Otto Weininger. The prosperous business man, we are told, enjoyed his astonishing fame with the innocent wonder of the amateur: did it not, indeed, justify his passive philosophy that all positive intentions blunder and that our success, our happiness, our virtue itself, settle in us by chance, though not by indolence and indifference? As Renato Poggioli's acute introduction to *Zeno* pointed out, Svevo's novels are about people in their empty, off-time or leisure, the hours they have been longing for as they watched the crawl of the hands of the office clock; yet they strike us by a driven and unceasing busyness. Svevo's mind wears itself out like the grasshopper, sings endlessly like the needle of a machine.

Nearly half of Svevo's not very long life lies between *As a Man Grows Older* and *The Confessions of Zeno*, and all the difference between failure and success. Self-improvement is the obsession of his unlucky heroes, and, as Svevo's life went on, they do improve. Their anxious analysing of motives, their eagerness for illusion, their inevitable failures, and their anxiety to understand and to arrive at a sane attitude to life gives them the pathetic air of miming clowns: they talk so much that it creates, by a paradox, the pathos of dumbness. But they become as wise, gentle, restful in their indetermination as the Chinese and walk with the fullness of the super-annuated. It has been their curious fate to learn the lesson of life backwards, becoming younger and more apt for life as they grow older; so that if they were to look back upon their youth, and even their middle age, these would seem to them like a puzzling sleep from which, little by little, they have been permitted to awake.

As a Man Grows Older can be considered as a half-awakening from Svevo's grim, earlier novel *Una Vita*. *Una Vita* is the story of a bank clerk's fatally insincere love affair which ends in suicide: the lovers have destroyed the meaning of their lives. An austere smile appears between the lines of the next book: the exactions of conscience are severe, but it is perhaps comical that they are self-inflicted. Brentani, a clerk in an insurance office, is too poor to marry and indeed has to support his plain and delicate sister. He is literary, dreamy, a victim of that disease of the sentiments which is called Bovaryisme, which Paul Bourget defined as *"le mal d'avoir connu l'image de la realité avant la realité"* and which, tinctured by puritanism and snobbery in English literature, produced certain heroines of Scott and Dickens. Brentani has never had a love affair, for he evidently satisfies himself in dreams and repents in analysis; and when he at last decides to fall in

THE EARLY SVEVO

love, he makes the worst possible choice in a young, beautiful, hopelessly deceitful working-class girl. The cynicism of the affair owes something to the curious social customs of middle-class life in Trieste at the turn of the century—in general they resemble those of the Mediterranean, where the demi-monde has a precisely defined economic status—but Brentani absurdly encumbers his own path with hallucinations about the girl, unpredictable jealousies and the cruelties of his conscience. A love affair that would not have wrecked his extraverted friend Balli, is fatal to the introverted Brentani; and the effects of the affair are not merely to exalt him or drive him to despair, but to create the desire for love in his sister. A shaded and faltering creature, she conceives a sincere passion which is unrequited; she is taken ill and dies and Brentani is made to see that his impossible behaviour has been the cause. Or rather—for the egoism of Svevo's characters is unfailing and is the source of their comedy—Brentani chooses to think he is the cause; and marrying the delicate image of his sister, to the passionate one of his now discarded mistress (who has run off with a bank thief) he has now a new "image of reality" to dream about, console himself with, and no doubt to impose with results just as devastating, on the next adventure, if he ever has sufficient strength or wilfulness to undertake one.

When I first read *As a Man Grows Older*, some years ago, it seemed to me one more trite little tale about the "little mistress", a grey and listless exercise in Viennese subtlety. I had been carried away by the comic Italian dazzle of *Zeno*; and the only virtue I saw in this earlier book was Svevo's gift for writing innumerable short epitaphs on the nuances of human feeling. I was wrong. In the first place the story of *As a Man Grows Older* has the emotional fullness which is the reward of perfect form and internal balance. How discreetly the cold mists, the sudden rains, the rough seas of the Adriatic port, the glimpses of the city—its business quarter where beautiful women are stared at if they should happen to pass, its empty walks by the sea, its hard-faced flats lit by candles and oil in the poorer quarters, its café meetings—are made to break into Brentani's unstable, never to be self-trusted, yet self-aware mind. In its way, this book is as complete a case-history as *Adolphe*, has the same lucidity, and its analysis the same ruthless serenity, but touched by the clear-headedness of the mad. Here is the passage where Emilio Brentani, in his jealousy, makes his friend Balli, the natural man, promise not to attract his girl who is already betraying him:

> "I am sick with jealousy, nothing else but jealousy. I am jealous of the others too, but most of all of you. I have got accustomed to the umbrella maker, but I shall never get accustomed to you." There was not the faintest touch of humour in his voice; he was trying to arouse pity so that he might the more easily get Balli to promise what he wanted. If he had refused Emilio had made up his mind to rush round to Angiolina at once. He did not want his friend to profit by a state of affairs for which he himself had been largely responsible.

Balli promises, out of pity. But a dreamy look in his eye betrays the natural hunter, tempted by the very fact of having given his word. Balli says he has long wanted to make a sketch of the girl "because I thought you would like to have it." Emilio sees through this at once. With ludicrous anxiety he cries out: "You have promised me, you can't go back on it. Try to find your inspiration elsewhere." And when Balli calms him, the base consequences of an apparently disinterested idealism are slyly shown:

> Emilio began lamenting his sad fate with an irony of self-analysis which removed from it every trace of the ridiculous. He said that he wanted all his friends to know how he looked at life. In theory he considered it to be without serious content, and he had in fact never believed in any of the forms of happiness which had been offered him; he had never believed in them and he could truly say that he had never pursued happiness. But how much

less easy it was to escape suffering! In a life deprived of all serious content even Angiolina became serious and important.

Half the beauty of Svevo's work lies in his cunning gift of throwing away his lines. Were it not for his pain, Balli reflects, Emilio's situation would be ridiculous; and it is in the subtle balance of the delicacies of pain with the load of comedy that the excitement of the book lies.

The scenes of action are brilliant, freshly observed and as concrete as anything in *Madame Bovary* and a good deal better-natured. It is unforgettable when Amalia, the sister, puts Balli's cup back in the cupboard when she discovers her dream of love will not be realised. There is the long, and really gripping account of her illness. Svevo's scenes of illness are among the most dramatic in any literature, for they observe the struggle of the mind with the body; is not life itself an illness, and sickness one of its more highly-coloured, poetic and even thrilling acts? The love scenes with Angiolina are all excellent, for the Svevo heroes discover women as if they were a new species. These heroes are the kind of men at whose behaviour women smile. And when Angiolina pushes Brentani out of bed with the words "Get out, my beauty," she has said everything. Brentani for her is "a beauty and no mistake." Awed by a love quite beyond her and which would drive her out of her mind if she were to take it seriously, she quickly sets about deceiving him.

Social criticism has been at work on Italo Svevo and there is an interesting account of his work from this point of view by Edouard Roditi. But the weakness of this school of criticism is that, while it analyses the roots, it can only do so by disparaging the flower. And it falls into conventional judgments. It is no doubt true, as Roditi says, that Svevo and his heroes are "culture-snobs" and that "in a bourgeois society of culture-snobs illusions of intellectual grandeur thus compensate social or emotional maladjustment." What of it?

Don Quixote was a culture-snob. The type exists within and without the bourgeois order. Illusions of social grandeur compensate contemporary Russian writers for their spiritual failure. Renato Poggioli's introduction to *The Confessions of Zeno* is illuminating on the question of Svevo as a bourgeois. Here is an acute passage:

> Exactly because he does not judge the bourgeois spirit, Svevo amuses himself, tremendously and naïvely, by looking at it. A perfect bourgeois as a man, as a writer, he is almost alone in not looking like one. Instead of descending or condescending to the bourgeois spirit within his soul he raises it and uplifts it along with himself to the sphere of imagination, to a world of fancy and dreams, which is at the same time the world of reality itself. Once Stendhal asked for a literature written by bankers and industrialists able to understand, lucidly and cynically, the economy of life, the business of society, the value of man. Svevo was certainly a writer of this brand, and furthermore, endowed with such bourgeois honesty and commonsense as to refuse to transform his indulgent egoism into any set of theories, any "egotism". A kind of innocent wisdom was the real source of his greatness and originality.

Possibly Svevo's independence sprang from his Jewish background, from his plural personality—as Roditi shrewdly says—as an Austrian, an Italian and a Jew. When the 1914 war came Roditi says, Svevo "treated the whole business as a sort of supreme Jewish joke in which all humanity is involved in the role of the unreasonable Gentile." Svevo found "normal" behaviour desirable but not reasonable. It was too easy. Like the blameless clown, he preferred the difficulty, the busyness of trying all the wrong roads first.

6

Galdós

THE 19th century was the great age of the novel but, in Spain, Peréz Galdós is the only novelist who escapes to some extent from Spanish provincialism and can be compared with the European figures. He has a large range of scene and character; he has been beyond the Pyrenees; he is a social moralist. His masters were Balzac, Dickens and Cervantes and his huge output—he wrote forty-five historical narratives in addition to a number of ambitious novels, one of which is longer than *War and Peace*—composes a kind of Spanish *Comédie Humaine*. How is it that he is so little known outside of Spain, and so little translated? In the long and warm analysis of Galdós' work which Mr. Gerald Brenan gives in his *Literature of the Spanish People*, he makes several points which suggest an explanation. The first is a "lack of temperament" in Galdós. Then

> we look in vain in his portrait gallery for outstanding figures . . . One reason for this is that he never treats his characters in isolation, but always as members of a class or group or family. He is a social historian who aimed at giving the pattern of a society and, what is more, of a society which he regarded as corrupt and frivolous, rather than as an individualist.

Galdós was born in the Canaries and spent his long life in Madrid essentially as an observer, or as a kind of visiting doctor who comes in to diagnose an illness. In consequence, he keeps an objective eye on what he sees and his characters never exceed life-size: "most of his characters"—I quote again from Mr. Brenan—"are mediocrities, some are almost painful in their lack of personality." If, like the Russian novelists, Galdós gains in evocative power by testing his characters against "the national predicament" he has not the Russian desire to magnify the key figures. He aimed, as he once wrote, at a special kind of naturalism which would be salted by Spanish irony, and though his psychological perception is fine, we have a little the impression that his excellence depends for us on our feeling for the peculiarity of Spanish life in his time. In Spain, Galdós was greatly read, though there has always been some clerical opposition to his work and he has been very much forbidden. Under the present régime, I have been told, new editions of his work suffer from excisions by the censor. This is not surprising. Galdós was a liberal, an enemy of the ultramontanes. He made damaging fun of certain kinds of Spanish piety and of the perennial political corruption of the official classes.

The English reader has now the opportunity of starting on Galdós in Miss Gamel Wolsey's translation of *La de Bringas* (*The Spendthrifts*). The characters of his novels reappear in other works, and this one follows *Tormento* and *El Doctor Centeno*, though it is quite independent of them. *The Spendthrifts* is a brilliant, well-constructed comic story, blooming absurdly out of the political realities of its time. The translation preserves the tone of the period and flows simply and naturally along. The immediate theme of the novel has the Balzacian mark of the theory of the dominant passion: a woman's passion for clothes. This is not a trivial subject. It leads Galdós to the heart of a society which has a mania for display at all costs. Indeed, the greater the poverty of the country, the greater the social and political corruption, the more important public display becomes. Refugio, the courtesan, who has tried her hand at dealing in dresses and hats smuggled through the customs, says towards the end of the tale:

> Here, except for half a dozen families, everyone is poor. Façade, nothing but façade. These people have no idea of comfort in their houses. They live in the streets; and so that they can dress well and go to the theatre, some families eat nothing but potato omelettes all the year round.

Where does the money come from? From bribes, sinecures, official swindles and an eternal tragi-comedy of cadging, sponging, borrowing and plain stealing—for half the people do not pay their bills. And the whole system has the lazy, generous, careless figure of the Queen at the top of the pyramid. Galdós has caught the comedy in the last year of Isabel's reign, and by the end of the book the *coup d'état* has occurred and the whole pack of cards comes down.

The Bringas are a modest but rising family in the upper official class. The husband has a place in Court, the family lives in a wonderful menagerie of royal hangers-on, on the top floor of the Palace. Bringas has a horror of debt and has become a miser who watches every penny in the household accounts. He has succeeded in preventing his wife from entering society by keeping her without fashionable clothes. If clothes are her fantasy, Bringas too has a peculiar fantasy of his own. Like everyone else he owes his position and his son's advancement to "influence", keeping important persons sweet, and tacit bribery. The boy has, for example, been given a government job at the age of sixteen, though in fact he is still at the university and only goes to the office to collect his salary. For this and other advantages Bringas wishes to show his gratitude to his benefactor in a spectacular way. He sets out to make a "hair picture" as a memorial to his benefactor's dead daughter. The Spanish cult of death has never been so comically treated. Bringas' picture is a fretwork horror, a landscape of tombs, angels, willows, lakes and distant Gothic walls, set in an oval frame eighteen inches across; but it is woven from the tresses of the dead girl, with some help from the hair of her mother and her sister. The task is minute and monstrous; each thread of hair has to be picked up by tweezers, snipped by scissors into tiny pieces no larger than the smallest stroke of an etching, and is then gummed to the plate.

While Bringas sits half the day absorbed in this sepulchral folly his wife is gradually infected by a ridiculous friend with the mania for dresses. Soon she is caught up in debts and cheated by friends who borrow from her. When the crisis comes, a stroke of luck saves her: the minuteness of her husband's work has made him temporarily blind. She is able to sell candlesticks and tamper with his cash box without being seen. Eventually she finds herself helplessly drifting among a group of ruined and lying women, all borrowing from one another, and turns to take a lover for help. We see the gradual downfall of a nice, faithful wife, her humiliation at the hands of her lover, who politely evades helping her after his success and, finally, her total humiliation at the hands of a courtesan who claims to be a member of the family.

So far this is no more than a story by Maupassant, dry and ironical in its beginning, steely and inexorable in its end. But Galdós is far more interested in character and the density of human relations, than he is in pure plot. His moral is never merely neat. There are two ways of looking at Rosalia Bringas and her husband. We can see them as a good, devoted, pious married couple bringing up their children well; if Bringas is close with money, that is merely because he is determined not to live the silly life of pretence and debt around him, and the moment his sight goes Rosalia is the soul of care. They live clucking together like a couple of funny, anxious ducks on their little domestic island. Rosalia's passion for clothes is native, feminine and imaginative; her vanity is part of the ancient comedy of women's lives; her piety is appropriate. The dream of clothes is Don Quixote's dream in another idiom. But Galdós has prepared us, in *Tormento*, the earlier novel, for a Rosalia who has been poisoned by society. Envy, family pride, class pride are in her. She will stick at nothing in keeping up her social position; she will fight tooth and nail to keep the inferior woman out. Her religion is ignorant and vulgar hocus-pocus; it is also a financial drain. When her lover tricks her, when the courtesan—who claims to be a relation—makes her crawl for a loan and pours contempt on the respectable married woman and her "superior" morality, Rosalia's Spanish violence comes out. She instantly thinks of murder. And far from being chastened, she reads her lesson otherwise. She hardens. For after the intolerable August in Madrid where she has been obliged to stay—and in this kind of atmosphere Galdós is admirable; he is the novelist of a city—the *coup d'état* comes, her reactionary husband is ruined, her safe place in the Palace has gone: and she gets a thrill of power as she realises that it is upon herself that the family will now depend. The lesson she has been taught is that it is important to go after the men with the big money; and she has learned how to do it. The tempted fool has turned into a formidable and spirited expert.

There are many good portraits in the book. Doña Milagros with the smart parties she cannot pay for, her self-deceit, her emotional lies, is at a stage more advanced than Rosalia. Doña Cándida, the simple, mad, harmless cheat, or Refugio, the courtesan, are at further stages. There is a delightful Proustian politician in Don Manuel Pez, the serene dandy and adept manager of formulae who expresses all his ideas in triplicate:

> "It's impossible, it's very difficult, at least, it would be risky in fact to hazard an opinion. The revolution we have laughed at so much, joked about so often, jeered at so many times. . . ."

And so on. Pez, the urbane centre of the bribery system, the system of influence and introductions on which the Spanish state was based—and still is—was soon back after the *coup d'état*. No Committee, not even a revolutionary one, could work without him and his enormous army of friends and relations. How else could the system of free railway passes, wholesale smuggling from France, and jobs for the needy, be managed? In the minor portraits, the children are excellent: they play their part, indeed the compositions of Galdós are orderly, despite touches of Dickensian extravagance.

There is a mildness in Galdós, in spite of the vigour of his mind, which brings the reader back to Mr. Brenan's remark on his lack of temperament. The historian broadens the note of the novelist who lacks the intellectual edge of the French novelists of the time or the English sense of theatre. There is a certain idleness in the Cervantesque irony, as if we were listening to the shrewd brain of a lazy mind. But to feel his full effect, it is necessary to see this novel in relation to others, to see it as a corner of his large, sad speculation on the Spanish predicament. There is no "Spanish soul" to compare with the "Russian soul", in the same kind of novel, nor does Galdós feel that he is making a natural history of human nature. Galdós is deep in Spanish egoism. But he was sufficiently a European to explore that; he wrote at the time of intellectual revival; he is free from that "typical" regionalism which travels so poorly in literature. He has the certainty, sharpness and power of the novelist who is saturated in his subject. If, as they say, everything in Spain is personal, then Galdós is the novelist of this kind of society which destroys every idea and issue by the thickly involved personal concern. In Galdós one is deeply involved in 19th-century Spain, yet *The Spendthrifts* itself is one of his novels which seems to be about the present day.

7
A Portrait of T. E. Lawrence

WHAT was the character of T. E. Lawrence? I have been reading a selection of his writings which Mr. David Garnett has put together with the aim of making this character reveal itself. The book opens with a sardonically expert letter written when Lawrence was eighteen, goes on to his archaeological journeys in England, France and Syria; and then chronologically to the *Arab Bulletin* and *Seven Pillars of Wisdom*. It ends with extracts from *The Mint* and some of the final letters. Lawrence's Cairo reports were described by an official as "observant, pungent in style and character" and these qualities made him a swift, singeing narrator, a sound and irreverent analyst of situations which were on the move. When situations do not move, when he is describing the static life of the Army and the R.A.F. in peacetime, as in the passages from the unpublished *The Mint*, Lawrence strikes one as being deeply bored by his material. He tries to make it vivid by fixing it with his eye. In doing this he becomes mannered and bitterness gives his writing a thick and embossed effect, which is not the best side of a talent made for fluency and variety. We can judge, of course, from extracts only; the impression made by the whole of *The Mint* may be quite different. But since T. E. Lawrence's time there has been a good deal of documentary or disinterestedly observant writing about the airman's and soldier's life, and it has been soberer in tone, less egoistical in sensibility, less plagued than Lawrence's is by horror of the mass of men or, at any rate, instinctively forgives them. Lawrence felt cut off from them, especially—as he put it—from their carnality. Beside this writing—and I think of things like Alun Lewis's *Ward* 03(*b*)—T. E. Lawrence sounds studied and precious. It is the end-result of the abstract and ascetic bias in Lawrence's mind, a gift he had learned to apply to men when he wished to use them in action.

Forgetting all one has read and heard of T. E. Lawrence, what portrait can one build up from his writings? He has the total, sanguine, efficiency of genius, of course. After that, the Anglo-Irish and Highland Scottish parentage makes a bold and distinctive general outline. Courage, militancy, imagination, clear separation of close-packed thought from withdrawn feeling, the ability to get "inside the skin of the participants" in an action—which Sir Ernest Dowson noted —without losing oneself in the process, a dizzy sexless energy, irony—but that is the militant tradition—an instinct for mischief and intrigue, vanity and a core of diffidence, weakness, insecurity. History suggests that their insecurity as the lonely conquerors of a savage and treacherous country is a profound element in the general character of the Anglo-Irish and (as Lawrence's brother thought) the weakness provoked in T. E. Lawrence that transcendent will which is incessant in men and women of genius. Other Anglo-Irish traits are suggested by a comparison with Bernard Shaw. There are the continuous histrionic touch and the remorse that follows—an unavailing remorse because it, also, is theatrical. There is the merciless mental energy which pours out endlessly in words or action, and turns upon the character with humiliating self-criticism. There is the special kind of idealism: ascetic, bodiless, rational, unromantic, and it keeps a place for the inevitable cynicism of tactics. Unlike English idealism it is unsentimental and without hypocrisy. Lawrence's guilt about betraying the Arabs could not be dissolved by useful moral arguments; it was hard. An objective thinker cannot get rid of the objects he sees or deceive himself by turning them into something else. Lawrence's dislike of Imperialism was traditional; on the other hand, he was drawn irresistibly to the military fascination of Imperial power. Thus, to hold Alexandretta for ever is vital; to lose British soldiers for Mesopotamian oil is squalid and wicked. In this kind of judgment Lawrence may have been a strate-

A PORTRAIT OF T. E. LAWRENCE

gist and not a political economist, but he was chiefly a kind of aesthete, plumping for abstract power which was, in some way, connected with honour. It had nothing to do with the squalid, practical interests of the oil trade. (His reading at this time is suggestive: Homer, the *Morte d'Arthur* and Blake; the epical, chivalrous and mystical.)

At any rate the attitude of Lawrence is not that of a 19th-century Romantic. Nor is there any Rupert Brooke in him. Of all those who wrote about the first World War, he is the only one to go into it with his eyes open. He had been studying castles, military science, the actual terrain of his war and its people in his youth scientifically. The disillusion of the other war writers of that generation arose because war was not what they thought it would be; the strong ruling and military bent of the Anglo-Irish seems to have preserved Lawrence from illusion. What he experienced after the war was the disgust of success, the disgust following intoxication; perhaps the affront that he was no longer a king-maker; and, of course, the frustration of the guerrilla soldier's ideal of freedom for a race of soldiers.

I do not say this to whittle down the sincerity of his desire for Arab Freedom, but to underline the importance of the idea of honour in his character. It goes back to the Elizabethans in Ireland, not to the English public schools; and his feeling for the Arabs—though there was always some part of him that was the observer—seems to have been a natural response to people who lived by honour, the corruption of honour by eternal quarrels, and its ironies. It is an exquisite moment in *Seven Pillars of Wisdom* when Feisal discreetly shows that he has guessed Lawrence is doctoring the telegrams from Mecca; there is an Elizabethan taste for the conceit, for the subtle arabesque of innuendo. When Feisal says to Lawrence "You always prefer my honour to your own," the words have the ambiguity of a verse cut by the diamond of a betrayed Tudor. For, as Lawrence said many times in the *Arab Bulletin* and *Seven Pillars*, he *used* the honour of the Arabs; he was stronger because he had a motive unknown to them. He had the demon inside him, the will of the Allies; and he was strong also because he had to make an enormous moral effort to live with his own guilt:

> In compensation stood my energy of motive. Their less-taut wills flagged before mine flagged, and by comparison made mine seem tough and active.

The precocious Lawrence who, as a boy of five, could read a newspaper upside down, who became a technician, an archaeologist and an historian while he made himself into a deep and original military thinker, was a "thought-riddled" man. He was the kind of man of action who did not value what men of action valued. He was made to bear the Hamlet-like burden of the double role; he became a legend, perhaps because he was a new and prophetic prototype. The guerrillas of the 1939 war, the equipped individualists, the educated men or the sensitive who had to stick out the promiscuous living of the Nissen huts, were foreshadowed by him. He stands, rather flamboyantly guilty, at the beginning of a new age to which the conflicts of *Seven Pillars* were to become soberly familiar. In everything, from the hold-ups, the executions, the intrigue and the tortures to the final nihilism, he was the first guinea-pig of the underground. What a guilt-eaten book *Seven Pillars* is and how subtle. True to the feeling of his period (for the book is very much of the Twenties in its artifice, its mastery and egoism) and true to his own nature, it is theatrical; but it has to be so to make its corrosive mark as a new, progenitive kind of mind in war. *The Mint* was a good title for its successor, because it was Lawrence's place to stamp the hurt contemporary face on the new coin.

The theme of *Seven Pillars* seems to be ecstasy, guilt and suffering. In action, that means the satisfaction of the well-laid mine, the provision of timely loot, excitement and slaughter for the tribesmen; it means blood-guilt; and it means the martyrdom of leadership—having to shoot a man oneself in order to prevent a blood feud—and a curious moment like the one when, after a massacre, Lawrence went round and arranged the dead in more seemly positions. The self-questionings have the rhetorical touch—later Lawrence criticised the "foppishness" of his mind—but the manner he adopted, one feels, was simply his device for screwing the last ounce out of sensibility, or a kind of flagellation:

> The practice of our revolt fortified the nihilist attitude in me. During it, we often saw men push themselves or be driven to a cruel extreme of endurance; yet never was there an intimation of physical break. Collapse rose always from a moral weakness eating into that body, which of itself, without traitors from within, had no power over the will. While we rode we were disbodied, unconscious of our flesh or feeling; and when at an interval this excitement faded and we did see our bodies, it was with some hostility, with a contemptuous sense that they reached their highest purpose, not as vehicles of the spirit, but when, dissolved, their elements served to manure the field. . . .

Or:

> I seemed at last approaching the insensibility which had always been beyond my reach; but a delectable land: for one born so slug-tissued that nothing this side fainting would let his spirit free. Now I found myself dividing into parts. There was one which went on riding wisely, sparing or helping every pace of the wearied camel. Another hovering above and to the right bent down curiously, and asked what the flesh was doing. The flesh gave no answer . . . a third garrulous one talked, wondered, critical of the body's self-inflicted labour. . . . Telesius, taught by some such experience, split up the soul. Had he gone on, to the furthest limit of exhaustion, he would have seen his conceived regiment of thoughts and acts and feelings ranked round him as separate creatures; eyeing, like vultures, the passing in their midst the common thing that gave them life.

BOOKS IN GENERAL

The pages on self-surrender, obedience and abasement are, in their way, religious and, indeed, were observed among believers in a warlike religion. The final desire is for physical solitude. Lawrence could not bear to be touched, unless, one supposes, he was hurt.

And so one could go on about this strange actor whose aim—realised only among the Arabs—was to be notable for being unnoticeable, an actor both morally and physically. His self-analysis is not really the best part of *Seven Pillars*; what holds one is more than the story; it is the brain. Travellers have told before how they have stopped a quarrel by a well-turned tale, especially (one seems to remember) in the East, the home of convenient formulae; but Lawrence giving an impromptu parody of an Arab story-teller, at a bad moment, to an audience who (he tells us) had never heard parody before, is superb in assurance. Or again, Lawrence dominating his illness by thinking out his campaign, shows us the will at work hour by hour. Throughout a swift, masterly narrative, packed with action, character and personal emotion, we have the extraordinary spectacle of a brain working the whole time. It is as if we could see the campaign thought by thought. The close texture of genius in action has rarely been so livingly done by an active man; it has been left, as a rule, to the self-watching invalids. And this density of thought was present from the beginning. If there had been no war in Arabia, and no epic to live, Lawrence would still have been a vivid, trenchant and sardonic historian. Hardly classical in manner (for that was "out" in the Twenties and writers were looking for manners which would bring home their nervous singularity) *Seven Pillars* is the solitary classic of the self-conscious warrior, as Doughty is of the great self-conscious traveller.

8

The Notebooks of Henry James

THE notebooks of the great authors are the idlest kind of reading as, for their writers, they have so often been the idlest kind of writing: in the forest of life they mark the trees to be felled. It is always a moment this, delicate and touch-and-go, when a piece of life is chipped off and is still neither life nor art, a fragment with the sap, the tang, the freshness still on it, to be picked up and considered. We are at a beginning, and there is a kind of pathos in knowing that presently this bright bit will be lost to life and become an anonymous, altered and perhaps undecipherable piece in the forbidding structure of a work of art. To some minds, and especially the critical, there will be a pleasure in tracing the history of that chip from the time when it flew off the axe until it found its present home in what Henry James called "the real thing"; to lazier minds there is the pleasure of being there as the first stroke rings, even when it rings flat and untrue. "A good deal might be done with Henry Pratt", wrote Henry James, recalling an evening with this friend of his in Venice. How one responds to that suddenly decisive and injudicious cry. Hurrah, the woodman has not spared the tree! Bring Henry Pratt in here. Let us *all* look him over. Let us keep him here, with the soil on his roots, while we make up our ingenious minds. That is one pleasure of notebooks: they are dramatic. A character, a scene, a smudge of scenery, half a dozen lines of talk, a few epigrams with no visible means of support, are caught in all their innocence. The other attraction is the strangeness of the workshop. Here are not only the acceptable ideas but the unacceptable, the discarded, the litter of a profession, the failures.

The Notebooks of Henry James belong to the working kind. Even the opening judgment on his first twelve years as a writer is done to clear the mind and not to indulge his memory. The great are monsters of efficiency, the mills work day and night. What strikes us is how much James's notes were used. Hawthorne's long notes, for example, seem to have been a studied alternative to his real subjects. Dostoevsky's—as far as we know them by quotation—generate fog rather than precision, though we may regard Dostoevsky as a note-writer whose object is to work up a fog of the right density. With James the matter is all literal: the American genius is technical and for production. The *Prefaces*, the anecdotes that have come down to us, show that nothing was lost: James was presentable and publishable in his very socks. His life was an arrangement in words, born to circulate.

These *Notebooks* of his were begun in Boston when he was thirty-eight and when he feared that he had let too many impressions slip by, and they cover thirty years. They confirm that the word was totally his form of life, as if sentences rather than blood ran in his veins. Outside of words lay the unspeakable:

> Meanwhile the soothing, the healing, the sacred and salutary refuge from all these vulgarities and pains is simply to lose myself in this quiet, this blessed and uninvaded workroom, in the inestimable effort and refreshment of art, in resolute and beneficent production. I come back to it with a treasure of experience, of wisdom, of acquired material, of (it seems to me) seasoned fortitude and augmented capacity. Purchased by disgust enough, it is at any rate, a boon that now I hold it, I feel I wouldn't, I oughtn't to have missed. Ah, the terrible law of the artist —the law of fructification, of fertilisation, the law by which everything is grist to his mill—the law in short of the acceptance of all experience, of all suffering, of *all* life, of *all* suggestion, sensation and illumination.

And again:

> To live *in* the world of creation—to get into it and stay in it. . . .

THE NOTEBOOKS OF HENRY JAMES

This is a language, with its "inestimables", its "alls", its "boons" and "beneficences", which oddly recalls the otherworldly language (so blandly assuming solid rewards on earth) of his contemporaries, the American Transcendentalists: like them Henry James was tuning in to a private Infinite which would give the painful American gregariousness a sense of privacy. His words to Logan Pearsall Smith who had described a desire to excel in literature (I quote from Simon Nowell Smith's *The Legend of the Master*) are the proper conclusion:

> There is one word—let me impress upon you—which you must inscribe on your banner, and that word is Loneliness.

Loneliness, like a pair of empty eyes, stares between the lines of this volume. We see the empty silent room, the desk, the lost, blank face of the well-dressed writer. Already as he takes his pen, he is far away from the dinner party he has just left. He is caught by "the terrible law." As fast as Emerson he is turning matter into spirit. Nearly every note is made after a meeting with people whose words, or what he knows of their lives, have provided him with one of his "germs", and at first sight, these pages might pass as the record of a vast sociability, a discreet mass of anonymous gossip. James himself, once attacked by Alphonse Daudet for frequenting people below his own intellectual level, might appear like another Thackeray ruined by dining out, or like the Major in *The Real Thing* with "the blankness, the deep intellectual repose of twenty years of country-house visiting." (The American editors of the *Notebook*, F. O. Mathiessen and Kenneth B. Murdock, point out that the French critic exaggerated: Henry James had a great many distinguished friends and some of the notes clearly are prompted by them. It is an illusion that a novelist needs high company continually, unless that happens to be his material; the conditions of the intellectual life are dangerously inclined to cut the novelist off from ordinary people who expose themselves less guardedly than the intellectuals do.) But examine a typical note carefully: the memoranda of Henry James are not jottings and reminders. They are written out, hundreds of them, at length. They are not snatched out of time, but time is in them; already the creative process has begun. A glance shows how much of James's life must have passed in the immense labour of almost continuous writing, and writing out in full detail, as if to fill the emptiness of the day with the succulence of its lost verbatim. The earliest reference to *What Maisie Knew*—a story which may be followed from behind James's shoulder in many entries in this volume—is not a hurried shorthand. It might be a minute passed from one civil servant to another:

> Two days ago, at dinner at James Bryce's, Mrs. Ashton, Mrs. Bryce's sister, mentioned to me a situation that she had known of, of which it struck me immediately that something might be made in a tale. A child (boy or girl would do, but I see a girl, which would make it different from *The Pupil*) was *divided* by its parents in consequence of their being divorced. The court, for some reason, didn't, as it might have done, give the child exclusively to either parent but decreed that it was to spend its time equally with each—that is alternately. Each parent married again and the child went to them a month, or three months about—finding with the one a new mother and the other a new father. Might not something be done with the idea of an odd and particular relation springing up. . . .

James's method is uncommon among writers and explains why his *Notebooks* are more fertile than most others we have been allowed to see. A full, superfluous, self-communing phrase like, "Might not something be done . . ." slows down the too bright idea, roots it in the mind, gives it soil. The slower the process of note-making the more likely it is to have sap and growth. James passing minutes to himself,

James in colloquy, writing himself long and intimate letters: the note becomes one of those preliminary private outpourings, a "voluminous effusion . . . so extremely familiar, confidential and intimate—in the form of an interminable garrulous letter addressed to my own fond fancy." Not only is his material the subject: he himself is in it, adjured, egged on and cozened. Strange cries, like the whimper of hounds on the scent, comically, not without mockery—and yet touchingly and even alarmingly: "I have only to let myself go"—break out. In life he is an outsider, but not in letters:

> I have brought this little matter of Maisie to a point at which a really detailed scenario of the rest is indispensable for a straight and sure advance to the end. Let me not, just Heaven—not, God knows, that I *incline* to!—slacken in my deep observance of this strong and beneficent method—this intensely structural, intensely hinged and jointed preliminary frame. . . .

The coverts are drawn:

> What is this IX, then, the moment, the stage *of*? Well, of a more presented, a more visible cynisme, on the part of everybody. What *step* does the action take in it? *That of Sir C's* detachment from Ida——

Then comes the view:

> Ah this *divine* conception of one's little masses and periods in the scenic light—as rounded Acts; this patient, pious, nobly "vindictive" (vindicating) application of the same philosophy and method—I feel as if it still (above *all*, Yet) had a great deal to give me, and might carry me as far as I dream! God knows how far—into the flushed, dying day—that is! *De part et d'autre* Maisie has become a bore to her parents—with Mrs. Wix to help to prove it.

And so from field to field he runs, down to that kill, so protracted, so lovingly delayed lest one thrill of the chase be lost—"Do I get anything out of Folkestone?"—where Mrs. Wix at last *"dit son fait* to—or about."

We could not ask for a more explicit statement of the compulsive quality of the creative process; in fact, one could say that any other quality is excluded from these notes. There is little that is casual or speculative. "Writing maketh an exact man." The conception is musical or mathematical. Method has become a divinity. There are few descriptions of places though there is a warm evocation of what London meant to him in the early and almost pathetically impersonal summing up of his life at the beginning of the book. Our picture is continually of crowds of people, in clubs or drawing rooms; but not of people seen—for they are not usually described—but of people being useful to Henry James, in some way working for him, wired in unknown to themselves and all unworthily to his extraordinary system of secretive illumination. The lonely man lends them his foreign mind. Abstract notions occasionally are flashed to him: "What is there in the idea of Too Late?"—the idea of a passion or friendship long desired? But, generally, the information is trite. Even where the neatest plot is boxed, we see how the deliberate endeavour to heighten consciousness which contains the whole of Henry James's art, has transformed it at once (after, we can ask how much this very deliberateness lost for him as a novelist). Situation, dilemma rather than character, except in a very general way, mark the *Notebooks*; there is little portraiture and one would not gather much of James's richness in this respect, a richness which displaces for many heretical readers the metaphysical interest of the double and triple turning of the screw upon them. How many readers, like hungry, but well-provided spiders, run carelessly over that elaborate and mathematical web, shimmering with knots and subtleties from one beautifully trussed fly to the next.

For other novelists the value of Henry James's *Notebooks* is immense and to brood over them a major experience. The glow of the great impresario is on the pages. They are unwearyingly readable and endlessly stimulating, often moving and are occasionally relieved by a drop of gossip. (It is amusing to see him playing with the plot of *Trilby* which was offered to him by Du Maurier.) Of no other stories and novels in the language have we been shown that crucial point where experience or hearsay has suddenly become workable and why it has. We see ideas taken too briskly; we see bad ideas and good ones, we see the solid mature and the greatest ventures, like *The Ambassadors*, spring from a casual sentence. The ability to think of plots and to see characters is common; the difficulty is that one plot kills the next, that character sticks in the mud, and the novelist is motionless from sheer ability to see and to invent too much. What made James a fertile writer was his brilliant use of what, as I have said before, can only be called a slowing-down process. His material begins to move when the right difficulty, the proper technical obstruction or moral load is placed on it. The habit of imposing himself, rather than the gift of a great impressionability appears to have been his starting point; there was a conscious search by a consciousness that had been trained. For the kind of writer who stands outside life as James did, who indeed has no *life* in life, has to create himself before he can create others.

9

Butler's Notebooks

THE period of excitement over *The Way of all Flesh* has passed. This novel anticipated the outburst of parricidal fury which was so strongly felt in England after the 1914 war; but there is an insensibility in Samuel Butler—the result of an injury to sensibility, really,—which is beginning to make him seem arid and even pedantic as the Victorian controversies fade. His *Notebooks* stand out as strongly as ever. They have the crankiness of nature, the stubbornness of personality. They store up Butler as a character, a minor of the Johnsonian school. They are the sketches of a mind and its habits, year in year out; and, taken together, they make an intimate portrait of a peculiarly English type of Worthy: the man who sets out to make recalcitrance respectable—even demure.

Behind those who make a cult of Common Sense we are usually, though not always, entitled to suspect the wounded heart. Benjamin Franklin, for example, was hardly an injured character; puritanism and self-interest fitted him like a glove and he had the urbanity of his period. But Butler, we know, was a hurt man. The love he must have proffered at one time to his father and which, on some stern conception of principle or duty, was rejected, rebounded and became the comic anger of satire. Feeling was cut short, pruned back in Butler and its full expression is rare; one remembers only the lines supposedly written about his love for Pauli and his remorse after the death of Miss Savage. But the latter was expressed with a defensive touch of brutality and our lasting impression of the emotional Butler is a wistful and misanthropic one. The ridiculous and ironical make their protective gestures. He is dryly aware of a dull, edgy, armed neutrality in human relationships and he has the stubborn air of a man too sensitive to private pain. And so sensibility is shut off, the spirit of perversity wakes up, the comic eye aggressively winks, and if imagination is there—but there was more dialectic than imagination in him—it is soon nipped by the sobering eye for fact. Though fact itself (in Butler's kind of character) is liable to be turned into fantasy, caricature and the bizarre. The members of the parricide club have only one emotion and that is too original.

The amusement we get out of Butler comes from his stand for Common Sense, Equanimity, Worldliness and the Plain, and from comparing its downrightness with its underlying timidity; one sees the cult at work in his criticism of Bunyan:

> What a pity it is that Christian never met Mr. Common Sense with his daughter, Good Humour, and her affianced husband Mr. Hate Cant; but if he ever saw them in the distance he steered clear of them, probably as feeling that they would be more dangerous than Giant Despair, Vanity Fair and Apollyon all together—for they would have stuck to him if he had let them get in with him.

Like Shaw, Butler is without humbug. Possibly it was a form of humbug on Butler's part to pretend to be unrespectable and rebellious, when he was in fact a conservative and rather prim and tetchy character. He was a true Victorian —far more Victorian than a man like Bagehot who hardly belongs to his time at all, or Clough who seems to us now contemporary; and yet, having said that we begin to doubt its truth, for Butler is not easy to catch. One thinks of him as a Victorian because he sallied into the great wars of religion in the 19th century but he turned them into private wars, fought with home-made weapons of his own invention. He attacked church religion with autobiography. He attacked it with his personality. Like a minor Johnson, he is pithy, downright and scathing. But where Johnson is orthodox, tragic and frontal in his declarations, Butler drops into the ill-wearing habit of paradox. He is out for dramatic effect and one often feels that when he has turned things upside down, it will only mean that someone is going to have the bother of turning them right way up again—and possibly that someone will be Butler himself:

> A drunkard would not give money to sober people. He said they would only eat it and buy clothes and send their children to school with it.
> An idiot is a person who thinks for himself instead of letting other people think for him.
> Truth does not consist in never lying but in knowing when to lie and when not to do so.
> Lord I do not believe, help thou my unbelief.

In Butler one sees the exasperations of the intelligence; in Johnson the baited bear, the growls that can become the roar of unanswerable moral rage or emotional agony. Then, one feels, Butler was unlucky in his time. He had, as it were, been forced into the Victorian age against his will; he seems to have been born to parcel out the Moral in the fashion of the 18th century, and not to gnash at its unsightly conversion into the conventional morality of the Victorians. And, in fact, their profession and their inherited wealth preserved the whole Butler family from any notion of what the Industrial Revolution did to England. He really wanted, one suspects, what the earlier century had had: a respectable cut and dried and formal God who, except for holidays with the Wesleyans, left the world alone.

Butler's science harked back to that humane period and his attitude to his interests has the versatility, the whim and the egocentric touch we see in the 18th-century amateurs; people like Maria Edgworth's father, solid and yet crankish, who lapped up Rousseau, became practical philosophers, invented extraordinary mechanical and scientific devices. Butler broke into the fields of the specialists with the unholy joy of the independent nuisance, demolishing one kind of father-figure, eloquently erecting others, knocking down

Aunt Sally and rigging up Aunt Handel; and he did this out of the love of the natural man which was his inheritance from the Enlightenment. Unlike the late-Victorian pessimists and agnostics, he is permeated by a discernible complacency, or rather, by a determination not to cry down his satisfactions; he has seen the devil who has told him that God is neither as black nor as white as he is painted, and is assured that the world is gradually becoming more sensible and more comely. Only one thing haunts the human comedy —the loneliness and the pathos of it, the price we have to pay for our good sense. There is a sad note on his half-wish for a son of his own to be hated by, which he turns off with a joke.

Butler's failure in his own lifetime does not seriously affect his spirits; it makes him more phlegmatic and a little touchy, that is all. The *Notebooks* suggest a packed life, the sword never back in the scabbard. Life in whatever *cul de sac* he gets himself into is so dense in its interest, so transformed by his personal curiosity and by his disagreement with it all, that he is more sorry for the bewilderment of the reader than perturbed by it. A parricide cannot fail to be fascinated by his own charmed life. Eccentrics gather round Butler. The upsets with his sisters are delightful in their tedium: the way they look twice at his cheques, get ill when their father gets better and recover when he gets worse! The family letters with the things that had better not be mentioned! They read like negotiations between governments. Around this family row, which Butler could never bear to leave alone, are the Cockney characters, the demi-monde of servant life with its ripe sayings:

> He is generally a little tight on a Saturday afternoon, he always speaks the truth, but then it comes pouring out more.
>
> Boss said that Mrs. Honor would drink everything she could stand upright and pay her money for.
>
> Boss said she wished the horn would blow for her and the worms take her that very night.

Alfred, the note-writing valet, is the strangest of this trite London chorus who, at times, seem to be the ageing Butler's only audience and public. One can think of no more charming scene from the peculiarity of London life than the one where Butler and Alfred are in the British Museum rubbing out the pencil marks the author had made on the letters of Dr. Butler. The notes passed by Alfred were generally practical reminders about things like buying a hat, changing socks. There was once a request for a geranium; but as he worked beside his master in the British Museum Alfred slipped this to him: "You cannot rub out half so nice as Alfred can."

Butler's notes have a dry, almost scientific and specimen-like quality. Compressed, worked upon, shaped, made economical though not elegant, they are uttered without comment. It is the vanity of the aphorist. The good-and-evil, vice-and-virtue themes seem now the poorest, and to a contemporary taste the jokes about religion no longer shock and even require—what damns an epigram—an explanation. In an edition done by Geoffrey Keynes and Brian Hill, one or two new notes have been discovered. They are Butler's irritable accounts of collisions between rival vanities—a meeting with Augustine Birrell who is presented as an egotistical old bore; and a very wary note on Shaw. Butler's one-man war against the Victorian age led him to believe he was the only important writer in it. Of Shaw, he wrote:

> I have long been repelled by this man though at the time attracted by his coruscating power.

In their absurd meeting Shaw cried down Handel, praised the disgusting Ibsen, but agreed that the Odyssey was "obviously" written by a woman—

> but I cannot forgive Bernard Shaw for sneering at Shakespeare as he has done this morning. If he means it there is no trusting his judgment—if he doesn't mean it I have no time to waste on such trifling. If Shaw embeds his

plums in such cakes as this, they must stay there. I cannot trouble to pick it out.

Did the lowering, mistrustful old man apprehend that this sportive disciple was going to beat him at his own game and eclipse him? Worse—did he suspect that Shaw had that command of his own talent, that heaven-sent sense of proportion, which Butler could so rarely rely on having to hand? Where Butler lost himself in the craftsman's acrimonies, in the carpentering of belief, nailing down a joke or sawing off an outrage without an audience, Shaw was soon dancing to applause on the stage above. The fault of Butler is that he goes on arguing too long, that he chisels a joke until it vanishes.

Except in the *Notebooks*. In these he hit upon the form most congenial to him: a system of recording guesses about life. The great damage done to Butler in his childhood gave this able, virile and tender man of immensely original curiosity, a craving for the "normal", and the normal could be surmised only by posing extreme statements and from their collision extracting the mean. His wisdom is a kind of practical guesswork and it has a power to move or convince when we feel the hourly puffing and blowing of his experience behind it.

It is not by what a man has actually put down on his canvas, nor yet by the acts which he has set down so to speak on the canvas of his life that I will judge him, but by what he makes me feel that he felt and aimed at.

That is pure Butler: the doctrine of the conflict, the fantasy, the guess and the growing point.

10

A Victorian Child

AFTER we have looked through the drawings of Cruikshank, we find ourselves haunted not by the gargoyle figures of the males, nor by the ethereal or comely silliness of most of the women; but by that other Victorian race, the pygmies in adult fancy dress, grave-eyed, elderly-headed, wraithlike, marked already by a Gothic intimation of delicacy and death: the children. They are, as we know, survivors who have escaped the large Victorian graveyard; and in their foreheads, we seem to detect, a knowledge—or is it an innocence?—beyond their years. In the violence of Victorian life these, and the poor, are the victims; and perhaps the attitude of the main body of Victorians to their children reflects an attitude to the appalling poverty upon which the fathers' prosperity was built. In the mellifluous and also blistering lecture Ruskin delivered in 1888 to a middle-class audience in the prosperous boscage of Tunbridge Wells he told them they were less attractive than the Borgias whose crimes, at any rate, had been crimes of sudden passion and not unknown to remorse. He was attacking the moral oppression of the deserving poor:

> Be assured, my good man—you say to him—that if you work steadily for ten hours a day all your life long, if you drink nothing but water, or the very mildest beer, and live on very plain food, and never lose your temper, and go to church every Sunday, and always remain content in the position in which Providence has placed you, and never grumble, nor swear; and always keep your clothes decent, and rise early, and use every opportunity of improving yourself, you will get on very well, and never come to the parish.

A VICTORIAN CHILD

Is that very different from their injunctions to the deserving child?

The large untaxed profits of the middle class, the startling rise in their standard of living—at Herne Hill, in Ruskin's time, the rich shopkeepers kept powdered footmen and lived in enormous ostentation—was a violence which exacted a stringent virtue in the oppressed in order to balance the rapacity. The blessings of obedience, faith and peace, Ruskin said in *Praeterita*, were implanted in him in his childhood by his father, the sherry merchant who saved half his income every year and who, beginning without a penny, died worth £120,000. What was desired was the industrious apprentice, the obliging workman and the unchild-like child, as respectful and unperturbing as the trusted assistant of the counting house. The elder Ruskin (the son said) even chose a wife as he would choose a clerk.

In this the martyrdom of the rich child was as bad as the martyrdom of the poor, if not worse; better to be Oliver Twist than Paul Dombey. John Ruskin's life is an exemplary criticism of his time; and he knew it was. His education was forced by an ambitious mother who saw in him a future bishop. The family was isolated by her snobbery; she cooled off her humble relations and was too uncertain of herself and too proud to know those above her in station. In this delicate game the Ruskins never discovered any equals, from too much looking up or looking down. He was emasculated by her possessiveness and her fear for his innocence, and the whole scheme of his upbringing was calculated to enlarge the conceit and coolness of his nature if it did not create them. To this upbringing he traced his calamities in love and marriage; and it eventually provoked his savage attacks, culminating in madness, upon the society that had formed his parents and himself.

After the public disaster of his marriage, Ruskin understood his situation: the evil had lain in the perfection of his childhood and it was incurable. *Praeterita*, the autobiography which he wrote in the shortening intervals of sanity at the end of his life, is his final submission, the confession (as Sir Kenneth Clark says in a really admirable introduction to a new edition of the work) of defeat. For here the struggle is given up. Only those things that are innocuous in memory are set down. His marriage is not even mentioned; there is only a passing reference to Rose la Touche; there is only a glance at his conversion to socialism, which was as dramatic and violent as Tolstoy's religious conversion and as tremendous a satisfaction of the ego. (Socialism was also a revenge: he had been derisively rejected by the daughter of his father's Spanish partner, Adèle Domecq, and when, later on, she made a fashionable marriage, he was stirred to condemn her indifference to the peasants in her father's vineyards). In the last years, when reason flickered in his long-maned head and "uninvited phantoms" came to disorder the slippery tongue of the eloquent old prophet, only the happy things were to be recalled.

What a bishop was lost in her son, Mrs. Ruskin said. What a novelist was lost, said Miss Thackeray. *Praeterita* almost confirms her. The simple engagement of memory, the wandering precision of his picture of the sherry merchant's house at Herne Hill, the limpid, delightful portraits of cousins and friends, the ironical judgments, have no didactic nag; nor have they that too beguiling eloquence which brought tears to the eyes of his parents when he dutifully read his day's writing to them. Now Ruskin was no longer a middleman; he was an artist. Here is one of the Perth nephews:

> A stumpily made, snub or rather knob-nosed, red-faced, bright-eyed, good-natured, simpleton; with the most curiously subtle shrewdness, and obstinate faculties, excrescent through his simplicity.

The occasional miniatures of this kind hang beside the grander studies of Papa and Mama. There is an evocation of the pleasures of suburban life which is droll, delicate and

A VICTORIAN CHILD

affectionate and astutely examined as they are brought up glittering in the net of time. We see again that fateful visit of the Domecq family, with their ravishing English-speaking daughters who flung him unprepared into "the fiery furnace" of his first, sudden and unhappy passion. As he remembered it, what struck him was, characteristically, that "nothing more tragic in the essence could have been invented by the skilfullest designer in any kind." He thought, we note, of the pattern, the design. A galaxy of witty Andalusian beauties, in the brief excellence of their race, convent bred, in Paris clothes, tantalised a young man who was a combination of Mr. Traddles, Mr. Toots and Mr. Winkle.

> While my own shyness and unpresentableness were further stiffened, or rather sanded, by a patriotic and Protestant conceit, which was tempered neither by politeness nor sympathy; so that, while in company, I sate jealously miserable like a stockfish (in truth, I imagine, looking like nothing so much as a skate in an aquarium, trying to get up the glass) on any blessed occasion of tête-à-tête, I endeavoured to entertain my Spanish-born, Paris-bred and Catholic-hearted mistress with my own views upon the subjects of the Spanish Armada, the Battle of Waterloo and the doctrine of Trans-substantiation.

The character of Mrs. Ruskin has so often been drawn by writers who, as Sir Kenneth Clark says, have gutted *Praeterita* and left no suspicion of Ruskin's mastery of the intricacy of portraiture. Unluckily she is the kind of Victorian who lends herself to caricature. We cannot help seeing Mrs. Ruskin in black and white; the prudish and ambitious Protestant, managing and policing her house, mistrustful of her neighbours, shut up in an acquired intellectual pride. We see her taking her son six times through the Bible, settling him primly in the corner; after, Papa reads Shakespeare or Byron aloud for hours, whipping the boy when he falls downstairs to show him the folly of falling, allowing him nothing to play with but a bunch of keys and a box of bricks, commending his seven-year-old imitations of Pope. We see a cold and finicking Grundy who held up her marriage for ten years and even then, from prudence, would have delayed it. We cannot say that Ruskin's portraits of his parents are done with love for, as he himself says, he did not know what love was; nor even are they done with affection; but rather with that tranquillity of habit which might pass for affection. So that Mrs. Ruskin is set down with the fidelity with which he would watch a stone, an irresistible view, a Venetian building or the formation of a tree. There is only the negative affection of forbearance in the portrait.

Sir Kenneth Clark suggests that the simple style of *Praeterita* is not the artlessness of an old man's writing, nor even is it to be interpreted as a final serenity and resignation; it is a conscious simplicity assumed by Ruskin to show the world that he had not lost his reason. And indeed, Ruskin was a master of pastiche. Here is a passage of near-Carlyle quoted by Collingwood in his *Life*:

> All the fine ladies sitting so trimly, and looking so sweet, and doing the whole duty of woman—wearing their fine clothes gracefully; the pretty singer, white-throated, warbling "Home Sweet Home" to them so morally and so melodiously? Here was yet to be our ideal of virtuous life, thought the *Graphic*! Surely we are safely back with our virtues in satin slippers or lace veils; and our Kingdom of Heaven is come again *with* observation, and crown diamonds of the dazzlingest. Cherubim and Seraphim in toilettes of Paris (bleu-de-ciel, vert d'olivier de Noë, mauve de colombe-fusilée) dancing to Coote and Tinney's band; and vulgar hell shall be didactically portrayed accordingly (see page 17) wickedness going its way to its poor home, bitter sweet. Ouvrier and petroleuse, prisoners at last, glaring wild on their way to die.

Captivated as we are by the technical skill of his hands on the keys, we become restive when we realise that we are the instruments on which he is playing. We suspect the resourceful Celt. Where Shaw has the art of saying unpleasant things without making enemies, so Ruskin had the art of transporting unpleasant things into entrancing metaphors and flattering his readers and audiences by intoxicating their imaginations. In Tunbridge Wells they must have been delighted to be told that they had planted a poisoned asp in the bosom of society, especially when, in the previous sentence, they had been compared, in the most vivid colours, to the Borgias. Does he not make us feel, sometimes, in his political writing, not that injustice, wickedness and stupidity must be put down, but that indignation, anger, and the wrath of God's chosen, are themselves palatial and satisfying edifices to dwell in? When we compare the simple exactitude of Tolstoy, the other great convert, in similar writings, with Ruskin's, we see the difference between the saint and the saintly conjurer.

11

The Carlyles

THE Universe, so far as sane conjecture can go, is one immeasurable swines' trough, consisting of solid and liquid, and other contrasts and kinds;—especially consisting of the attainable and unattainable, the latter in immensely greater quantities for most pigs.

Moral evil is unattainability of Pig's wash; moral good attainability of ditto.

We are back in the Animal Farm of the Victorian Age, among the Pig Propositions of Carlyle's *Later Day Pamphlets*. We are at the stage before Orwell, before the unattainable has been made attainable by revolution and has been distributed. So the Victorians haunt us for we are still not out of the mess they were in. But what a difference of tone lies between Orwell and Carlyle! A stoical bitterness has succeeded to the rage of frustration. There is all the distance that lies between the Calvinist's pulpit vision of disgust and doom, and the betrayal in the trench. What was literature, vision, or exhortation to Carlyle, we have had to see with our own eyes.

And history has been unkind to the preaching historian. We now pick up *Heroes & Hero Worship* gingerly: we have had to crush one or two dictator-heroes. Carlyle's ultimate contempt for the masses, his dream of an aristocracy of the wise, his call for a labour corps, take us back twenty years into Fascism. In England, where social injustice has been effectively attacked and constructively dealt with, the honour goes to the continuous, practical, rational efforts of the heirs of Bentham and Mill, and not to the mystics and supermen. Carlyle could describe the battlefields of the past, but he had no notion that war was the superman's chief

THE CARLYLES

export. He denied thinking might was right; but his statement that right is might "in the long run" is comfortless; he certainly thought that might in the long run becomes right which was pleasant enough to believe in the long Victorian peace, but to our generation it seems to be one of those question-begging pieces of rhetoric which lead us straight to the concentration camp. It is not surprising that even at his most irascible and sadistic, Carlyle was pre-eminent among Victorian prophets: he embodied the energy and the pathos, the aggression and the guilt, of those who had exchanged belief in God for belief in themselves alone and, in many ways, Carlyle's attitude to religion is far more sympathetic than that of other apostates, for it was deeply tinctured by the tragic imagination and the sense of human pain. He never lost, as more optimistic or more accommodating figures did, the powerful morbidity of the Romantic movement into which, as a writer, he was born.

The Carlyle we have had in mind during the last thirty years or more is a very different character. We see a crabbed and complex person, a neurotic made for the problem-biography. Like Tolstoy, he is now almost more famous for the struggle of his married life, than for his doctrine; he is one of the keys to Puritan marriage. Turning to his work we see that his pungency, his incomparable physical portraiture and power of image-making, might have made him a supreme satirist, a writer as great as Swift, if he had lived a hundred years earlier—or perhaps in some more solid period ahead of us. His literary fame lies, for us, in his *Reminiscences* and above all in his letters. Carlyle is one of the supreme English letter-writers, and there is something tragically fitting in that—for there he was a great artist because he was no longer kicking against the pricks and was perfectly assimilated to life and his material. We must add, I think, that *Sartor Resartus* is a masterpiece of the grotesque; the strain of sanity, like the strain of simple religion and pure poetry, never dried up in him, and they worked together to make him a wonderful comic writer, one of the great clowns who are subtle with self-irony and who are untainted (on the whole, in a book like *Sartor*) by the poisons of satire.

But are we entering a new period when the kind of portrait we have just been looking at will require modification? Professor Willey, in his *Nineteenth Century Studies*, has inquired with sensibility and sympathy into the question of Carlyle's religion; and in a new, deeply considerate biography Mr. Julian Symons has patiently gone into those social and political prophesyings which, most of all, had horrified liberal and what may be called Fabian thought. He has put himself into Carlyle's shoes and has related his life to his writings in a revealing and often delightful way—for Carlyle's pitiless, unsparing, almost photographic memory of his own life has preserved incomparable material for the biographer—and in tracing the course from Chartism to contempt for the masses, he has scrupulously looked at this from the point of view of Carlyle's own time. This is, for a change, a non-theoretical book about Carlyle; I mean that there are no dramatic theories about the notorious questions of his dyspepsia, his sexual deficiency, and there is no *parti pris* on the marriage to Jane Welsh. The human Carlyle is there in his incredible stoicism, bearishness, tenderness, pathos, in his generosity, his rages and his remorse; and to the intellect, when the exaggerations are washed away, are restored the force of his remarkable insights.

The main insight, on which Carlyle was to build both sane and—in his frustration—violent and sadistic conclusions, was into the power-basis of human societies. Mr. Symons writes:

> In a time when most thinkers believed that the world could be changed by good will, he understood the basis of force upon which all modern societies rest. In a time when political economists thought that the industrial revolution must bring automatically increase in prosperity he realised that it would involve the overturning of established society. In a time of continual abstract arguments about the amount of liberty that might reasonably be allowed to

human beings, he saw that liberties are obtained by one social class at the expense of another and that they are not abstract ideas but concrete realities.

It is inevitable to argue that Carlyle's cult of the hero sprang from his own pride, from the need to find a mystical father-surrogate and an alternative to the lost Biblical God of his childhood. It is impossible not to see that the individual who had been released from its classical chains by the Romantic movement, was moving, unchecked, towards megalomania. It is natural to smile when, famous at last after years of grind, loneliness and suffering, Carlyle began to believe in the wisdom of the aristocracy who had taken him up and whom he had once nicknamed Gigmanity and Imposture. But Mr. Symons reminds us of the simplicity of Carlyle's character and the major cause of his social frustration. Looking at the condition of Victorian society he longed for action; looking at chaos he thought that it called for decisive authority. Dangerous talk. At bottom, it is clan talk. Carlyle's mind was formed in a society which still lived in the mental climate of the 17th century. One more imaginative, fanatical, dogmatic Scot had failed to understand English compromise, or our unprepossessing, semi-religious veneration of inertia. That we prefer worry to drama.

Carlyle, says Mr. Symons, was a great magician who rubbed the wrong lamps. I have a suspicion that even in his Chartist days, when his voice rings most truly, Carlyle's effect was not political in the sense that he added to the practical or theoretical thought of politics. He added, rather, to that part of the inner life of people, to the imagination above all, which may take them to religious or political action. His objection to Bentham and Mills was fundamentally the poet's or the preacher's: they had ignored the soul, they had ignored the individual's need for a vision of his own drama and significance. The most satisfactory of Carlyle's revolutionary acts was the creation of his enraging prose which, as Mr. Symons says, was an act of genius:

nothing more calculated to break the smooth classical reign, than this Gothic and Gaelic confection. It takes us back to Sterne, Mr. Symons says; but I think really it goes back to the language of another Puritan in whom the violent pressures of Puritanism had created an intense extravagance of fantasy: to the writing of Milton. I do not think Mr. Symons makes enough of the Biblical strain. It is not the canting or whining of the dissenting tabernacles, or the uttering of magical passwords. It is a hybrid in which the Gaelic and Hebraic minds are joined. Energy, rather than the moral force of Milton, binds this writing which has all the Gaelic artifice, acting and love of decoration, all the intoxication of image with image, and the peculiar Gaelic cruelty. Carlyle was a Gaelic pagan with the Biblical rhythms thumping in his head and the German absurdities cavorting inside him "in every conceivable sense." Exhausting as we may find a style as consciously allusive as *Finnegan's Wake* is, we cannot but feel our imagination enlarged. Humility vanishes, acceptance goes, egoism expands. We live no longer in the prose in which it has pleased God to call us, but suddenly have the rights of our wild poetic intuition. We recognise our genius. In other words, we become human souls. Was that not at the heart of the tragic struggle of the poor peasant Calvinist: the struggle to become not a citizen but a human being in an iron age.

*   *   *   *   *

And the marriage of the Carlyles? Because sex is the predilection of the 20th century, we have to turn to the late 18th century for the analysis of love, and to the Victorian Age for the specialists in marriage. We go, that is to say, to the professionals. For that is what the Tolstoys and the Carlyles are. No doubt enters their minds as to married monogamy being the only way and the most engrossing; their groans from the treadmill are part of their pleasure; they have the satisfaction of those who have chosen a Fate. Like Fundamentalists they live by the Book. Deeply they sus-

THE CARLYLES

pect any attempt to ameliorate this or that condition of their married life. When Geraldine Jewsbury wrote a novel which argued for the "right" of a woman for freedom to choose her love but within marriage, both the Carlyles were indignant at the "indecency" of the notion. Were they any different, one must ask, from the lovers of the 18th century, the figures of the *Liaisons Dangereuses*, of *Manon Lescaut*, or *Adolphe*, who held on just as tenaciously to the pain of their free condition; or from ourselves who cling to the privileged wounds of sexual aberration. The professional knows that part of the satisfaction is in the struggle, in the price to be paid daily. If the Tolstoys paid with their reason, and the Carlyles with their health, that is the compulsion of extremists. Their tragic genius enables us to appreciate, at its full worth, the mere talent for marriage of, say, the Brownings; just as the strategy of the *Liaisons Dangereuses* illumines the talent for the naval warfare of love in Jane Austen; just as Lawrence is the turbulent prophet of the sexual bliss, which has become free for all at any clinic.

What was it that bound the Carlyles, the most touching of unhappy and clinging couples? Sincere love and long affection, admiration, too; but that says all and nothing. Getting her blow in first, as usual, Jane Welsh said that habit was stronger in her husband than the passions. And she herself had, or came to have, short patience with them in other people. The pitiful side of her story is well-known; its sexual misery is guessed at but not certainly known; but it has always been clear that she was not the downtrodden Victorian wife. The Carlyle marriage was a marriage between equals. On the negative side, difficulty must have been a bond between these arduous Scots; Scottishness, also, with its dry appreciation of the angers and humours of domestic recollection. The couple would be just a little tough about the miseries created by bad nerves, bad health, bad temper. On the positive side, the bond was surely their tongues; they had a common taste for satire, malice, exaggeration and everything that was singular, a zest for scorn and the damaging, picturesque images it could be expressed in. At their worst moments, in the absences brought about by their disagreements or their health, each could be tantalised by the thought that the other was seeing, saying, thinking or writing exaggerations of the most intimidating piquancy. Each would be feeling the hypnotic challenges of the other's wit.

There is a quality here that makes both of them arresting. Mrs. Carlyle is one of the best letter-writers of the 19th century. He writes large and she writes small, but she rules her page, as certainly as he does his, like a circus master. Her exaggeration is conscious, too; it is not the helpless, personal hyperbole of a bosom too full. She was always fashioned to the subtle, disguising whalebone of common sense. She picks her subject and electrifies her brain. It is all irony. Why did she not, with her Jane Austenish tongue, become a novelist? Here, it is instructive to compare her with that disturbing gusher, Geraldine Jewsbury, of whom she said,

> her speech is so extremely insincere that I feel in our dialogues we are always acting in a play, and as we are not to get either money or praise for it, and not being an amateur of play-acting, I prefer good honest *silence* . . . she is as sharp as a meat axe—but as narrow.

With all her quick, fantastic interest in people, Mrs. Carlyle did not become a novelist and the gusher did. Mrs. Carlyle was too interested in hitting people off, and in keeping on top herself, for the novelist's life; she totally lacked that Messiah-producing and soulful inner glumness of the pregnant artist; or the inner silence which a Jane Austen had.

The good letter-writer has to be an egotist with a jumping mind. Even at nineteen Jane Welsh was the born boss of the notepad:

> Allons ma chère!—let us talk of the "goosish" man, my quondam lover.

He came; arrived at the George Inn at eleven o'clock at night, twelve hours after he received my answer to his letter; slept there "the more soundly" according to his statement "than was to have been expected, all the circumstances of the case being considered" and in the morning sent a few nonsensical lines to announce his nonsensical arrival. . . . In a day or two after his return . . . there came a quantity of music from him. (Pour parenthese, I shall send you a sheet of it, having another copy of *Home Sweet Home* beside.)

If Carlyle howled like a dervish, and went lamenting about his house like the Wandering Jew, when the cocks crowed or the dogs barked in the Chelsea gardens or the piano played next door, Mrs. Carlyle had a tongue. It missed nothing. One evening, the impossible Mrs. Leigh Hunt "behaved smoothly, looked devilish and was drunkish." Plain drunk would have been more amiable. When Mr. Leigh Hunt, after the same party, went downstairs and gave a lady a couple of handsome smacks as he left and whispered "God bless you, Miss Hunter," Mrs. Carlyle, with her "wonted glegness", heard! Poor Mr. Severn, so devoted to his wife, goes off to Italy alone with the sting that "people who are so devoted to their wives are apt from mere habit, to get devoted to other people's." What a power, "beside a fund of vitality" Mr. Sterling had of "getting up a sentiment about anything or nothing." And Geraldine, the never-spared, gets a letter with the immortal beginning: "Dearest Geraldine, I am sending you two men." The only way to get even with a lady as sharp as this was to use her own methods and make her laugh at herself; and this happily she could do. A young Charles Buller who had been snubbed by her on the sound Annandale ground that he was an expert philanderer and unkind to his parents, was not going to be put down. For two days she held out against him without a smile—and her face with its fine but sullen brow, its full-orbed eyes and hard mouth could look formidable— until a brilliantly silly idea occurred to him. They were all standing in the hall watching the rain fall on the Norfolk garden when the young man exclaimed, "I will shoot a hollyhock" and did so at once, bringing her the trophy with all the solemnity (the learned and topical lady writes) of Mr. Petrucci in the character of Heraclitus. She was obliged to laugh, "to the disgrace of her originality." The immoral Mr. Buller had subdued a fantastic satirist, by a fantastic act.

Mrs. Carlyle was the most amusing woman in London. Everyone with any brains came to her house. She astonished Tennyson by allowing him to smoke; she gave Mazzini many a dressing down. D'Orsay called twice: "at first sight his beauty is that of the rather disgusting sort which seems to be like genius of no sex." But he had wit and sense on the first occasion; they had diminished by the second. No longer dressed like a humming bird, he had cleverly subdued his finery to the recognition that five years had made a difference to his figure. She was quite aware, in spite of a flutter of pretence, that people like seeing her as much as they like seeing her husband; and when Carlyle was beguiled to Bath House by Lady Ashburton, there was a lively salon in Cheyne Row to put against it. And put against it it was. With the acid relish of inner loneliness, she was a great deal out and about observing the human comedy. The born letter-writer sees incident or absurdity in the smallest things and picks out what will divert the reader. This was written for the scornful preacher in Carlyle:

> A Mrs. Darbyshire, whom you saw once, came the night before last to stay while I stayed. She seems a sensible *gentlewoman* enough—a Unitarian *without the* Doctrines. But I could not comprehend at first why she had been brought, till at last Mrs. Paulet gave me to understand that she was there to use up Miss Newton. "Not," she said, "that my sister is an illiberal person, though she believes in Christ, and *all that sort of thing*. She is quite easy to live with; but it will be pleasanter for herself as well as for us that she should have somebody to talk to of her own

sort—a **Catholic or Unitarian, she doesn't mind which.**"
After this initiation I could hardly look with gravity on
these two shaking heads into one another's faces and bum-
bumming away on *religious* topics, as they flatter themselves.

And she was capable of folly. There was the wonderful
party when Dickens did his marvellous conjuring tricks,
where the crackers went bang and the champagne flowed.
She had been green, bilious and ill with her terrible nerves
when she left Cheyne Row, but here in the uproar, she was
suddenly cured. She talked mad nonsense to Thackeray;
and at the climax Forster

> seized me *round the waist*, whirled me into the thick of it
> and *made* me dance!!! Like a person in the treadmill who
> must move forward or be crushed to death! Once I cried
> out, "For the love of heaven let me go; you are going to
> dash my brains out against the folding doors!" to which
> he answered, "Your brains! Who cares about their brains
> here? Let them go."

There were other lettings go of the brain. Obviously,
taken in by Geraldine Jewsbury, she had let herself go too
far for a moment or two. She was on the verge of a "crush".
There was the Father Matthew episode, a pure case of hero
worship, when she rushed to his meeting in the East End,
and, climbing on to the platform, fell flat at the priest's feet.
She gripped his hands, burst into tears and after a few chok-
ing words gave him a memento of herself, and went home
sick and mad with exaltation. After her husband, the
Father was "the best man of modern times." But here the
ironist returned: "Had you any idea your wife was such a
fool?" And there was the sobering reflection that "the
Father got through the thing admirably."

There must have been a good deal of "getting through
the thing" at Cheyne Row. It was, for all its ready sociability, a fort, with the old warrior upstairs, bloody and

unbowed, and herself the sentinel below. They had, in this marriage, the belligerence and tenderness of soldiers. Her letters amuse like a novel because they catch the hour-to-hour life, the alarms and domesticity of this peculiar garrison. We are spared the hysteria of a Countess Tolstoy, for Jane Welsh and her husband were stoics; when the woe, the illness, the insomnia, the loneliness, the jealousy come through, and the wary hardness that followed their insoluble differences, it comes through a mind capable of some self-criticism. Strangely, it is not the *suffering* that moves one—only by an effort can one sympathise with neurotic or imaginary suffering, for one is always aware of how strong and relentless the neurotics are—rather, the happiness, the devotion, the love and the deep deposit of friendship that accumulate in a marriage, and the exquisite pain of the passage of time, that bring tears to the eyes. How quickly the early excitement goes; how warmly the devotion expands; how strong the ties between the contestants become. The Carlyle marriage becomes an archetype of the marriage of genius. We owe to Mrs. Carlyle an intimate picture of a remarkable man caught, as in the Laocoon, by his own gifts; not once is there any attempt at that reckless, destructive criticism of his work, which animal jealousy and mania aroused in a woman like the Countess Tolstoy, unless the journals Mrs. Carlyle destroyed contained such outbursts.

If both the Carlyles had a terrible power of speech—when one regards them from the Marriage Council point of view—they took a comic pride in the dramatic effect of their silences. Carlyle said hers was terrifying: and he would know, for he has given us a notion of his own when he speaks of resting on "the iron pillar of silence and despair". Mrs. Carlyle denied she was a jealous woman when Geraldine Jewsbury was invited to stay, but the over-quickness of her denial, her clever turning of jealousy into what she could claim was ordinary worldly percipience about the effect of pushing young women on distinguished men, give her away.

THE CARLYLES

She was an exceedingly jealous woman. Carlyle, similarly, appears not to be a jealous man: she had far more men (and women) in varying states of passion for her, than he had women. He never objected. *His* jealousy was directed outside the home, at other writers. We owe to him the most brilliant, destructive, ill-tempered portraits of the chief figures of his time: Lamb sodden with gin, Godwin vacuously playing cards, Emerson thin as a reed and with a head like a starved cockerel's. He could pretend that these caricatures were quintessences caught by an infallible artist in the godly or the grotesque, and not the jealousy of a tormented egotist. Her caprice must be matched by his manias; his determination to hold the floor, by her determination to manage the table. It was sufficient to give either of them a present or to offer money, to insult them. If he saw through every other writer she saw through every woman, especially every married woman, the moment they opened their mouths. If she made a dead set at the husband of every woman who came into the room, especially if he were famous, Carlyle, just as possessive as a prophet, took possession of every major aspect of the fate of England.

There was fire in both of them. There was also porridge—the curious, flat, short-tasting gift for finding nourishment in daily, domestic ironies which, when one looks back on the lame attempts to describe love in Scottish novels, appears to be its sentimental substitute. How the Carlyle marriage recalls those domestic scenes (so often placed in the sculleries, kitchens, and backyards) of the novels of Scott and Stevenson, where scolding, clatter, a gift of tongues, retort and counter-attack are the language of love, and raised from squalor by the wanton bellicosity of the Gaelic imagination.

The archetypal marriages—and the Carlyles' was the archetype of the wedding of wit and genius—owe their position to the outspokenness of the parties. The Tolstoy diaries! The Carlyle letters! Can human happiness survive so much forthrightness? The Carlyles were saved because they admired each other's wit. Their worst agonies seem not to have come from their common hypochondria, her jealousy or his monstrous selfishness, but from not getting letters from each other on the day they were expected when they were separated. It is the most moving thing about them: their craving for the other's voice. But behind her skill and humour, behind her simplicity, behind the habit of a certain obdurate competition with each other lay something one can only call primitive. Like some couple out of a novel by D. H. Lawrence—some anti-phallic couple one must say and Carlyle, oddly, uses the word—they had built, open-eyed, a contest of essences and prides.

12

Boswell's London

THE discovery of cache after cache of Boswell's manuscripts, journals and letters at Malahide and Fettercairn between 1925 and 1948 is one of the truly extraordinary events in the history of English letters. It gave us the original journal of the *Tour to the Hebrides*, before the war and now we have a totally new manuscript, appearing 180-odd years after it was written. This is the London journal which Boswell wrote in 1762 and 1763 when, twenty-three years old, he came to London to get a commission in the Guards, and, failing in that, met the man who was to be his god, his subject and his insurance of fame. What, we wonder, will be the state of our old editions of the *Life* of Johnson when the manuscripts yet to be seen are published? The *Life* has been a kind of lay scripture to the English, for it contains thought in our favourite, pragmatic form, that is to say, masticated by character. The book has been less a biography than a sort of parliamentary dialogue containing a thundering government and an adoring and obliging opposition. It will be strange if the proverbial and traditional characters are altered, though in the last generation the clownish Boswell has risen in esteem, and beyond Macaulay's derision. He has changed from the burr on the Doctor's coat-tails into an original blossom of the psychological hothouse.

Here we get on the dangerous ground of Plutarchian contrast. If Boswell created himself, we must never forget that Johnson made that possible. We lean to Boswell now because we have been bred on psychologists rather than philosophers, and love to see a man drowning in his own contradictions and self-exposures. The Doctor, who believed in Virtue, believed inevitably in repression, where we have been taught that it is immoral to hide anything. Boswell's very lack of foundation, his lack of judgment, are seen merely as the price he pays for the marvellous fluidity, transparency and curiosity of his nature. Dilapidation is his genius. Yet if Boswell is a genius we cannot forget that the Doctor is a saint, a man of richer and more sombre texture than his parasite. He is a father-figure, but not in the mechanical fashion of psychological definition; he is a father-figure enlarged by the religious attribute of tragedy. It was the tragic apprehension that was above all necessary for the steadying of Boswell's fluctuating spirit and for the sustaining of his sympathetic fancy.

The marvel is that at the age of twenty-three Boswell was already turning his gifts upon himself in the *Journal*. Professor Pottle, his lively American editor, thinks that his detachment is more complete than that of Pepys or Rousseau. Boswell's picture of himself has indeed the accidental and unforeseeable quality of life which better organised, more sapient or more eloquent natures lose the moment they put pen to paper. Boswell's detachment comes from naïveté and humility. He was emotionally surprised by himself. To one who had been knocked off his balance by a severe Presbyterian upbringing the world is bound to be a surprising place. To those who have lived under intense pressure, what happens afterwards is a miracle and release is an historical event. If the will has been destroyed by a parent like Lord Auchinleck, it may be replaced by a shiftless melancholy, an abeyance of spirits, and, from that bewilderment, all life afterwards will seem an hallucination, when a high-blooded young man engages ingenuously with it.

There is an obscure period in Boswell's youth when he joined the Roman Catholic Church. We do not know whether passion, giddiness, his irrational fears, or his tendency to melancholy, moved him to this step. But native canniness got him out of the scrape which socially and materially would have been a disaster in that age, and we can be grateful that the confessional did not assuage what Puritan diarising has preserved. For that confession contains more than an account of his sins; it contains his sillinesses, his vanities, moods, snobberies, the varying temperatures of his aspirations. "I have a genius for Physick," he says. For what did he not think he had genius? If only he could find out how to develop it! No symptom was too small when he studied the extraordinary illness, the remarkable fever, the very illusion of being a Self, James Boswell.

Exhibitionism? Vanity? The *Journal* was not private. It was posted every week to a friend, one of the inevitable devotions of the hero-worshipper. It is amazing that a young man should be an ass with such art, that judgment should not sprout anywhere. How rare to see a fool persisting in folly to the point of wisdom. One of the earliest comedies in the book is his lamentable affair with the actress Louisa. Calculation is at the bottom of it. Meanness runs through it, yet it is an exquisitely defenceless tale. In time he hoped to have a mistress who was a woman of fashion, but social inexperience and poverty—he is wonderfully stingy, a real hungry Scot of the period—held him back. As an actress Louisa could *cheaply* create the illusion of the woman of fashion. All this is innocently revealed later by introspection; at the beginning he is all fine feeling. To emphasise the fineness of the feeling, he astutely points out, in his first timid advances to Louisa, that love is above monetary considerations. Presently he begins to believe his own propaganda; he is in love and to the extent of lending the woman £2. In the seduction, his sexual powers at first disappoint and then suddenly surpass anything he (or Louisa) has ever heard of. The next time he has a shock. Love has vanished. He is an unstable character. Presently he discovers she has introduced him to the "Signor Gonorrhœa." Despair, rage, moral indignation—can he have left the path of Virtue?—hard bargainings with the surgeon, melancholy, the ridicule of friends, nothing to do but to stay at home and read Hume's *History*. Philosophy calms him until the surgeon sends his bill. (In the matter of cash, the dissolving selves of Boswell always come together with certainty.) He writes to Louisa, points out what she has cost him, and asks for his £2 back, and says he is being generous. The doctor's bill was £5:

> Thus ended my intrigue with the fair Louisa which I flattered myself so much with and from which I expected at least a winter's safe copulation.

To be so transparent, thinking neither of the impression he makes upon himself nor of the figure he will cut before his friend, is possibly to be fatuous. But Boswell's fatuousness, which seems to arise from a lack of will or centre in his life, is inspired. Instead of will, Boswell had that mysterious ingredient of the soul, so admired in the age of sensibility: "my genius", or, as we would say, his Id. On that point only is his *amour propre* unyielding. Drowning in midstream, unable to reach the shore of Virtue and swept back into Vice and Folly, he clings to the straw of his "genius" and spins round and round until, what is he but a frantic work of art?

"How well I write!" he exclaims, after flattering a peer in six lines of doggerel. How wonderfully "facetious" he is with the Earl, how wonderful are "the sallies of my luxuriant imagination."

> How easily and cleverly do I write just now! I am really pleased with myself, words come skipping to me like lambs upon Moffat Hill; and I turn my periods smoothly and imperceptibly like a skilful wheelwright turning tops in a turning loom. There's a fancy! There's a simile.

Sheridan punctures him brutally, but Garrick comes along:

> "Sir," said he, "you will be a great man. And when you are so, remember the year 1763. I want to contribute my part towards saving you. And pray, will you fix a day when I shall have the pleasure of treating you with tea." I fixed the next day. "Then Sir," said he, "the cups shall dance and the saucers skip."

Like Moffat lambs, no doubt; fancy has been at work on Garrick's talk. Boswell continues innocently:

> What he meant by my being a great man I can understand. For really, to speak seriously, I think there is a blossom about me of something more distinguished than the generality of mankind.

If only it can be left to grow, instead of being chilled by "my melancholy temper" and dishevelled by "my imbecility of mind." The extraordinary thing is that a man so asinine should be so right.

The words of a man fuddled by middle-age? No, we have to remind ourselves, they are the words of a coxcomb of twenty-three. Hypochondria, as well as the prose manner of the time, has doubled his age. "Taking care of oneself is amusing," he says, filling his spoon with medicine. Life is an illness we must enjoy. In goes the thermometer at every instance. How is the genius for greatness? How is the fever for getting into the Guards, for chasing after English peers and avoiding the Scottish—if their accents are still bad—the fever for the theatre, for planning one's life, for wrecking the plan by the pursuit of "monstrous" whores or by fanciful fornication on Westminster Bridge; the fever for wit; for being like Mr. Addison; for a trip down the river; for lashings of beef; for cutting down his expenses and for freedom from error and infidelity in the eyes of Providence? Boswell goes round London with his biography hanging out of his mouth like the tongue of a panting dog, until the great climax comes. "I am glad we have met," says the Doctor, and the dog with the genius beneath the skin has found its master.

Boswell's picture of life in London drawing-rooms, coffee-houses, taverns and streets is wonderful. It is done by a man much alone—and such make the best observers—to whom every word heard is precious. Listening to the plays, listening to the ordinary talk at Child's, he makes his first experiment in that dramatic dialogue which later was to give the *Life* its crowning quality. His ear is humble at Child's:

> 1st citizen: Pray, doctor, what became of that patient of yours? Was not her skull fractured?
> Physician: Yes, To pieces. However, I got her cured.
> 2nd citizen: Good Lord!

Transparency is his gift of nature; affectability turns it into art; his industry, above all, fashions it. For Boswell stumbled soon upon the vital discovery that experience is three parts hallucination, when he made up his diary, not dryly on the spot but three or four days late. He had, as his present American editor shrewdly points out, a *little* foreknowledge His "genius" taught him to prepare the way for surprises which the reader could not know. It is one of his cunning strokes—he was not a regular theatre-goer for nothing—to repeat to Louisa, at the calamitous end of the affair, the words she had primly used at the beginning of it: "Where there is no confidence, there is no bond." And he is plotting, too, for that moment—surely handed to him by his Genius and not by Life—when she will send his £2 back in a plain envelope without a word. To illustrate, no doubt, his genius for stinginess. By the end, when the Doctor comes, the *Journal* overlaps the *Life*, but until then this is new Boswell, disordered and unbosomed.

13
Swift to Stella

THE literature of common sense is a gift of the early 18th century; it derives from the citizens' view of life. Hence, after reading, say, Swift's *Letter to a Very Young Lady* our pleasure and our restlessness. What excellent advice and yet, what a slaughter of the innocents—the innocent instincts and emotions—has been committed before the advice could be uttered. In Swift, at any rate, common sense has been arrived at, only by a lifelong pruning of the random buds, a ruthless cutting back; in the end we have the impression of reading epitaphs on human hope, and what is displayed as the sensible view of life, disturbs us with an underlying suggestion of anger, mutilation and misanthropy. There is a double sense in everything Swift wrote that imposes a strain upon our reading of him; we feel the rod of an over-ruling will and it is only at those times when we ourselves are capable of rancour, passion and the spleen that the iron touch in his simple, deceptive writing can really be endured for long. Swift's words arrive on the page with the regular tap of a day's rain, monotonously clear, and positive in its sting; but they shut us into our own house, and it is not until we, too, have reached his point of bitter claustrophobia, it is not until we think of all that we have lost by having to sit inside, that the spell begins to work.

Once we are shut in and can gaze at the foolish world from which we are cut off by contempt, Swift can affect us; but before that happens his habit of reducing everything to the plain terms of personal business makes the *Drapier Letters* a labour to read and *The Tale of a Tub* sound like a tedious piece of fantastic personal litigation, an old case flogged by a rasping and pedantic lawyer who cannot bear a hatred to die or an old folly to be forgotten. The very plainness is the argument for Swift's innate madness; so that even when his imagination is at its most savage or its most freakish, in *Gulliver* or in *A Modest Proposal*, he distracts us by the smallness and homeliness of his means. Is this the new minute method of science or the pestering of the local archaeologist? Is he putting on the knowing humdrum of the careerist politician who knows how to hammer the homeliest instances into the thick, self-infested head of the plain man? Or is it the humanism of the century?

Questions like these must harass the inquiring reader as he listens to the dry Dean cracking his facts and his arguments, as the busy Franklin dished out his endless proverbs or the plain Defoe put his draper's yardstick on human circumstance. But after reading a Defoe or a Franklin, nothing happens to us; after Swift, also, for a little while; and then, old wounds begin to burn, old sores to open, and old infirmities awaken under our skins. He has revived in us our personal hatreds, he has revived and exacerbated angers that we thought we had forgotten; out of his local instances he has raised the universal pain. And with such undermining violence does his simple method work, that our pain is, as it were, reflected back upon his own character and his legend: the Swift legend walks again, haunting and terrible. Like him, when this power of his falls upon us, we cry "I am a fool" and will our money to the madhouse. He has retaught us our personal megalomania.

When the Dean's legend begins to walk in our thoughts, the exact impression of him vanishes. Any lie, any anecdotal invention, any imaginative guess about a legendary figure seems more acceptable and revealing than what the strict evidence will concede. This is especially true of Swift. He was a careerist and a secretive man. Now it is true that secretive men are often without interesting secrets and that careerists are surrounded by enemies only too eager to suggest that they have; but even the least suspicious of biog-

SWIFT TO STELLA

raphers would have to concede that certain mysteries of Swift's life make him unaccountable.

Was he impotent? Was he the bastard of Temple? Was he Stella's half-brother? Was he married to Stella, as early biographers believed? Did Vanessa challenge Stella with this story in that dramatic scene which Scott has described? Was Vanessa his mistress? Can the little language be so interpreted as to mean, in two direct references, that he thought of Stella as his wife; and are the very blots and evasions in the manuscripts part of a double secrecy in their code? Such questions go to Baconian lengths of fantasy; we have to reject them as fabrications and tittle-tattle, as Mr. Bernard Acworth does in his latest study. And yet we do so with reluctance because they would give us a Swift less inhuman than the monster who rises from the strict evidence; they would soften an egotism or a pride which are appallingly self-contained.

Mr. Acworth's interest is to discover in Swift the Christian and the moralist. Swift's relation with Stella is presented as a perhaps presumptuous but, at any rate, a noble attempt to advance the minds of women to a higher plane; but Mr. Acworth might also have pointed out that Swift's great power over women may have been due to his profession and his rudeness to them. The book is readable but it has the weakness of Christian urgency and I cannot believe that Mr. Acworth has taken the most revealing approach to Swift's genius. The scholarly discretion of Mr. Harold Williams in his new, meticulous and exhaustive edition of the *Journal to Stella* is more rewarding. With him the legends vanish at once; what cannot be proved he will not have. We are not likely, for example, loosely to accuse Swift of changing his party for reasons of power or favour, before weighing this against Swift's purpose in coming to England; on the other hand, even after reading Mr. Williams's defence, the character of Swift himself strides into our minds. Had he no appetite for power, the man who would make the great Harley come half-way to meet him? He hated faction, but why? He was an intolerant High Churchman; was faction a vice because it interfered with his friendships or because it thwarted his despotic nature?

The cool-headedness of Mr. Williams's summing up is a severe preparation for a book so intimate, so revealing and yet so unbetraying as the *Journal*—unbetraying in the sense that it keeps the shell of Swift hard and can be quoted like Scripture, for and against. The *Journal* is the complete picture of a man managing himself, managing the full team of his affairs with the rein in hand—career, friends, love and health all trot together; none can get out of his hard and playful grip:

> Morning. I am going this morning to see Prior who dines with me at Mr. Harley's; so I cant stay fiddling and talking with dear little brats in a morning, and tis still terribly cold—I wish my cold hand was in the warmest place about you, young women, I'd give ten guineas upon that account with all my heart, faith; oh, it starves my thigh; so I'll rise, and bid you good-morrow, my ladies both, good morrow. Come stand away, let me rise: Patrick, take away the candle. Is there a good fire? So—up a dazzy. At Night. My Harley did not sit down till six, and I staid till eleven; henceforth I will chuse to visit him in the evenings, and dine with him no more if I can help it. It breaks all my measures, and hurts my health; my head is disorderly, but not ill and I hope it will mend.

And money is there too—how often money trots with the successful team. Are we to think him avaricious? Mr. Williams thinks not; is it then an aspect of the exhausting matter-of-factness of his nature?

> Lord Halifax is always teazing me to go down to his country house, which will cost me a guinea to his servants and twelve shillings coach hire; and he shall be hanged first. . . .

or something else to be cunning about:

SWIFT TO STELLA

I dined with Mr. Lewis of the Secretary's office at his lodgings: the chairmen that carried me squeezed a great fellow against a wall, who wisely turned his back, and broke one of the side glasses in a thousand pieces. I fell a scolding, pretended I was like to be cut to pieces, and made them set down the chair in the Park, while they pickt out the bits of glasses: and when I paid them, I quarrelled still, so they dared not grumble, and I came off for my fare; but I was plaguily afraid they would have said, God bless your honour, wont you give us something for our glass? Lewis and I were forming a project how I might get three or four hundred pounds which I suppose may come to nothing.

The portrait that we build up from this prattle is not of the madman or the terrible Dean; nor indeed of the man who had flayed the soul of Varina with his words:

> I shall be blessed to have you in my arms, without regarding whether your person be beautiful or your fortune large: cleanliness in the first, and competency in the other, is all I look for.

but of a man, without mysteries in his life, spryly attending to his business. The childishness of the little language:

> Well, well, we'll have day-light shortly, spight of her teeth; and zoo must cly Lele and Hele and Hele aden. Must loo mimitate pdfr, pay? Iss, and so la shall. And so leles fol ee reetle. Dood Mollow.

comes as expertly to him as the way to handle a Prime Minister or terrorise a Duke.

Why do we read on and on through these 700 pages? Their events are reduced to shorthand. Compared with the letters to Pope or the great array of lords and bishops (letters more polished, far richer in judgment or comedy, even in masculine affection) the *Journal to Stella* is a ragbag of jottings about people we do not know. We are in the candle smoke of the great world, but we have to rack our memories of history to place the quarrel of St. John and Harley, to fit in the orgiastic figure of Marlborough and to remember which European war they were arguing about. Who are all these supplicants at the Court, why is this Duchess less important than that? One looks to Mr. Harold Williams's notes: they are as mysterious as Debrett is to the uninstructed. And yet, one does read on. What is the fascination? It is, I think the fascination of the magnifying glass. Swift puts it into our hands and, behold, everything is out of proportion; a corner of a room becomes larger than the room itself, an hour at the coffee house fills a day: the entrancing, minute glimpses of London life in the 18th-century crowd out the generalities of history; we are given the intensely distorting glass of private life into our hands. The boredom we have felt has not been the boredom of dull writing, but the charming ennui of the busy life itself. The lackey is drunk again. Have I strained my thumb, or is it the gout? It rains, it snows, it blows. Now the sun shines. Here is a bit of gossip only you will understand. Guess who is thinking of whom now. I dreamed that I was in Ireland without my clothes: "Oh, that we were at Laracor this fine day! The willows begin to peep and the quicks to bud."

So the trivialities enlarge under the glass of this extraordinary egotism: they are the threads of an ambition, the iridescence of a success. Here rather than in the diplomatic bag of Swift's correspondence with his contemporaries—correspondence which was measured and cut to the fine fashion of the period—will be found the affray of his genius; for here he is in Lilliput itself, now large and hard with power, now small as Tom Thumb acting his part. Here, too, in the very objectivity of the writing, its sudden jump not from thought to thought but from thing to thing, we see the mark of his isolation: all things, for the egotist, the madman of tomorrow, are related to one another only through him. Only he knows; only he controls; only he has the sense, the clarity of mind, the sanity. But, when we turn from the

Journal to some other piece of his writing, we feel the temper rising as the clear prose rains down in its regular drops, and our legend making begins: for only Swift knows the price of that appalling pride and in what mysterious transactions of his life, he paid it.

14

The Unhappy Traveller

THERE is one in every boat train that leaves Victoria, in every liner that leaves New York, in every bar of every hotel all over the world: the unhappy traveller. He is travelling not for pleasure but for pain, not to broaden the mind but, if possible, to narrow it; to release the buried terrors and hatreds of a lifetime; or, if these have already had a good airing at home, to open up colonies of rage abroad. We listen to these martyrs, quarrelling with hotel keepers, insulting cooks, torturing waiters and porters, the scourges of the reserved seat and viragos of the sleeping car. And when they return from their mortifications it is to insult the people and the places they have visited, to fight the battle over the bill or the central heating, again and again, with a zest so sore that we conclude that travel for them is a continuation of domestic misery by other means.

Character that provokes fuss or incident is valuable to the writer of travel books, and it is surprising that this liverish nature, so continuously provocative, has rarely been presented. I do not forget the hostile travellers who, after being cosseted by the best hotels, turn round and pull their hosts to pieces, but to those who travel because they hate travelling itself. Of these Smollett is the only good example I can think of, and after 180 years his rage still rings out. Why is he still readable? Literature is made out of the misfortunes of others. A large number of travel books fail simply because of the intolerable, monotonous good luck of their authors. Then, it is a pleasure to be the spectator and not the victim of bad temper. Again, Smollett satisfies a traditional and secret rancour of the English reader: our native dislike of the French even when we are francophile; and recalls to us the old blisters of travel, the times *we* have been cheated, the times *we* threatened to call the police, the times when *we* could not face the food or the bedroom. But these are minor reasons for Smollett's readableness. We could, if we wanted to do so, let out a louder scream ourselves. Smollett is readable because he is a lucid author—as the maddened often are—writing, as Sir Osbert Sitwell says in his well-packed preface to a new edition, "in a beautifully clear, easy, ordered, but subtle English, a style partly the result of nature, and partly of many years of effort." It is the sane, impartial style which makes his pot-boiling *History of England* still worth dipping into and *Humphrey Clinker* nutritious to the end.

There is one more explanation of his instant readability. There is an ambiguity, always irresistible, in books of travel if in some way the unguarded character of the author travels with him like a shadow on the road. Smollett draws his own dour, stoical, irascible character perfectly. It is vital, too, that the author should have an interesting mind. Smollett has. He is not a gentleman on tour, but a doctor, and he carries the rash habit of diagnosis with him. His observations, like his quarrels, are built up with light but patient documentation. His passions are not gouty explosions, but come because his sense of fact, order and agreement has been in some minor particular outraged. It is laughable, but before the end we feel a touch of pity. If (it had slowly been borne in on him by the time his journey was done) he had been content to be cheated a little, to pay a trifle extra, to forget the letter of his bargains, if he had not bothered about the odd sous, he would have travelled faster in comfort and happiness. Alas, it was impossible. The one-time ship's surgeon who had made his own way in the world on little education, whose sense of inferiority had not been reduced either by a rich marriage nor by great monetary success in his profession, who had been thrown into prison (and very rightly) for libel after an outrageous attack on his admiral, and had sought out gratuitous quarrels with every English writer of his time, was not the man to allow others any latitude. The quarrel was what he wanted. Since the author of *Tom Jones* was not on the Continent Smollett took it out of the innkeepers.

It began on the Dover Road where

> the chambers are in general cold and comfortless, the bed paltry, the cooking execrable, the wine poison, the attendance bad, the publicans insolent; there is not a tolerable drop of malt liquor to be had from London to Dover.

It continues in Boulogne where the people are filthy, lazy, "incompetent in the mechanical arts", priest-ridden, immoral, their wine bad—he drank no good wine in France—and their cooking worse. Smollett, who was travelling with his wife and servants, five persons in all, preferred to buy and prepare his own food, such were his British, albeit Scottish, suspicions of the French *ragoût*. As for the French character, vanity is "the great and universal mover of all varieties and degrees." A Frenchman will think he owes it to his self-esteem to seduce your wife, daughter, niece and even your grandmother; if he fails he deplores their poor taste; if you reproach him, he will reply that he could not give higher proof of his regard for your family:

> You know Madam [Smollett writes to an imaginary correspondent], we are naturally taciturn, soon tired of impertinence, and much subject to fits of disgust. Your French friend intrudes upon you at all hours: he stuns you with his loquacity: he teases you with impertinent questions about your domestic and private affairs; he attempts to meddle in your concerns; and forces his advice upon you with unwearied importunity; he asks the price of everything you wear and, so sure as you tell him, undervalues it, without hesitation: he affirms it is bad taste, ill-contrived, ill-made; that you have been imposed upon both with respect to fashion and the price. . . .

Has this race of egotists and *petits-maîtres* any virtues? They

THE UNHAPPY TRAVELLER

have "natural capacities" (it appears) but ruined by giddiness and levity and the education of the Jesuits. It is, however, unfair to describe them as insincere and mean:

> High flown professions of friendship and attachment constitute the language of common compliment in this country, and are never supposed to be understood in the literal acceptation of the words; and if their acts of generosity are rare, we ought to ascribe that rarity not so much to a deficiency of generous sentiments, as to their vanity and ostentation, which, engrossing all their funds, utterly disable them from exerting the virtues of beneficence.

No, there is nothing to be said for the French. Their towns are often better than their inhabitants and in the descriptions of places we see Smollett's virtue as a writer. Clearly, like some architectural draughtsman, ingeniously contriving his perspectives, he has the power to place a town, its streets, its industries, its revenues and even its water supply, before us like a marvellous scale model. We get a far clearer notion of what a French town was like in the 1760s than we can form for ourselves of an English town today. Smollett was a sick man on this journey, he was travelling in search of health, and he brings to what he sees the same diagnostic care that he brought to the illnesses of others or his own; but he had grown up under the matter-of-fact and orderly direction of his time. Even when one of his inevitable rows begins—he swears he has been given bad horses, bad servants, bad meals, made to wait beyond his turn at the coaching stations and so on—they are conducted with all the sense of orderly manœuvre which he must have observed in his life at sea. We know exactly where he sat and where the innkeeper stood when the row began, and how often the doctor banged up the window of the coach and—one can see his ugly, peevish, stone-yellow face, for in a fit of repentance he describes it—refused to budge until the bargain was fulfilled to the letter. The astonishing thing is that he is always defeated; but petulance has no authority.

BOOKS IN GENERAL

Here is a typical upset at Brignolles—it was followed by worse at Luc: there the whole town turned out to see the defeat of the Doctor:

> At Brignolles, where we dined, I was obliged to quarrel with the landlady, and threatened to leave her house, before she would indulge us with any sort of fresh meat. It was meagre day, and she had made her provision accordingly. She even hinted some dissatisfaction at having heretics in the house; but I was not disposed to eat stinking fish, with ragouts of eggs in onions. . . . Next day when we set out in the morning from Luc, it blew a north-westerly wind so extremely cold and biting that even a flannel wrapper could not keep me warm in the coach. Whether the cold had put our coachman in a bad humour, or he had some other cause of resentment against himself, I know not; but when we had gone about a quarter of a mile, he drove the carriage full against the corner of a garden wall and broke the axle tree.

"Resentment against himself!" Smollett would understand that. It is the antidote to Sterne.

A useful and detailed *Life* of Smollett has just been written by a conscientious American scholar, Mr. Lewis Mansfield Knapp. One sees that Smollett, caught between Grub Street and the gentleman writers, a commercially popular professional who made enough money to employ ghosts and hacks, was a man of hyper-sensitive, jealous yet remorseful temper, ardent and generous, yet easily stung and quick to sting. His sensibility has led to the suggestion that the passages of grossness and brutality, his chamber-pot humour, are not the broad comedy of a man who liked a dirty joke and the writing on the lavatory wall, but disclose a horror of the flesh, the wincing of the man with a skin too few. Like many doctors, he jokes brutally about the body because it shocks him. Up to a point this seems to me certainly true: to deny it is to deny the double mind of many eighteenth-century writers who were not less moved to

THE UNHAPPY TRAVELLER

reform manners because it happened to pay them to be gross and licentious in presenting the case. Smollett in his *Travels* is a fastidious man; he has the doctor's dislike of filth and the eighteenth century (as we see again in the case of Swift) saw the beginning of a hatred of filth in the person and the home. The bad temper of Smollett, though it was aggravated by ill-health, became, to some extent, a protest against the squalor, incompetence and cruelty which impeded the sensible desires of the civilised man. He liked decorum. He hated the raffish, the Bohemian and the wild. He was, in short, one of the earliest respectable men, when respectability was a weapon of reform; when it meant that you were jeered at for objecting to capital punishment, flogging, the public exposure of bodies broken on the wheel by the roadside, and the maddening disorderliness of a system of travel which belonged to the middle ages and not to 1763. Smollett's temper was, in some respects, a new, frost-bitten bud of civilisation, of which sick, divided and impossible men are frequently the growing point.

15

Maupassant

WHEN, as a young man, Maupassant sat in the talkative company of writers and was asked why he was silent, he used to say, "I am learning my trade"; and that is what the hostile criticism of his work comes down to in the end. That he learned, and some better writers never have. He is one of the dead-sure geniuses, a hunter without a blank in his magazine. What one means by Maupassant's genius—for he was very limited in his range and depth of subject—is hard to say. The opening chapters of *Une Vie*, and many of the Seine stories, are Tolstoyan: there is the same limpid, timeless animal eye, alert without innocence to every movement, to every blink of light and shadow. There is the same crisp lick of the feathered surface by the perfect sculler. The difference is that Tolstoy is a man and Maupassant is a male; that Tolstoy is a man who can repent, Maupassant a machine that can only wear out. Or we might say, as Henry James did, that Maupassant is unable to reflect and that the existence of an inner life astonished him and struck him as being a surprising pathos. Conrad said "such is the greatness of his talent that all his high qualities appear in the very things of which he speaks, as if they had been altogether independent of his presentation." Life itself seems to be writing his best stories, to have inked itself upon the page; the only thing that makes one wish to qualify such a statement is that Maupassant was fly enough to say something of the kind himself in one of his letters which is quoted in the *Louis Conard* edition of his works. He is too consciously the successful writer to be trusted:

> No, my spirit is not decadent. I am quite unable to look inside myself; I am dominated by the unceasing, involun-

tary effort of penetrating the souls of others. Really it is not I who make the effort: what is around me penetrates and possesses *me*. I am impregnated by it, I give myself to it, I drown in the flow of my surroundings.

A feminine and passive analogy. It was learned from Flaubert and many writers have since professed it. One has noticed that the writers who train themselves to *be* life in this way become, in fact, less than life; and when Maupassant says he is unable to look inside, that is to say to record the human wish to enlarge life (as Chekhov did), one suspects he means he is unwilling to succeed: one must limit one's objectives. There, possibly, we have the hint that Maupassant's genius was not inclusive, like Tolstoy's, but selective and taught.

Like pretty well all Maupassant's work, *Une Vie* is a story from a life very close to his own. The book is his first novel. It arises from Maupassant's strongest emotion: his feeling for his mother. Jeanne, transposed into a Flaubertian key, is Laure Maupassant. Jeanne is a Madame Bovary who is not drawn to adultery by reading romances, but who is made obstinately innocent of the world by them. She receives one brutal shock after another in a life of virtue which seems touching but obtuse.

Laure Maupassant was a woman of more nerve and brain than Jeanne, who is at heart the conventional upper-class bride of the period; but Jeanne's story is Laure's in essentials. In the first place Jeanne is given a family rather more distinguished than Laure's. On both sides, the Maupassants came of moneyed mercantile families. It was Maupassant's father who quietly interposed the aristocratic *de* with its touch of the Trade Mark. Jeanne's father is, however, noticeably not a parvenu when Maupassant tells *her* story. He is the agreeable, spendthrift country gentleman whose fortunes are dissolved by the impulses of eighteenth-century philosophy. The Maupassants who moved into the chateau in Normandy were climbers who overspent on the way up;

they were hard as the rich bourgeois are; they were committed to success, and were drily scornful of the aristocracy of the old regime who creaked like marionettes taken out of the cupboards of their damp and solitary houses. Maupassant, who was trained by his mother to hate his womanising father, hated him far more for giving him no money and making him work as a poor clerk in a government office. The clerking injured Maupassant's pride, and it irked the sense of efficiency which is the strongest instinct of the self-made rich.

It is impossible to know what hardens the heart, what checks the impulse to "look inside." In a general way we can surmise that the broken home of the Maupassants had fixed the detachment, the watchfulness, the habit of *surveillance* in the child; hardness of heart comes, perhaps, from being forced by one's imperilled situation to be continually on the look out. When Laure left Maupassant's father, the son stepped into his place in the home, and there are instances of iron-willed impudence in his childhood which show that he was precociously aware of his powerful position as the supplanting male. Again and again (as Mr. Steegmuller, an American biographer has pointed out) his stories are of humiliated women and cuckolded men. There must have been precise scenes that remained in his memory all his life; perhaps that scene in *Garçon! Un Bock!* where a man recalls how, as a frightened child, he secretly witnessed a violent quarrel between his father and mother in which the mother is struck to the ground. Such scenes awake double emotions in a child, and they are not a pleasure to recall. They certainly fix in the child's mind a precocious, ungraduated and crude conviction that human relations are to be reduced at once to a question of animal dominance. To see life naked too young is never to observe, later on, that, characteristically, life is dressed. The animal watchfulness of Maupassant is the watchfulness of a childhood not outgrown; his cynicism is the recognition that he is like the father whom he can never cease to hate. And why should he "look inside", in any case?

Evil, the child has seen, comes from the outside. It is the outside that must be watched and, towards the end of his life, the very title of *Le Horla*—"what is outside"—shows that the horrors come from an outside world that cannot be trusted. In the last stages of syphilis, this was Maupassant's terror: that the world would crash inwards upon a nature which, for all its assiduity, could not make itself hard, efficient, drastic, sealed off and settled enough.

Time is the subject of *Une Vie*. It is the pervasive theme of a large number of his stories. The early destruction of his moral sense—which was replaced only by an acceptance of the conventional moral sense of his class—led Maupassant to see the teeth of time eating up everything. It is disgusting of the Vicomte to betray Jeanne, but as time goes by Jeanne's virtue becomes something like stupidity. Live and let live; life will turn out to be neither as good nor as bad as we think. If we live long enough we shall see things turn into their opposites. So strong and harsh are these passive sentiments in Maupassant that it is strange that time is bungled in *Une Vie*; after the miraculous clear and truthful picture of a girl's awakening to love, at first painful and then mature, after the shock, the novel scrambles hurriedly over the years, in too great a haste to point the moral and turn the irony. There is evidence that Maupassant altered and corrected the plot many times; he was at home only in the disconnected episode. His nervous nature needed to work in a limited field; his intense feeling for time is a feeling for its minutes which became, as it were, concrete. The more slowly his narrative moves, watching dream change to love and love to desire, the more certain is he to put his finger upon the exact shiver of change. Out of this is born his wonderful awareness of the feelings of women who are more sensitive to the climatic changes of feeling than men are. Few chapters in any love story can equal Maupassant's descriptions of the marriage night and the honeymoon of Jeanne; for it is the sense of change in sexual experience, the sense of the hours or the days going by, which enables him to write of sexual experience explicitly. In his preoccupation with the sexual act in every conceivable circumstance from the brutal and the comic to the ecstatic, there is always an unruffled observation of the changes of mood that make the act possible and the changes that are part of it. To those who value sexual conquest, the stages are as important as the conquest, and Maupassant, who is often hypocritically reproached for this excellence, may be compared with those sportsmen who love the creatures they kill. He has a natural sexual curiosity and he is, in consequence, freed from that obscuring zeal for personal and vicarious participation in the coupling of his characters, that ruins the descriptions of inhibited writers. There is not a woman in the sexual episodes of Maupassant's stories who does not come to life because of them.

Maupassant's open vanity in his submission to life is softened by his patient sense of time. The launch of a boat, a drink in a café, an empty afternoon anywhere, the preparations for a shoot, the inquiring hours when lovers sit side by side unable to speak, are not matters to be hurried over. He is so slow that the minutes become dramatic. Every word is an event. The most banal thoughts can be so placed that ecstatic happiness is conveyed by them: "It seemed to her that there were only three beautiful things in the whole of creation: light, space and water." Or again—"They felt happy—each thinking of the other." Time breathes in such simple sentences; they have the turning of the earth in them. Just as they have in innumerable minor observations in this novel. Everyone grows old in *Une Vie*, yet each in a distinctive way. The day itself and not some constructing, self-imposing author might have written a passage like this:

> In the morning Jeanne would set out to meet him, with Aunt Lison and the Baron, who was gradually growing bent and who walked like a little old man with hands clasped behind his back as if to prevent himself from falling flat on his face. They went very slowly along the road,

sometimes sitting down at the edge of the ditch and staring into the distance to see if the rider were not yet in sight. As soon as he appeared, a black dot on the white line, the three of them waved their handkerchiefs. Then he would break into a gallop and arrive like a hurricane, which always made Jeanne and Lison shudder with alarm and produced an enthusiastic 'Bravo' from the grandfather who cheered with all the enthusiasm of one whose active days are over.

Only one or two Russians, Tolstoy above all, have surpassed Maupassant in describing happiness, the delicious sensation of simply being alive; and it is done by fidelity to what is passing, by making concrete the sense of evanescence in ordinary things.

I have possibly been too summary in my comments on Maupassant's character and have also tended to move too speculatively between the man and his work. Let us look, as much as possible, at the work alone. What are his chief interests? Sex, animal delight, of course; more important, I think, the effect of poverty and circumstance on character. Life is made endurable by sexual love and by usage; only these relieve the meaningless and unremitting irony of circumstance. It is interesting, here, to compare Maupassant's novel *Une Vie* with Arnold Bennett's *Old Wives' Tale*, which, one recalls, was prompted by Maupassant's book and which patiently attempts the same attitude of mind. Immediately one is struck by a strain of dry triviality and perfunctoriness in Bennett's masterpiece, a connoisseur's diffidence which keeps his people at a certain distance, whereas in *Une Vie* one is struck by the nearness of Maupassant to his Jeanne, the unguarded and sincere intimacy of his observation of her as a character. He is sexually aware of her. And his picture of her sexual reserve and of how, unexpectedly, it dissolves and she becomes a woman is the mark of Maupassant's superiority to Bennett as an intuitive artist. Jeanne is an obscure woman, but she is never trivial. The pessimism of Maupassant is pitying, sympathetic and humane.

Listening to the criticisms of his stories that have been made chiefly since the rise of Chekhov, one is given the impression that he was simply a brilliant conjuror or special pleader. He has been held up as the arch-exponent of the trick plot, the cynical moral and the surprise ending. Nothing could be less true of his best work. Where is the trick in *La Maison Tellier* or in *Une Fille de Ferme*? The test of the artificial story is its end. Do you, at the end of a story, feel that the lives of the people have ended with the drama of their situation? Do you feel that their lives were, in fact, not lives, but an idea? That is the artificial story. All short-story writers produce stories like this, for, like the sonnet, the short story is liable to become a brilliant conceit. But a large number of Maupassant's tales, and especially those which deal with the lives of the Normandy peasants, do not belong to this group. The ends of these tales are, so to speak, open. The characters go on living. They are beginning to live their way into a new situation. Rosa, in *La Maison Tellier*, will not be quite the same woman after she has taken the child into her bed. The *fille de ferme* is at the beginning of a new story when she tells her husband about her illegitimate child. The triumph of custom—the custom of avarice—justifies the girl in *L'Aveu*, who sleeps with the carrier in order to save her fare, and you see her at the story's end, grown into the cramped, terrifying world of peasant poverty. It is a growth, not an end. It is true that in all these stories the characters are dominated by a strong, dramatic situation; but to call this method arbitrary, when one compares it with Chekhov's, is a mistake. Chekhov's subject was life, life breaking and running like a chain of raindrops upon the window. Now the drops run and pool together, presently they part, slide off on their own and momentarily catch the light in some new, fragile and vanishing pattern. There are meetings and partings, crises and respites. For Chekhov life is an arpeggio of moments. But when Maupassant looks at the life of one of his characters he is a moralist thinking of the custom of their life. One has the sensation of seeing not merely the crises in *Boule de Suif*, but all of the lives of the people in that story. We come back to Maupassant's French respect for usage. The peasant comes out in him. There is a negative virtue in our acceptance of fate. There are certain permanent things, he seems to say: poverty, hard work, the obligations of work, the begetting of one's kind, the scheme in which a life has been set. And into this circle the heart brings its untidy animal fire, often trodden down, but never quite extinguished. Moments are a reality in that life—the *fille de ferme* will never forget the moment when, dazed by the sunlight, she lay down on the straw in the barn and woke to strike the farm hand who crept up to touch her; nor will Jeanne, in *Une Vie*, forget that time, long after her marriage, when her miserly young husband suddenly, inexplicably, became desirable to her—but these moments are part of the grave and fatal pattern of their respective lives. There is indeed an appetite for life, a robust reaching out to life in Maupassant, and especially a love of animal life, innocent and lazy in the country scene. Suppose, for a minute, that *La Maison Tellier* is a joke. I mean, suppose Maupassant did not originally intend to go beyond the farce suggested by the notice on the door of the brothel. And now look at the story again. How quickly he leaves the farce of the original idea behind. His animal spirits warm up, his heart expands; how quickly the idea ripens and becomes life itself. The description of the carriage ride through the dusty, dazzling countryside flashes with poetry; but it is an earthy poetry, written out of the heart and not twanged and tweaked on the nerves:

> Une lumière folle emplissait les champs, une lumière miroitant aux yeux; et les roues soulevaient deux sillons de poussière qui voltigeaient longtemps derrière la voiture sur la grande route.

La Maison Tellier dazzles one like a May morning; but in the harder story, *Une Fille de Ferme*, one also sees the same pagan love of nature. When the girl runs away from the farm before dawn, thinking to drown herself, one sees the strange, mad aspect of the countryside before sunrise. The moon appears at its unexpected and crazy slope in the sky, and the fields lie in a yellowish light, and only the warm smell of the earth in the odorous Normandy morning and the play of the leverets in the furrows remind the girl that man may be mad but the earth is not. Maupassant's feeling for nature, a feeling that went back to his childhood, is the assurance of his sanity and his heart. And nature for him is the nature of a man close to the work of the land, close to the hunter—there he reminds one of Turgenev—and close to use. How simply, too, this nature distracts and heals the human sufferers for a while: the little boy who runs away from the boys who are jeering at him, and forgets his shame in playing with a frog. And, as I said before, I think it is from his closeness to the peasant's knowledge of nature that Maupassant got his sense of the pattern of fate or necessity in life.

The morbidity, the mere ingenuity and sentimentality of Maupassant have been explained as the bad wages of the doctrine of art for art's sake, but that criticism is not very valuable. Writers write badly when they write too much; possibly Maupassant's physical disease ensured that he would write with a frenzied facility. At his second best he is still enjoyable simply because he has that gift which no theory can explain—original talent; and that quality which cannot be obtained by taking thought—sincerity, which I take to be clarity and singleness of mind. Whatever the idea of the moment, however poor or flippant, Maupassant gives himself up to it. I think this is true of a mechanical story such as the one where the man blows his brains out because he is afraid to show his fear of fighting a duel, or in that cynical story of the prostitute who attracts her customers in the cemetery by weeping at the grave of an imaginary husband. Maupassant has a wide range of character-anecdote, if not a very wide range of character or situation, because of his

MAUPASSANT

curiosity. And "art for art's sake", plus curiosity, is a formidable combination. Usually, when this useful doctrine is attacked, the critic forgets that Flaubert, who was Maupassant's master, insisted that great curiosity was indispensable. The weakness of Maupassant's mind is that its atheism was cynical. It was a personal despair unsupported by any great intellectual structure—a quality in him which, oddly enough, as Mr. Desmond MacCarthy has reminded me, attracted Tolstoy: "What is truth if a man dies?" This atheism was not damaging to Maupassant when he was writing about the pagan Normandy of his childhood, but outside of that world, cynicism left him isolated and he was reduced to seeing small, ironic, moral conundrums everywhere. There are accidental resemblances to Turgenev, who was also an atheist, in Maupassant; but he has neither the feeling of the sensitive aristocrat for his people nor anything to correspond with the mystical Russian cult of the humble. And he made no political judgments about his country, as Turgenev did. Maupassant was a child of the disaster of Sedan, and that line from the opening of *Boule de Suif*: "L'angoisse de l'attente faisait désirer la venue de l'ennemi," reads like his epitaph, the inscription of an isolated and haunted man.

16

A Love Affair

IT seems to be true that the love affair is not a subject which, for its own sake, can engage the exclusive interest of the English novelist. We have little or nothing in our literature to compare with books like *Adolphe* or *Dominique*, with Daudet's *Sappho* or Colette's *Chéri*, or with a novel like Svevo's *As a Man Grows Older*. I do not think this is entirely due to the puritan tradition and, in any case, many contemporary writers who are free from this tradition have attempted the subject and yet have failed to convey immersion in it. The inability to transplant this admired continental genre arises, I think, from a permanent habit of mind. We tacitly refuse to abstract or isolate a subject or to work within severe limits. The love affair, with us, is regarded as a chance to illustrate something more than itself: to lead to some kind of action, to cause manifestoes (D. H. Lawrence), to make religious, social or satirical pronouncements, to provide opportunity for our special taste in the comic, the romantic or the bizarre. It appears to be impossible for the English writer to treat love as an idea in itself, to confine himself to the meteorology of the emotion, to believe that it can be thought of as a climate in itself to which every other consideration must be, for the time being, subservient; for departmentalisation is a method which a northerner is bound to resist. A native instinct warns him that he could learn more than it is good for him to know. He could learn, for example, final fatalism and acceptance; whereas the last card the northerner always relies on is something very different: it is action, eccentricity, extravagance, even personal tastelessness and the absurd. There is an ageing English cocotte in Daudet's *Sappho* whose case illustrates the point. Where her French companions have compounded with their

A LOVE AFFAIR

fate and have turned into tyrants, gossips or melancholy alcoholics, the Englishwoman rails at the *injustice* of being rejected by a lover because her face is ugly while her body is still beautiful. Something ought to be *done* about it! It is enough to drive one, she says—vulgarly undoing her dress—to walking naked in the street; it is a pity that convention prevents one from doing that. The awful probability—we reflect—is, that one of these days, the sense of injustice will in fact drive her to just this exhibition, and one more English eccentric, lonely, hard-bitten, naïve and unassuaged, will be born

For the English reader Daudet's *Sappho* is an easy introduction to the genre. It is not too abstract, nor too exacting, and it is a story busy with Daudet's invention. "Fineness" was above all Daudet's quality—it was he who rebuked Henry James for living among people who were "moins fins" than himself. But, as Mr. Hodge says in his introduction to a new edition, we admire not the invention alone, but the grace with which Daudet's powers are used and the ease with which he passes from comedy through irony to tragedy. Perhaps tragedy is too strong a word for a writer who strikes one as being a weather prophet of the climate of passion rather than a native and victim of it, but it is true that Daudet moves as quickly as the mood itself. He is one of the magicians of the surface of life, one of the masters of the moments of the heart. He has also a genius for selecting the small Dickensian *milieux* of petit bourgeois society: the absurd picnic, the vulgar boating party, the boarding house where the droll boarders are more respectable than the retired demi-mondaines who run it, the holiday shack on the outskirts of Paris, the gay and idiotic fancy dress "do". Yet all these distractions are here to extend our knowledge of the love affair which is the only subject of the tale, to establish not only the changes it goes through in the course of five years, but how these are conditioned by something we hardly ever see mentioned in English fiction: the *kind* of love affair it is.

Sappho, or rather Fanny Legrand, is the Bohemian mistress, the model who is "educated" by a number of distinguished lovers who have been artists or writers, who has the reputation of being a clinger, but who does not expect to marry. She is given many of the bourgeois virtues, she is gay, kind, intelligent; but she is sexually accomplished and, therefore, she is a damned soul. When she takes up with Gaussin, she has quietened a little, she has lost her first youth, and he is the first lover to be a great deal younger than herself. In a rather alarmingly cosy state of mind, she prepares for a peaceful, if temporary, liaison, until the time comes for him to pass into the Quai d'Orsay, marry and go abroad. We must note, here, the conventions of Daudet's period. Since this is an irregular union its nature must be lust. Daudet's philosophy is that of "the romantic agony" reduced to the prosaic; love is known only in marriage to a girl of one's own class. Sexual talent will move inevitably to jealousy about previous lovers; and, after the first quarrels, from physical modesty to unbounded physical indulgence and perversion. The greater the physical pleasure, the less respect for the person; the body infects the soul. Here, the confused reader may well blink and wonder if he is not reading Tolstoy's account of regular, conjugal love in *The Kreutzer Sonata*. But the acceptance of a convention does not, in any way, injure Daudet's practical sensibility to every moment of the affair, or the subtlety of his psychological judgments. Jean Gaussin is a homely version of Adolphe. He is less of a moralist and more the fearing, bewildered, entangled young man at the mercy of his youthful generosity, his hatred of scenes and his dislike of causing pain. Fanny's desire to hold him begins when he changes from an impulsive youth into a guilty, worried and complicated young man like the rest. She loves and he does not, and guilt as usual takes on the clothes of jealousy. Within a few months his jealousy has become the real bond between them, for it releases their unreasonableness. From that moment he has the right to suffer and to accuse and she has

A LOVE AFFAIR

the right to let fly all she has learned in her life. She can become a slut, a howling termagant, screaming out obscenities and then collapsing into remorse. There is an excellent scene—which Mr. Hodge rightly points to—in which Jean obliges her to burn all the letters she has kept from her previous lovers. But with the desire of jealousy to add to its own tortures, he insists on reading each one before it is thrown into the fire, and interrogating her line by line. Her reticence pleases him no more than her candour. There is such a letter-burning that night, that the chimney catches fire, the fire brigade is called, and the wretched lovers find their misery turned into farce, and then back into the ferocity of reconciliation. But they have gone too far, and temporarily the lovers part.

Daudet shows wonderful skill in this story, by pausing to take breath before each stage of the affair. In these pauses lies the happiness of the lovers. What is their happiness? Daudet has a natural and continuous delight in the detail of life and he does not find it impossible to describe happiness nor is he embarrassed in the description of desire. His method is, so to say, to filter the longing and the physical passion of his characters through the commonest events of their lives. The love is in the eating, the shopping, the furnishing, the sitting apart in a room, the looking out of the window into the noisy streets by the Gare de l'Est, as well as in the scattered clothes of the bedroom. It is an obsession with things; to things it has given an inescapable part of evocation. When Jean leaves Fanny to visit his parents in Provence and hopes that the sight of the good life will appease and cure him, Daudet writes with simple truth:

> The seductive image of her loomed before him whenever he went out; it walked with him, it echoed in the sound of his steps on the wide, lofty staircase. It was to the rhythm of Sappho's name that the pendulum of the old grandfather clock swung to and fro, her name that the mind whispered in the big stone-paved, chilly passages of this summer dwelling, her name that he found in all the

books he opened in his country house library, old worn volumes with red edges and binding out of which crumbs fell, crumbs he had dropped there as a child nibbling cake. And her obsessive memory pursued him even into his mother's bedroom, where Divonne was doing the sick woman's hair, drawing the beautiful white tresses back from a face that was still rosy and peaceful in expression in spite of the unceasing pain that racked all parts of her body.

"Ah, here is our Jean," his mother would say.

But with her neck bare, her little coif, her sleeves turned up to do those things that only she could do for the invalid, his Aunt reminded him of other awakenings, other mornings, called to his mind yet once again how his mistress used to spring out of bed in a cloud of smoke from her first cigarette.

Daudet is the master of the inner juxtapositions of love, as he is also of life's devilish yet apparently innocent supply of warning or ironical contrasts. There is Dechelette, Jean's idea of what a cool-headed lover ought to be, who suddenly loses his head over a mere chit. Dechelette has left dozens of women, knows the art of separating—but this time he blunders. The chit throws herself out of his window. Then there is the grotesque example of the bourgeois Hettémas. Amorous, gluttonous, lazy, sordid, endlessly amiable, continually eating and drinking, the Hettémas are the picture of bovine contentment. But that is the awful thing: the good, gross, motherly woman is a reformed prostitute and Hettémas is a fool. He does one brilliant thing, however. Tired of the quarrels of Jean and Fanny he buys a trumpet to drown the noise. At Rosa's pension—Rosa is a cocotte who has retired from the circus—where Fanny goes to help during one of the breaks in the affair with Jean, there is the same sort of disturbing insinuation in the comedy. Fanny is being pure and respectable; but it soon occurs to Jean that Fanny is not called Sappho for nothing and he notes her dread of the old courtesan. Not only that, he sees in Rosa's elderly

A LOVE AFFAIR

lover who cannot escape from her, though he hates her, a glimpse of his own future. The end of the book is tremendous. For when at last Jean steels himself for the appalling scene he dreads so much and goes through with it, he enters into a false freedom. Daudet has the rare capacity to describe grief and loss, and it is a master stroke that Jean goes back when he hears that an old lover of Fanny's has returned. Jean strikes her in his rage and it is her triumph; he loves her at last. The time for her to break with him has come.

How cleverly Daudet turns the struggles of pride, of wills, of jealousies, of vanities, into life; how continually he converts insight into incident, and how astonishingly—and a moved and alert astonishment is the continual feeling we have in the book—he frees his people from the oppression of his own criticisms of their passion. If Fanny is such a disastrous woman, how delightful she is made to appear; the tricks and cheapness and slyness in her, are part of her attraction; her honesty is complete and one is satisfied by a complete portrait and one that has not been marred by "good trouper" sentiment or by the rather turgid melancholy which French romantic guilt was inclined to apply thickly to the demi-monde. Here, indeed, is Baudelaire without tears. If Daudet is apt to settle the difference between love and lust rather too neatly, his sense of physical love was not accompanied by the automatic disgust, which many novelists have taken out as a kind of insurance policy. He is warm and disinterested in his candour and gaiety, he bows—the accomplished anecdotalist—to life alone. He is one of the small, fine superficial masters whose touch is quick and perfect within the undisturbing limits in which they work.

17
Zola

THE novel seeks whom it may devour. It reaches out to more and more people, greedily assimilates them to the likeness of the writer, and when a Flaubert truthfully or half-truthfully says "*Madam Bovary—c'est moi*" we bow obsequiously to our ruling monster. We are the natural fodder and we have the pride of slaves. Only when the novelist openly writes of himself do we begin to eye him with suspicion, for then he subtracts something of himself, and if he should turn to his fellows in the other arts suspicion is likely to become protest. A monster is inclined to be overfond and professionally soft when he turns to his own kind. He has ceased to be at one remove from his material. The pretensions of the novelist are too great, the seductive impurities of literature are too easy; too fluently will he assume that other arts can be described in his loquacious terms and will pompously forget that all arts directly describe themselves.

It was Cézanne's opinion that his paintings were their own description. He had suffered enough from journalists; he believed his personal life to lack importance. But, more secretive than the journalist, the novelist hunted him. He was to come under the industrious, hammering pen of Emile Zola. The solitary was to be auctioned off by the great auctioneer who drew his breath from crowds; the visionary was to be weighed by the constructor; the "failure" was to be judged by the "success"; the friend of a lifetime publicly exposed to affection, understanding, pity. God protect us from those who praise us! We know, of course, from Zola's own notes on *L'Œuvre* that Cézanne was not the only model for Claude Lantier. We are assured by research that the portrait of Claude was not the cause of the breach in a profound friendship, which had lasted since Zola and Cézanne were schoolboys in Aix; though one critic, John Rewald, has made the point that Cézanne must have been wounded by the pity Zola displayed. Zola had never written articles about him, as he had of the Impressionists: now he saw why —Zola had not thought him important enough! But the two had quarrelled many times and Zola, on his way to ever vaster and more rhetorical panoramas and notorieties, ascending to apotheosis in his frock coat, was already distant from the painter who stared at nature in a solitude which could never be too intense, and where the difficulties could never be too great. It was less and less likely that the writer whose needs drew him to the orgies of the public stage and the painter who had been ridiculed, ruined and persecuted in them, would have anything to say to each other. There was nothing to bind them but the strongest tie—the passionate memories of their young days together—and, as the successful years go by, nothing snaps like a strong bond. The irony of Zola's novel remains all the deeper. It is the irony of an irrelevance.

What Cézanne may have felt, we can suspect, is what painters have commonly felt about literature: a sardonic anger at being, as it were, swallowed alive by another art. It is true that what is swallowed is usually a dummy. But, even by proxy to have swelled the maw of that Romantic glutton, to see paterfamilias (rather brilliantly) fattening himself so that *you* become *him*! To see him, above all, disposing of his private doubts by transferring them to yourself! For that Zola very curiously did in his portrait of Claude Lantier. "The struggles of the artist with nature"—we hear the novelist chugging out his notes like a great puff-puff— "the effort of creation", "blood and tears." He is going to "give his flesh." There are to be battlings with truth, wrestlings with the angel. "In a word", Zola explodes, "I shall recount my own intimate life as a creative artist, the everlasting pains of childbirth." What an appalling thing the thought of intimacy with Zola is. It suggests the dreadful intimacy of a prosperous laundry greedy for one's dirty linen. Why, then, pick upon poor Claude Lantier? Zola has already planned his own portrait in Paul Sandoz, the slave of the pen, suffering from all the morbidities of success. If Claude is still required, why must he be after the same kind of thing as Sandoz-Zola—"the wish to execute huge modern decorative works, frescoes giving a complete survey of our day and age . . . At bottom he is a Romantic, a constructor." Why must Lantier-Cézanne paint novels by Zola? Why must Claude fail where Paul succeeds? It is true that until then Cézanne had in fact failed, and was still, as far as Zola could see, a pitiable Bohemian, without the talent for extracting his own genius. Zola, even though duped by his romantic notions about greatness, had some grounds for his judgment. But there is evidently a deeper reason.

There is a very pertinent comment on the plot of *L'Œuvre* in a new English translation of the novel done by Mr. Thomas Walton, and it reminds us that although a novelist may require this kind of plot or that as an urgent personal need, he will be inclined to take what is still fashionable or conventional in the wardrobe of literature. It is a paradox that the more "realistic" a novelist is with his right hand, the more, with his left, he reaches for the well-worn garments. Mr. Walton points out that

> the failure of the pseudo-genius, the "conquest" of Paris by the younger generation, the fatal attraction of the Capital, and the rivalry between Woman and Art, had been part of the stock-in-trade of French novelists at least since Balzac.

Why, we may pause to ask, did this subject become so suddenly obsessional in the 19th century? There must always have been pseudo-geniuses, there must always have been the desire for fame and its corruption, there must always have been some conflict between the interests of the artist and the woman. The answer seems to lie in the momentous changes that had taken place in French society after the revolution.

ZOLA

The Court and the idea of classical authority had gone. The individual had been "set free", and once he is free he deifies himself. There is, theoretically, no limit to the rights and potentialities of men and women, and they become known by their dominant passion to which no restriction from the classical moral or fatal order can be applied. Before each individual lies an ultimate goal: fulfilment or success, and the new morality denies that these are subject to the gods or that "absolute power corrupts." We are at the beginning, in French literature, of the morality of a commercial society—to put the matter at its lowest; but, to take a loftier view, the Artist is felt to be the only really free man in an ugly commercial world, and has replaced the ruler or the great man as the highest subject of spiritual drama. And, in any case, after Napoleon the individual can only be conceived of in Napoleonic terms. In individualistic societies all individuals are at war. The individual is not corrupted by himself, but by other individuals and Woman inevitably corrupts Man; yet, underlying this doctrine one detects in the theatrical view of Woman, an excessive protest. It looks like a guilt felt towards the discarded classical order; the opposite of success is mere failure and, compared with classical Comedy or Tragedy, failure has the indignity of a personal domestic mess. The theme of *L'Œuvre* is matched by Balzac's *Le Chef d'Œuvre Inconnu*. Claude Lantier has to bear the burden of Zola's own dread of his own Romantic tendencies and the guilt that eats at old friendships. Zola-Sandoz marries because marriage ensures order, peace and freedom from Woman for the artist; yet marriage rather disturbingly contains Woman, and who knows when She will not arise and manifest Her traditional jealousy of art, her hatred of a passion stronger than anything she can evoke? By transference, this evil can be placed upon Lantier who can also be made to bear another nightmare of Zola's, indeed of any writer's life; the fear of creative impotence. For Zola the passion for art is sexual. Chaste in life we are potent in art. And in this book, as in so many of his novels, the sexual motif and its symbols are blatant and orgiastic. They are also signs of deep neurosis. In *Germinal* we saw the broken engine of the mine raise its lever and fall in the last stroke of the sexual act, a stroke that indicates its death. In *L'Œuvre*, Claude is raped by his wife, made to renounce his picture, and then goes off in remorse at his betrayal and hangs himself before it. Its central figure, characteristically academic and promisingly shocking in the Zola fashion, is an ornate, splendidly indecent and luxurious female idol. And this (we hardly need a psychologist to tell us) was the loved and hated mother-figure which dominated Zola's sexual life, first in his own mother and then in his mother-wife.

Nothing is impossible, as we soon discover when we find our way into the secret lives of people. Suicides have been known to go in for an erotic decor. An obscure painter, who had killed himself because he was rejected by the Salon, is said to have put this final scene into Zola's head. There are jealous women who wreck pictures, tear up manuscripts, and head men off to the office. What displeases is the inevitable operatic note in Zola's story: the painter is obliged to fail at the top of his voice. He lives with visions which are well argued but which, upon reflection, look like poster advertisements. Yet, in the midst of it all, the one acceptable artist—and he is very convincing—is Paul Sandoz, working like a factory, faithful to his wife, charitable to his friends, worrying to death about his reputation, unable to believe or disbelieve in it, cozening the public, buying antiques, going respectfully to funerals and regularly to meals. How Zola's own death was to fail the theatrical formula! And yet, since he was working off the dread (as Mr. Walton says) of his unconquerable Romanticism, how gratifying to the Naturalist to be scientifically asphyxiated by the fumes of his stove! But Sandoz is a writer, and the writers must have a square deal. The good portraits of painters are the brief glum sketches of Bongrand (who is Manet) hating his early work because he fears he has been unable to surpass it; and the minor fry of cunning imitators. They are not burdened with a mystique which Zola, as his critical articles on Impressionism had shown, did not understand and was impatient of because it showed no signs of producing a "great" man—a fresco painter.

Zola is the novelist of simplification, inflation, drama, the large, slack, crowd-catching line. He seeks the pictorial. The weakness of *L'Œuvre* as a novel is that the content of one character is divided among two. We know it is beside the point—for Cézanne was still a failure, a ridiculed, persecuted painter, and easily presented as one of the *ratés* of a Murger-like Bohemia, incompetent in life as in art—but suppose Cézanne had, by this time, succeeded? Would this have persuaded Zola to stick to the facts of Cézanne's life? Or was failure romantically necessary to the novelist? What ham theatre, what Hollywood stuff it is when Claude "fights" his canvas, gazes at Notre Dame (of all places), watches his child die without concern! Or rather, how trivial it seems beside Cézanne's strange, busy, silent life: the efficient separations from his wife—he adroitly got her another room in Aix when she came back—his dependence on his mother and sister, his adoration of his son, his secretiveness with his rich father, the quiet cunning of his Catholicism. The drama of Cézanne's life is in the simplicity of his passions, the secrecy of an intense life that uses naïveté to veil the path of single-mindedness.

The Romantic dogma of death, failure and the hidden taint is responsible for the false twists in Zola's realism. Yet *L'Œuvre*, of course, does not fail to display his great gifts as a novelist. He is a master of large scenes. The crowded account of the Salons is brilliant; if the studio talk is unbearably jaunty and slangy, the general essay on the preoccupations of the artist's life is touching, tolerant and true. Claude's wife is well-drawn, especially when she is a modest young girl, and Zola modest and domestic is always superior to Zola repelling himself in scenes of physical passion, when he presents reality as if he hated it. There are reasons, indeed, to suspect his sexual capacity; the most convincing and pleasing sexual descriptions in literature appear in the comic writers in whom sensuality has the hunter's delicacy and the easy grace of appetite. There are dozens of small, tenderly observant touches in the portrait of Claude's wife, especially in the record of her changes of opinion about her husband and his work; these things go to the heart. Zola knew married life. He can convey sadness without sentimentality, resignation without the poison of an injected pessimism. *L'Œuvre* is a bad novel except in those passages where it is moved by that sad and universal music which stirs when we look back upon our youth and the friends of that time and see the changes that have been brought to hope, the transformations grotesque, beneficent or ineluctable, that experience has forced upon our desires. It is a novel about the injustice of time itself; and everything springing from that knowledge in it, is truthful and good. Claude himself, in those moments, is a friend, and friendship itself appears as a passion.

Yet—back to the novel factory at Medan. Art has been polished off in *L'Œuvre*. Science must be dealt with in *Dr. Pascal*. Back to the hell of success which, to be habitable, depends on the comforting knowledge that failure abounds. Back, indeed, to work for work's sake, despite the dismal suspicion that even the virtue of the treadmill is dubious, for posterity will not care a damn about these terrible personal conflicts. One goes out in an ugly scene at a cemetery with a random train-whistle going off. The terrible temptation towards one more operatic scene, one more orgy of sexual symbolism, visits the labouring Naturalist; he has covered the families, the professions, the industries, the passions. Megalomania points to the cities; perhaps if he enlarges enough, the weary rationalist will find a meaning to life.

*   *   *   *   *

L'Assommoir (*The Dram-Shop*) was the first novel of Zola's to have enormous popular success and notoriety. Henry

ZOLA

James, who crept very gingerly round the subject and who said one or two final things about it, put *L'Assommoir* beside *Germinal* and *La Débâcle* at the top of Zola's productions. It seems to me superior to *Germinal*, because it is not theatrical. Compare the famous mine engine of this book with the distiller's engine of *The Dram-Shop*: the former is a theatrical sexual symbol and throughout the book there is an obsessional preoccupation with sex, which comes dangerously near the ludicrous. The distiller's engine is merely a fascinating machine, perhaps a witch's cauldron, throbbing, bubbling and dripping its poison, which infects the life of the slum around it. That is no more than the plain truth: the delusions, the corruption, the diseases, the tempers, the fights, the murders and final madness of alcoholism are not fancies. And then the crowds which Zola excelled in describing are not poster-work. In *Germinal* one remembers the crowds described as if they were panicking and slavering cattle, as gluttonous and hungry maws; in *The Dram-Shop* there is nothing herd-like or anonymous in the hordes of the Paris slums; they are particularised with a delicacy which is unexpected in this coarse-grained novelist. For Zola had been wretchedly poor in his own youth and he understood that poverty individualises like a frost; it etches upon human beings lines and traits as refined in their way as those of happier sensibility. Coupeau the plumber, Lantier the hatter and Gervaise the laundress are not mere documentations for the purpose of illustrating the life of the industrial poor at that time; they are subtle, variable, extraordinary human beings. They are not more than life size, but we see more and more in them as we turn each page.

The Dram-Shop is a novel without a plot. We see the rise of Coupeau and Gervaise from abject poverty to the condition of prospering working people, enjoying the decencies of life. They work hard; they save; but they do not become miserly and oppressive. Then Coupeau has an accident. It ruins his character, for he discovers the pleasures of idleness, the ease of living on his admirable wife; and after an idyllic period this corrupts him. He gradually tipples, take to idleness on principle, invents every kind of rationalisation and drifts gradually into alcoholism. He takes his wife's former lover as a boon companion; between them they exploit her and bring her ruin, for the sweetness and goodness of her nature have rested on an element of acquiescence; and prosperity has corrupted her. No more than any other human beings are the poor freed from the seductions of success; poor Gervaise lets herself go and is soon whirled bewildered into sluttishness, laziness, blurred amiability, drunkenness. Coupeau dies of D.T.s; Gervaise, a tippler rather than an alcoholic, dies of starvation, and Lantier, her former lover, moves on to exploit another couple, an absurd gendarme and his wife. This is not a plot, in the usual sense of the word; it is a moralisation which must be slowly disentangled from the driftings and confusions of everyday life. If Zola is an indiscriminate writer, if he is mainly an appetite for life, people and conditions, this has an important compensation: any plot we care to see in *The Dram-Shop* arises out of daily life as his people knew it and is not imposed with the *parti pris* of the storyteller. It could be complained that we are too much submerged in daily life in this book, in all the goings on of the tenements, the interminable small quarrels, envies and chatter of the neighbours, of the bars, of Gervaise's steaming laundry; but out of this Zola produces two or three wonderful long and dilatory episodes.

There is the fight between Gervaise and another woman in the wash house, a terrible and heroic affair of animal fury and comedy. Far better, there is the wedding party of Coupeau and Gervaise, a superb piece of comic rambling: in which the climax is reached when the party fill in time before dinner by going up the column in the Place Vendôme in wild good humour, start quarrelling at the top and come down in silence:

> They all of them made their way to the top. The twelve members of the party had to climb the narrow stairway in

single file, and this they did with much stumbling on the worn steps, keeping close to the wall for safety. The interior soon became pitch dark, and there was a great deal of loud laughter. The ladies uttered little screams, because the men started tickling them and pinching their legs. But they weren't so silly as to protest, thinking it better to pretend that what they felt were mice. Anyway, it wasn't worth making a fuss about, because the practical jokers, they were convinced, wouldn't go too far. Boche produced a witticism which they all took up. Everyone started calling down to Madame Gaudron, pretending to believe that she had got stuck. Was there enough room, they asked, for her belly? A nice thing it would be if she got "took", and not able to go up or down! She'd be jammed in the fairway, and none of them would be able to get out! The belly of the pregnant woman gave rise to such hoots of laughter that the whole column shook. Boche, flushed by the success of his sally, was now well launched. They'd be in this chimney-stack, he said, for the rest of their lives! Wasn't there no end to it?—short of the sky? He tried to frighten the ladies by declaring that he could feel it move. All this while, Coupeau said nothing. He was just behind Gervaise, holding her by the waist. He could feel her leaning on him. He was just about to kiss the back of her neck when, suddenly, they found themselves in the open air. "A nice thing, I must say!" observed Madame Lorilleux with an air of outraged propriety. "Oh, don't mind us!"

Bibi-la-Grillade appeared to be thoroughly put out. "You all made such a damned row," he grumbled, "that I couldn't even count the steps!"

Like Balzac, Zola is the novelist of our appetites, especially of their excess in satisfaction or nausea, but he lacks Balzac's irony and subtlety. He is less civilised and less instinctively refined by the comic spirit. He excels until he exceeds, in atmosphere: the laundry of Gervaise is worked up until the point of sensual disgust is reached and we long to get out of that hot, damp room reeking of female sweat, filthy garments and dirty jokes. On the other hand, when he is not on his obsessive themes, he finely observes human nature.

Goujet, the good workman who tries hard to keep Coupeau straight, who has a serious political conscience, and understands the situation of the industrial worker, is not presented as the perfect man. Zola understood the wounds of human beings: Goujet is under the thumb of an excellent but stern mother and is paralysed in matters of decision in his private life. The variety of character in this novel is large, but even larger is the variety of mood and passion within the characters. Zola did not believe in the sacred working class; and, no doubt, this was the reason for the attacks on the book for being a travesty of French working-class life. Quite clearly, now, it was not: it simply contained everything; in it the poor ceased to be purely and simply the poor. They became individuals.

There are only two seriously false scenes in *The Dram-Shop*, and they occur towards the end, at the point where a novelist becomes over-heated by his own world and attempts to force the logic of events. The first occurs when Gervaise is told by her husband that she might just as well go on the streets. Gervaise sets out, starving, ragged, gross-looking and begs unavailingly in an awful night tour of the streets of Paris. At one point she runs into another starving being whom she has once befriended: this is excellent—starvation looks into starvation's eyes. But when she finally accosts the noble Goujet who had once loved her, the melodramatic cliché is too much. It is true that Zola's humane realism puts the episode right in the end, but it has been a strain on our trust. The second episode follows close on this one. Rejected by Goujet Gervaise throws herself at her neighbour in the next room, the drunken undertaker who is known as the Ladies' Comforter: not the comforter of the reader—he is an embarrassing symbol of the motif of Love-and-Death. Unlike the rich episodes of the wedding and the party, these incidents belong to the false, theatrical world of plot.

The argument for plot of that kind in the novel is, at its highest, the argument for meaning and value: but meaning

ZOLA

and value in Zola lie in the rendering of life itself. It was necessary, one might say, to write novels of this kind because the 19th century saw the dehumanisation of man. Christianity had become meaningless. It was necessary to write about conditions simply because the dominant class were trying to live without knowing what their life was based on. The marvel is that Zola came so close to the skin of his people. He was able to do so perhaps because of his peculiar vice: the idealisation of the ugly. His obsessive taste for the revolting, the dreary, the bestial was an energy, and put him completely at one with the dreadful spirit of the times; he was as ugly, disfiguring and, also, almost as ludicrous in his puffing and blowing as the early steam engines. But there is another reason for his success. Henry James gives us a clue to it when he reports, with a shock, Zola's decision to conduct research into popular speech, slang and foul language: Zola saw that this was not a barrier but the card of admission into the slum world. If he knew its language he would know its soul. A great deal of *The Dram-Shop* is written in an attempted vernacular—which Mr. Gerard Hopkins has tackled heroically in his translation with a very passable measure of success—and though Zola is far from contemporary feeling for common speech, he does make the first bold approaches. He succeeds chiefly where it is macabre and comical, especially when it is gross. It is a wonderful moment, for example, when Gervaise goes to the asylum to see Coupeau and finds him, temporarily cured, and squatting on the lavatory pan making jokes which are indeed lewd but are also very moving in their effect. Zola's following of bad words has led him, paradoxically, to the profoundest human feelings; and his own search for disgust and hatred is not proof against the surprising insinuations of the love that is mixed with the revolting—may even arise because of it. Finally, *The Dram-Shop* is free of that set Puritan piety which makes the moralising of Hogarth on Gin Alley or the Rake intolerable in the end. Human beings have the right to their tragedy; they have the right to be incurable. Zola's sense of corruption was, no doubt, based on specious scientific theories; but it was a larger, more humane sense than the Puritan moralist's trite preaching of domestic virtue and the merits of the savings bank.

18

A Political Novel

LUCIEN LEUWEN is a political novel, a novel about the effects of the class war upon manners and sensibility, about "the grand dispute which saddens the 19th century—the rage of rank against merit"; and, one might add, the rage of merit against mediocrity. It is a novel which startles by its frequent contemporary note, and a first English translation by H. L. R. Edwards under the title of *The Green Huntsman* is welcome. The book was begun in 1834 and written very fast at Civita Vecchia when the weather was not too hot. Stendhal was French consul. He was fifty-one, a hard-working official, bored and disillusioned. He put the novel aside in 1836 and for one reason and another never finished or revised it. He withheld it from publication because it contained contemptuous criticism of the regime that employed him. He could not afford to quarrel with his bread and butter and ironically foresaw the stupidity of the censorship. The present translation, though a shade Gallic here and there, is admirable; it crisply transmutes the hard, clear, nonchalant prose of Stendhal with its faint smell of gunpowder—the duellist's pistol has just gone off. The hardness is more noticeable in this novel than in his others because, as he said, it is still "an ossature"; revision would have cut the excess of detail; the flesh and the smile, as he said, would have been put on the skeleton. The book breaks naturally into two parts and Mr. Edwards calls the second half *The Telegraph*. The first has Lucien's life in the garrison at Nancy, his love affair with Madame Chastellar and ends with the grotesque episode which broke the affair and sent Lucien galloping back to his mother in Paris. The second part takes the reader inside the cynical French political machine under Louis Philippe and the

123

farce of a provincial election under the new democratic system.

"Character of this work: exact chemistry: I describe with exactitude what others indicate with a vague and eloquent phrase." So in his notes Stendhal described the method of *Lucien Leuwen*. The poetry was to be in the chemistry. Science and *logique*—and *logique* was surely petulance in disguise, as it so often is in men whose good sense really comes out of the pain of an old wound—ought to define what a man's attitude to the world was and to propound what it ought to be. This central preoccupation of Stendhal's is personal and egotistical: uprooted from his own class, gifted, ambitious but without means or rank, bearing the scars of father-hatred in his nature, Stendhal begins from an imaginary blank sheet to find out what "a superior man" can make of himself in a world hostile to high feeling. And so all his novels have the critical tone of experiments in autobiography. They are, more watchfully than in other novelists, the lives of possible selves. Detached writers are often more truly sensitive to the spirit of their time than the committed: revolution, war and *coup d'état* left Stendhal energetically disgusted. He became indifferent. What did persist with him was the sense of campaign: his psychology is generalship.

There have been a great many novels about what politics are about, but their writers have had little knowledge of politics in themselves. Mrs. Gaskell, George Eliot, Dickens, Zola, show us the social dramas; to Stendhal the social drama is chiefly the nourishment of politicians and, like some zoological keeper, he shows them to us at their feeding time. The soldiers, who had once fought with Napoleon, are reduced to the political trough, too. It is true that in *Lucien Leuwen* we are shown all this through the eyes of a young man who has the innocence of the very rich and that Stendhal's object is to give us a young man learning his lesson, not about politics, but about life. But it will not be the kind of lesson that young radicals were taught by the

A POLITICAL NOVEL

English novelists of the 19th century: Lucien will not end by acquiring "sound" political beliefs. His one abiding political belief is the love of liberty; but the only concrete notion is negative: to turn the army upon the workers is a degradation and a crime. Still, the working classes have hardly come into the political picture and, for all his hatred of tyranny, Stendhal is in a very similar situation to Voltaire's and he hated Voltaire. Lucien will end by giving up politics altogether. If he retains a kind of sneaking affection for one or two Republicans it is because personally they are energetic and mad; America, their promised land—the Russia of our time—will seem to him a sink of mediocrity and human indecency. What, then, will Lucien learn? That the highest life is beyond politics. It lies even beyond personal relationships—as Mr. Martin Turnell pointed out in his study of *La Chartreuse de Parme*. It is revealed at the height of love, in reverie and contemplation.

Lucien Leuwen is, as Mr. Edwards says, a milder figure than the working-class Julien Sorel or the aristocratic Fabrice. Lucien's amiable father has been too civilised, too sagacious and too good at business and politics. He is a figure of the 18th century; the son is at sea before such an admirable parent who can unobtrusively arrange everything from a box full of opera girls to an under-secretaryship. The 19th-century son requires difficulty, duty, conscience, puritan energy; he wants, above all, to keep his hands clean. His fatal disadvantage is wealth; it will take years, Stendhal points out, for Lucien to live that down. Lucien is a charming but conceited young prig, a hopeless mixture of ingenuousness and arrogance, premature worldliness and tongue-tied inexperience; absurd calculation and self-consciousness are combined with sudden affectability and spirit. In short he is a masterly model of the Young Man, in the drawing of whom Stendhal, to my mind, surpasses all novelists. Lucien, prickly with vanity and throwing his weight about as a young lieutenant in Nancy, practising irony, hauteur and frigidity in the mess, is engaging because he is almost unbearable. He is a charming, impossible puppy. We see him heroically giving up his money and deciding on exile: very fine, very spirited—but will he bring it off, we wonder, and in any case what precisely does he want to bring off? Here, the scientific observation of Stendhal comes in: Lucien is not a hero, he is the complete, intelligent wealthy young man of the period; and no doubt a daydream of imaginary autobiography. "Suppose I had loved my father and had been rich: how then would I have dealt with the fundamental issue of life—freedom!" so one can imagine Stendhal's thought.

The brilliant part of the book is the statement of the political situation in Nancy and of the plight of an unpopular army in a society that snubs them or hates them. Each character is planted in his political pot. When the rich young officer of the new army comes into the drawing-rooms of the "ultra" aristocracy, the young ex-officers of the old regime hang round, drooping and posing with airs of aggressive and calculated futility. When the Prefect sells a horse we see a young man just shot up into office by the new regime, arrogant, timid, and still learning what face to put on while one is feathering one's nest. The older soldiers who have seen the great campaigns and who have known what *la gloire* is, are wonderful artistic onions; peel off the top skin of political caution, peel off the next skin of military anecdote, and the next to find the man who will accept a tip or a case of liqueurs—and underneath one finds, at last, the puzzled, rancorous, bewildered human being. All these portraits are rich and marked by Stendhalian minuteness—"a face already crinkled with envy." The aristocrats, carefully listed, are not all of a piece; Stendhal has caught the moves of a coterie isolated and drying up in a futile class-hatred of the government.

He is equally pointed in his observation of the bourgeosie. Class-hatred had insulated the classes in Nancy and their outline is therefore clearer. The bourgeois who shouts his opinions almost verbatim from his newspaper is excellent,

A POLITICAL NOVEL

and so is Mlle Sylvanie, the shopkeeper's daughter and bourgeois beauty:

> A statue of Juno, copied from the antique by a modern artist: both subtlety and simplicity are lacking; the lines are massive, but it's a Germanic freshness. Big hands, big feet, very regular features and plenty of coyness, all of which conceals a too obvious pride. And these people are put off by the pride of ladies in good Society! Lucien was especially struck by her backward tosses of the head, which were full of vulgar nobility and were evidently meant to recall the dowry of a hundred thousand crowns.

This is a portrait done with irony, but without hatred; there is bitter envy in Stendhal, a good deal of it, but it is the envy of the outsider, of the observer, for the planted human being. Lucien may be snobbish about Mlle Sylvanie, but that other passionate, warmer part of Stendhal knows that she is life.

The most interesting portrait is of Dr. du Poirier, the brilliant intriguing demagogue of humble parentage, the non-stop talker and political agent who has got the aristocracy in the palm of his hands. Here talent and vulgarity, quickness and naïveté, intelligence and a touch of careerism are wonderfully mixed. Vanity makes him think he can turn Lucien in to an "ultra"; Lucien plays with him—a shade too maturely, I think, for a young man—and then, when du Poirier sees it, he brings his profound roguery to bear. Du Poirier is responsible for Lucien's disaster and for the most improbable scene which causes him to break with Madame Chastellar. It is said that Stendhal was nervous about this grotesque episode. It seems to me that novelists who are as detached as Stendhal was, run two major risks: dryness and a failure of judgment when they come to the grotesque and bizarre. Only a wild and minor Elizabethan dramatist—or perhaps a Richardson—could have brought off this scene, where the lady is falsely supposed to be in childbirth and a dummy child is brought in.

The loves of Lucien and Madame Chastellar are a mild but not wooden business. Stendhal is an expert in the hesitations, the misunderstandings, the trembling moments, the sudden meltings, freezings of love and—most baffling of all —its complete disappearance at the height of a love affair; but while we must recognise the master's hand, we must also be surprised by his refusal to give the lovers their heads and make them more interesting. Truthfulness has, of course, won, as it usually does with him; we are witnessing, I suppose, a classical case of love conceived in vanity or self-interest and which, owing to the inexperience of the parties, is likely to side-slip into confusion. Because he has the absurd incident of the false childbirth up his sleeve, Stendhal's "humour"—one suspects he called it "English humour"— holds him back. We cannot, however, judge the affair as a whole, for the novel was never completed; we can only say that in a dozen small moments the touch and the comedy of the lovers' conversations are exquisite. For Lucien the affair is one more terrible political test. Stendhal mocks at his first response.

> The suspicion that he was in love had filled him with shame; he felt degraded.

He feels not only that initial fear which is the sign of love (since conscience is everything in this young man) but another dread:

> "What a disgrace," suddenly exclaimed the opposite side of love. "What a disgrace for a man who has worshipped duty and his country with a devotion which he could call sincere! Now he has eyes for nothing but a little provincial legitimist, furnished with a soul which basely prefers the private interests of her caste, to those of all France. Soon, no doubt, following her example, I shall place the happiness of two hundred thousand nobles . . . before that of the other 30 million Frenchmen. My chief reason will be that these privileged two hundred thousand

have more elegant drawing rooms ... in a word, drawing rooms that are useful for my private happiness."

This double context in which Lucien's feelings are placed is characteristic of Stendhal's genius. There is always, in his novels, the extra dimension. This is Stendhal's version of the sense of general law upon which all the great French novelists have built, and which distinguishes them from those of other countries. They are the lawyers of the passions. Dry Stendhal often is, but his clear experiments in human chemistry give us the illusion that we have, for a glittering moment, seen what life is composed of before it becomes our daily bewilderment.

19

André Gide

"I DO not like your lips," Oscar Wilde said to Gide, when he first met the young Protestant with the Nazarene beard in Paris, "they are quite straight, like the lips of one who has never told a lie." In old age Gide's lips were still like a long truthful line ruled across a face to which experience had given that look of dominance and seduction sometimes found in the saint, the confessor and the actor. The penitents of this confessor were those who had committed the sin with which he himself had at times either struggled or ironically philandered: what he regarded as the sin of faith. He was, in the Socratic sense, a corrupter, one who liberated only to impose an infinitely arduous pursuit of virtue, and this made him a hard moralist as all the puritans are. For most of the moralists—Goethe and Montaigne are the exceptions who come to mind—have the attraction of working in a fixed climate from which there is no escape; they write us into an algebra which is a pleasure in itself, and gives us at least the relief of a sort of fatalism. But Gide's climate is changeable; the spring is defeated but the spring returns; the moral frontier, like the year, is open, exposed and dangerous. This calls for courage, the loveliest of the virtues; but, alas, also for diligence, the grimmest of them.

But, fortunately, the pastor in Gide is there to exacerbate Gide rather than torture the reader. We are not, unless we are theologians, involved in the religious issue as it presented itself to him, for its own sake, any more than we can now be involved in the historical state of Montaigne's faith. The issues of religion are universal; literature interests us by what they have imaginatively provoked; in Gide (as in Montaigne) the obsession has given us the psychologist and moralist, a spirit now lyrical, now scientific. We respond to

ANDRÉ GIDE

Gide's luminous curiosity about himself, which is less melancholy than Montaigne's, indeed not melancholy at all, for it extends beyond what he is at a given moment to what he is becoming. Here is, in fact, the trait which holds the secret of his extraordinary resilience and youthfulness; and when, after reading a translation of the last volume of his *Journals*, we notice his serenity, it is really youth prolonged. For he is always expectant. Like Stendhal (another master of his) he makes us feel more intelligent, more honest than we are without him, for he brings more into the light of day. He conserves the bite and gaiety of the intelligence; all that he says, even when he is bewildered, despairing or tragic, is on the side of life, for (he conveys to us) the pride of life revives, the intellect lasts.

The fourth volume of the *Journals* begins with the war in 1939 and ends ten years later. Mauriac has spoken of his "aggressive serenity", and if the radiant agitation of the earlier years is not here and Gide is inclined to be above his enemies where before he hit back, there is an astonishing vitality; and very little testiness. If he is more studied, more aware of his role, his power of ecstasy and joy is not lost; he still has those moments of being "born again" in the reading of a book, perhaps, or before some sight of nature. The intensity is now, naturally, of reflection rather than of action and feeling. Comparing, page by page, the younger *Journals* with this volume, we find in the earlier ones a sharper zest, a more cutting pain, a greater animation; but the new volume adds the indispensable and grave finale and its range is wide. Mr. Justin O'Brien's edition is well-edited and his introduction is very good; the translation is far from impeccable, though it serves. At the beginning of the war, Gide felt, as he had felt in 1914, that the duty of the writer was to be silent; he learned German and read Goethe. Presently, the disaster, the question of its causes, the moral situation of France preoccupied him and, if nothing else, the *Journal* is a remarkable record of an open civilised mind in agitation, trapped in political defeat. But I do not think this is the most interesting part of this book, and it is, in any case, for Frenchmen to argue about. Gide belonged to an essentially non-political generation. If he had fallen into "the trap of the social problem" (he said) he would have written nothing, and he wrote (he also said, with vanity perhaps but also with prescience) for "the next generation, not this." That seems to me true: the issues of freedom and authority, truthfulness and propaganda, are the only issues for Western people. Their drama moves from the outer to the inner life. What is interesting to a generation younger than Gide's is his fascination with authority and his obliquity in dealing with it. Gide was a resistance movement in himself, and the lasting impression one has of him is of a man who is working at a technique for freedom: it will be needed.

> I am reproached for my oblique gait—but who does not know that when the wind is contrary, one is obliged to tack? It is easy to criticise for you who let yourselves be carried by the wind. I take my bearing on the rudder.

Tacking is always Gide's method, for he is most alive when there is an opposing force and he draws as close to it as he can. The charge of vacillation was never just.

But Gide's true work is to paint the self-portrait of a free man determined on freedom and yet checking it, as if what he most wanted was intensity. The portrait itself is formidable and amusing. The old man afraid to waste a day; the old Protestant torn by the problem of idleness: is it worse to do bad work than none? He translates Vergil, he translates *Hamlet*, he reads Corneille, Koestler, Shaw, Browning, Johnson, Goethe, Pearl Buck, hundreds of writers good and bad, studies radioactivity, sea animals, a history of Moslem customs—reads and writes on what he reads. (He has always done so: he has gone to other writers continuously—for sympathy.) The judgments are very sharp: no patience with Conrad's *Romance*, a shrewd verdict on Johnson. Of a performance of *King Lear*: "It ceases to be human; it becomes enormous. Hugo himself never imagined anything more gigantically artificial and more false." And there is the sharp-eyed note: "Strange part played in that drama by papers and missives, presented, stolen, falsified; up to seven times, if I counted aright." (The device of the diary in *Les Faux-Monnayeurs*.) But reading, which has played a larger part in his life than it does in the lives of most imaginative writers, is for this puritan artist "the unpunished vice."

> By reading I seek to distract myself from myself, and whereas it would be essential to commune with myself, it seems that, almost without choice, I welcome everything that may help me to forget myself . . . it would be better to give (my mind) a total holiday than constantly to interpose a screen between it and God. I must learn to know solitude all over again. What I must take walking with me henceforth is not a book, but this notebook.

Conscience is the instrument he works and lives by; and the hypnotic effect of the *Journals* perhaps comes from the feeling we have of watching not a free man but a technician or tester of freedom.

The portraits in North Africa are fewer than in the earlier volume, though there are touching sallies into scenes of the past. One grotesque living figure stands out, during the time of the siege of Tunis: the awful boy Victor, a son of the family in whose house Gide was staying. The situation is piquant. The greatest living French writer is driven to the point of illness and flight by the tortures of this truly horrible adolescent. Victor has contempt for the master. Victor bosses the house, is rude, surly, silent, scornful, grabs the best fruit, eats his food with his hands like an Arab, sucks his fingers, lies with arrogance. He is hoarding bullets to sell as war souvenirs, has a secret cache of chocolate and gold coins to be sold at a profit, and has just joined the Communists. He is filthy in the lavatory. Several days a week he runs a gambling den for his school friends, where poker and baccarat are played from two till six p.m. "In principle" (he says) he doesn't smoke, but only in principle. This sudden appearance of a character from *Les Faux-Monnayeurs* hits Gide like a plague; and through the account of the bombardment the nasty comedy weaves its coarse human thread. A progressive child, Victor devours Rousseau, Diderot, Voltaire and seems to be heading for success as a gangster. It is, the more one reflects upon it, a terrible Jamesian story; almost, the enemies of Gide might say, a sardonic retribution; and, at one point, where the tortured sage is afflicted, as usual, by conscience and asks whether he himself is not to blame because he has not been able—nor ever has all his life—to suppress his instinct to reform others, one is on the point of tears. For Gide's irony, under the strain of the heavy air raids and illness, has left him for the moment.

The episode is short. We are back among the aphorisms, the ecstasies, the delightful quotations, the memories and the fine points once more. But we appreciate all the more, by the accident of this raw interruption, the enlarging intimacy we have been privileged to share with a mind that has observed its experience with more method and surgical curiosity than any other of its time, except Proust's.

Like *Ulysses*, that other novel to end all novels, Gide's *Les Faux-Monnayeurs*, has settled peaceably into literature; it is a criticism of the novel as it was, rather than an indication of what the novel might become. The generation of experiment has been followed by figures more harassed by life and less constrained by the metaphysical delicacies of literary form. Or perhaps we should say that the formal experiments of novelists like Sartre and Camus have not led to a question of how much more should be left out, but to the difficulty of getting much more in. When we look back now on Gide's notion of a novel about a novelist writing a novel, and engaged in reconnaissance along the frontiers between literature and life, appearance and reality, we recall the tourism of the untroubled decades before the wars of the Thirties. The problem for later novelists has been another, more dangerous frontier: the torn, sometimes secretive, sometimes blatant boundaries of private and public life, what could still be fermented into art and what would run out raw into journalism. When Gide was writing that man must play out his hand, it was forgivable to think that the Boulevard St. Germain would be always there to play it in; it was not imagined that the new trick might be the destruction of civilised man altogether. And so the fine experimental works, like the intrepid experimental living of that period, recede into isolation rather than show any strong influence on what has followed. Unless, in a general way, one says that the important novels of the last twenty years have been dominantly intellectual and critical in spirit, the daring defiance of the gods having been replaced by the habit of doing without either the gods or the stimulus of defying them. A dull and worthy lot has followed the brilliant rebels.

At the end of his introduction to *Oedipus* and *Theseus* Mr. John Russell catches the evasive genius of Gide for an instant in a good phrase: "it is only just to acclaim him, as he acclaimed Goethe, as 'the finest example, at once grave and smiling, of what man can wrest from himself without the help of Grace.' " That deftly defines a volatile yet methodical temperament. He is the good and the bad conscience of those who had thought to dispose of Grace; the most subtle and dangerous of the Calvinists who know—as his Theseus knew—that they are of the Elect. Gide has been compared to Rousseau and to Montaigne also, and his closeness to the latter is obvious, in the cast of his genius and in his historical situation: he is a Montaigne for whom a Protestant pastor replaces the melancholy of the stone and who has always stood his mind in the sun. But when we recover from the giddiness of making great comparisons, we cannot but feel we ought to be modest about our contemporaries. Like Montaigne's, Gide's work is an immense collection of scientific footnotes; but in Gide's the main text is missing. We cannot look above to the militant, passionate text of the

Faith, as yet unmutilated by the natural ageing of Western civilisation.

Les Faux-Monnayeurs (*The Coiners*) is manifestly a novel of footnotes, the text of life as it has been written by the novelists is assumed to be in our hands. We no longer ask whether the book is a novel or not; it is an egoist's enquiry, and yet it has the suspense of a narration. The shocking use of coincidence is brilliantly brought off, within the artifice of the book. The fatal reappearance of Boris's talisman, for example, which wrecks the security a careless psychoanalyst has given to the boy, was complained of in the past, but one might just as well complain of the story of Oedipus. In any case Edouard, the novelist, has made plain his taste for fables. The critic of Gide has the difficulty, when he makes objections, that he is dealing with one of the most clear-headed, the most alert, elusive and subtle of divided minds, who has usually guarded his main pieces. I agree with the French lecturer Hytier, who finds in the demon who clinches the fall of Vincent, and the angel with whom Bernard wrestles, the two small misty and unsatisfactory patches in the design. The devil and the angels rarely seem to be more than useful rhetorical arguments to the Protestant mind, and there is an insincere click of the lantern slide when they are mentioned. These two pieces are certainly open. Another point on which I am not sure is the character of Passavant. He is Edouard in reverse, a kind of double. What they have in common is disconcerting: amusement. Why can we be assured that Passavant's amusement is corrupting and Edouard's is not? In fact there are times when Edouard's amusement is shocking, for although we may trust him as a high-minded writer, are we sure we can trust him as a man? Perhaps we can, but as hostile critics of the novel have pointed out—those who have regarded Gide as a kind of Satan—*The Coiners* indicates what a good thing it is to steal people's suitcases, take their money and read their private papers in the certainty of finding something to one's advantage. The evil of Passavant is that he is a short-term man, buying and selling fast on the moral market; the virtue of Edouard seems to lie in little more than a longer view. He has the working security of those who can always fall back when in difficulties, upon the moral respectability of their personal conflicts. But an unlucky visitor might fall clean through that wide-open mind.

The stories of all Gide's young Julian Sorels are still affecting, but they are not to be compared with the portrait of La Perouse, where the realism Gide despises is brought to a high pitch; or with the stories of Laure and Douvier, of little Boris and the anxieties of the pastor's school. As usually happens in the novel, the characters that are not the author's desire and predilection are the best observed: "I lean with a fearful attraction over the depths of each creature's possibilities and weep for all that lies atrophied under the heavy lid of custom and morality." The true element of surprise in this novel is Gide's unveiling of these awkward characters who so dramatically expound the theme of the debased spiritual coin: Armand, desiccated by a harsh clowning that he owes to his puritan upbringing; the pastor deceiving himself with his energy; Rachel, who will have sacrificed herself in vain for a family which has been inevitably ruined by its narrow religion. The novel is a triumph of the critical spirit, for one dreads the extension of these people. One does not want to know more about Douvier than the crucial fact that he will not be loved, and that, however low his wife may fall, his desire to regard her as one above himself will make him abase himself still further. Gide's diagnoses are not, however, theoretical, too avid or simply arbitrary. There is always a recognition of the surprising in human nature: it is brilliant that Douvier's theatrical determination to find out the name of his wife's seducer exhausts itself in the mere excitement of making a journey. (*Amour propre*: it is the key subject, one is inclined to say of half French literature!)

The *Oedipus* and *Theseus* (the latter written in 1944) have been put together at Gide's suggestion. They interlock and they are fables growing out of the main division in his mind. Oedipus, the enlightened, godless man, who reaches forward to all that promises extra inches to his mind, is brought down by the gross intrigue of original sin. Even so he is not destroyed and he is certainly not reconciled to official religion.

> Is that what you wanted, Tiresias? In your jealousy of my light, did you seek to drag me into your darkness? I, too, gaze now upon the celestial dark. I have punished these eyes for their failure to guide me thither. No more can you overwhelm me with the superiority of the blind.

And when he is reproached for leaving Thebes to become an outcast and traveller among strangers, he replies:

> Whoever they may be, they are men. I shall be glad to bring them happiness at the price of my sufferings.

That is the Oedipus of 1930.

When he reappears in 1944 at the end of the story of Theseus his understanding of his disaster has become almost, but not quite, orthodox:

> I believe that an original stain of some sort afflicts the whole human race, in such a way that even the best bear its stripe, and are vowed to evil and perdition; from all this man can never break free without divine aid of some sort . . . perhaps I dimly forsaw the grandeur of suffering and its power to redeem; that is why the true hero is ashamed to turn away from it. I think that is the crowning proof of his greatness; and that he is never worthier than when he falls a victim; then does he exact the gratitude of heaven and disarm the vengeance of the gods.

Not quite orthodox, because Oedipus is allowed to be a spectator of himself: he has experienced, one would say, the

ANDRÉ GIDE

spectator's catharsis, not the victim's ruin itself. It is the great point in Gide that that particular hard core of human pride shall never be broken. The reply to Oedipus comes frankly from Theseus, a reply noble but worldly, not without a touch of the happy incurable cunning of the human creature:

> "Dear Oedipus," I said, when it was plain that he had finished speaking, "I can only congratulate you on the kind of superhuman wisdom which you profess. But my thoughts can never march with yours along that road, I remain a child of this world, and I believe that man, be he what he may, and with what blemishes you judge him to be stained, is in duty bound to play out his hand to the end. No doubt you have learned to make good use of your misfortunes, and through them have drawn nearer to what you call the divine world. I can well believe, too, that a sort of benediction now attaches to your person, and that it will presently be laid, as the oracles have said, upon the land in which you will take your everlasting rest."
>
> I did not add that what mattered to me was that this blessing should be laid upon Attica.

The mystic and the active man are unreconciled, but at least sit side by side united in their loneliness. The hostile moralists take the evening sun and have sacrificed to benignity some of their earlier edge. But the adventure of Theseus and the Minotaur has the clear, sensual joy, the laconic boldness, the sudden exhilarating refusals of the obvious turn of the story, or the received view of it, which Gide has always had at the height of his powers. The Minotaur is not a gross monster: the shock is that he is beautiful, drowsing, intoxicated, beguiled and witless in the delights of his labyrinth. The struggle is not against evil but against pleasure. There can be pleasure when Greece is free. The Theseus (of 1944) hesitates before he kills such a creature in such a divine place, in order to free his country. But the instinct that makes the hero choose freedom at whatever cost puts upon him the obligation to rid mankind of monsters. The application of the fable spreads like ripples from its first, obvious point.

20

The Early Dostoevsky

I HAVE worked but I put aside my chief production. I need more peace of mind. I jokingly began a comedy and jokingly conjured up so many comical circumstances, so many comical figures, and grew to like my hero so much that I abandoned the form of comedy, despite the fact that it succeeded, for my own proper satisfaction, in order that I might further follow the adventures of my new hero and laugh over him myself. This hero is somewhat like me.

So Dostoevsky, after he had been released from prison in Siberia and when, with his customary air of a stage conspirator uttering deadly secrets out loud, he was planning his way back to political favour and literary recognition. The comic book was *A Friend of the Family*.

All Dostoevsky's geese were swans. The tale does not succeed like its immediate predecessor, the exquisite *Uncle's Dream* which he despised; and is in many respects inferior to the novel *Nyetochka Nyezvanov* which was cut short by his arrest and imprisonment. A feeling of effusive insincerity and misguided over-confidence is occasionally and disturbingly purveyed by his writing; there is a kind of double-facedness which we may suppose comes from the anxiety that was fundamental in his life. Over the wagging pavement of that anxiety he sways like some suspicious, spiritual drunk. *A Friend of the Family* is a careless, exaggerated, complacent book, with a good deal of crude Gogol in its picture of provincial society. We know so well, by now, those masterful Russian widows, those "phantasmagorical" spinsters, those dull scheming young men and their half-baked conversations. The very smell of provinciality hangs about them all. Yet, the vitality of a master, spluttering, but in some passages irresistible, is there. Pride and humiliation—a point André Gide elaborated in his celebrated study—are Dostoevsky's "subject" and *A Friend of the Family* is written out of the cocksureness rather than the humility of the comic spirit.

The smallest works of Dostoevsky cast long shadows. The hero who is "somewhat like me": who is he? Is he Rostanev, the old Colonel of the Hussars? A man

> peaceable and ready to agree to anything. If by some caprice he had been gravely asked to carry someone for a couple of miles on his shoulders he would perhaps have done so.

The Colonel foreshadows the Meek figures of Dostoevsky, for he can speak evil of no one and submits, with remorse, to every injustice. He has the morbid sympathy of the hero of the *Notes from Underground* who, seeing a gentleman thrown out of a window during a fight in a billiard room, "envied him so much that I even went into the tavern and into the billiard room. 'Perhaps', I thought, 'I'll have a fight, too, and they'll throw me out of the window.' " With a shrewd native touch of the real Dostoevsky he later reflected that he was "not even equal to being thrown out of the window and went away without having any fight." The characters of Dostoevsky—and their huge garrulousness—are fantasies tried out, half-realised. Hence the confusion they at once create on the page. Rostanev has not the enticing slyness of the masochist, or of the great Meek figures. He has what is rare, we begin to suspect, in Dostoevsky's characters (for most of them have a dual nature), the quality of innocence. He is one of the few figures who does not know his own character and might pass for a Pickwickian Englishman in blameless deliquescence.

The other possibility is that Dostoevsky conceived himself to be the ludicrous and tiresome Foma Fomitch. Here Dostoevsky may have dipped his pen into the ink of his

THE EARLY DOSTOEVSKY

suffering in prison. Foma Fomitch is a Double. This grizzled and insignificant pedant with a wart on his chin, a hook nose, a sneering, imperious little head sticking out of his open-necked shirt—how brilliant are Dostoevsky's physical descriptions—has the arrogance of the slave turned master. (He is said to have been drawn, with Dostoevsky's usual malicious jealousy of other writers, from the Gogol of the mad period.) A bad writer turned toady, Foma had been the buffoon in the family of a General who played all kinds of torturing tricks upon him. Foma used even to be made to crawl round the drawing room on all fours. But now the General is dead and Foma, who had the sympathy of the General's wife and the other ladies in his humiliation, dominates the household, ruling it like a martinet, terrifying everyone by his tongue and reigning by his stinging exploitation of human weakness. He has become the casuist of abasement. There is a wonderfully comic scene, when Foma turns the tables on Rostanev who is the master of the house and has been trying to get rid of him. Foma soon has Rostanev begging for forgiveness; and, relentlessly sure of himself, goes on to bully the master into giving him the title, Your Excellency.

"Well, if I am worthy of it, why will you not say 'Your Excellency' to me?"

"Foma, I will, perhaps."

"But I insist. I see how hard it is for you, that is why I insist. That sacrifice on your side will be the first step in your moral victory; for—don't forget it—you will have to gain a series of moral victories to be on a level with me: you must conquer yourself, and only then I shall feel certain of your sincerity."

"Tomorrow then I will call you 'Your Excellency' Foma."

"Not tomorrow, Colonel, tomorrow can take care of itself. I insist that you now at once address me as 'Your Excellency'."

"Certainly, Foma, I am ready; only what do you mean by 'at once' Foma?"

"Why not, at once or are you ashamed? That's an insult to me if you are ashamed."

"Oh well, if you like Foma. I am ready . . . I am proud to do so, indeed; only its queer Foma, apropos of nothing. 'Good day, Your Excellency.' You see, one cant."

Until, arguing word by word, winning inch by inch, Foma has the Colonel apologising, blushing, bowing and uttering the words. Having succeeded, Foma doesn't want the success. He merely wants to demonstrate his power.

Foma is a little monster. He tortures the serfs by educating them, which they hate, but he educates only for the pleasure of seeing simple people tie themselves into knots. He finds out their secrets and then bullies them. One pretty young boy who has become the lapdog of the General's widow is a special victim. Foma discovers that the boy has only one dream: he always dreams of a white bull. No day is complete until Foma works up a scene about the feeble-mindedness of those who have only one dream. And yet, at the end of the book, when Foma is defeated and exposed, he is still triumphant. For after all, since everyone is happy now they are free of his tyranny, isn't he, in some way, the creator of their happiness? If he hadn't slandered the lovers, how would they have pulled themselves together and declared themselves? And so everyone cries out "Hurrah for Foma"; even the lovers he has nearly ruined; and Foma, with delighted vanity, leads the cheering.

The richness of Dostoevsky as a writer arises from the fertile uncertainty of his moods. A comic theme may become serious and then, transformed, become comic once more. The tragic theme may produce its comic undercurrent. As André Gide says, the schizophrenic has two contrasting personalities which operate at different times; but the double roles in Dostoevsky's characters operate simultaneously: love and hate, pride and abasement, cruelty and tenderness are not mingled but appear dramatically, incongruously side by side. Foma's defeat is an ecstasy. The effect is, of course, the notorious note of self-parody in Dostoevsky's writing, and yet those very parodies break off and assume a serious artistic life. We shall see Foma become, perhaps, Smerdyakov; in the meek Shatov we shall find a successor of the comic Colonel. The hysteric can laugh and weep at will. This inconsequence of mood has been an overwhelming advantage to Dostoevsky as a didactic writer, for it has taken the deadweight out of his teaching and has launched it on the confusing, chopping and changing currents of individual human life. Where other novelists state beliefs, put down the thing believed, Dostoevsky breaks belief down into its phases, as though the act of believing were a fate, an unsought suffering that has been thrust on us. Dostoevsky is able to catch the *process* of believing as it first stirs the entrails, as it breaks down the unity of personality: for his characters have all this dramatic propensity for turning into the opposite of themselves. One believes in their believing because, like the comic characters of Dickens, they live in the manias of the human solitude. The maniacal inner solitariness is all the more convincing because of the gregariousness of his people. A new character enters with his soul on his sleeve, but he brings all his quarrelling relations, his picaresque family history with him, and can be almost heard blatantly proposing a new novel. All the books are packed with short biographies and each dives with shameless irrelevance into the past. How important it is that Dostoevsky's psychological interests should be pathological and obsessed—as they are if we compare them with Balzac's—for without obsession, there would be no way through the hundreds of human lives that come on us in all their physical explicitness, suddenly, overpoweringly, like figures appearing dramatically out of a fog with the rime upon them.

The second tale, *Nyetochka Nyezvanov*, which appears in the same volume as *A Friend of the Family*, in Constance Garnett's translation, was left unfinished. It has two things which have the mark of Dostoevsky's genius. The first is the portrait of a drunken cornet player, who is tortured by the delusion that he is a great violinist, and who is driven to drink and the ruin of his wife and child, by his failure as an artist. Not only is this incomparably solid, raw and touching, but it is frightening too: Dostoevsky knew the artist's nightmare dread of failure, his fanatical isolation. But the richness comes from the knowledge of souls. The story is told as a reminiscence of childhood by a young girl and the wrong judgment of a child's mind give dimension, the sense of the ceaselessness and insolubility of human illusions. In Dostoevsky there is no time: time is simply the catalogue of illusion. For the child the tragedy is that she hates the wrong parent, and the tragedy of the father's life becomes more terrible when she realises she was deceived by him. The second and very astonishing distinction of this tale, is the story of this child's passionate, sensual love for a nobleman's child of the same age, a love affair inflected by all those sensuous desires for suffering, those agonising entreaties, those wars of pride in the heart and those lyrical ecstasies, which are seen in Dostoevsky's descriptions of adult love, and which seem more fitted to the mute, watchful, remorseless lives of children.

Putting these stories down, glancing afterwards at the great works, we cannot help wondering whether a good deal of our talk about the necessity of form and so on in the novel, is not, after all, nonsense. Dostoevsky is a force, ignorant of all the rules. He switches from the first person to long secondhand passages, written without change of voice. He pants back and forth just as he likes; he appears never to eliminate. He is far too garrulous and can never resist confusion. He relies on the dramatic urgency of what he has to say; he enormously relies on character and "characters"; yet he never misses or mauls the finest effect of a great scene, because the whole thing is never finished in his own mind, and it is certainly not preconceived—except in the vaguest sense. Exhausting and exasperating as this may be, it brings to us the sense that life is overpowering, full of a darkness which

THE EARLY DOSTOEVSKY

only he, at that time, can illumine; that we live on the point of Judgment Day and dissolution. As a novelist he is like some face on the screen which gets larger and larger, coming closer and closer to us, until frightened, exalted and perhaps a little disgusted, we are engulfed by the spongy, unhealthy face, laugh when it laughs and are submerged in its nightmares which shortly come to seem our own.

21

Tolstoy

OF all the Russian novelists Tolstoy has been the easiest to naturalise and domesticate in England; and he himself suggested there were affinities between the Russian and English characters. Whether he was remarking upon anything more than the character of the country gentleman in each country we cannot say; there is certainly a very English lack of intellectuality in Tolstoy, and he is nearer to us, if only because of his extroversion and energy than either Dostoevsky or Turgenev are. He is a gentleman of the family-loving kind, a farmer, a soldier and a sportsman. He is a puritan and an anarchist; a creature sanguine, class-conscious and egocentric and he has our particular Protestant madness: the madness of practical morality. The problem of evil is solved, quite simply, when we are drastically pure in private life. His genius for rendering the surface of life recalls to us the gifts of Scott and Jane Austen in their very much smaller scale, though in Tolstoy this genius springs from the classical tradition of Pushkin and from a primitive animality no English writer has ever had. We may even conceive the wild idea that a late novel like *Resurrection*, written when he was over seventy and enormously popular in England when his teachings were at their highest point of influence—was the last of our Victorian novels, the Victorian novel we failed to write but which some unblinkered Ruskin might have written.

Once again in *Resurrection* we can be deluded by Tolstoy's "Englishness" and imagine Tolstoy's Puritanism to be our own. But a great many Russian novels have come our way since 1905 when *Resurrection* was first translated. Now when Nekhlúdov begins his conversion and his long task of retrieving from penal servitude the woman he has seduced, our first thought is that, unknown to Tolstoy, he is mad; that the moral shock he suffers when he sees Máslova in the dock, a condemned prostitute, is something which the trite process of social reformation is inadequate to deal with. Here, we feel, after Dostoevsky, is a problem that has been stated without intensity, and has not been solved except by over-simplification. If Nekhlúdov is Tolstoy, he is Tolstoy without the spiritual pride and the love of his own lusts: Tolstoy as the Countess never saw him.

Nekhlúdov and Máslova are still left with their natures and their lives, and what they really are has never been spiritually or imaginatively grasped by the drastic old puritan who believed in simplifying life by chopping off its limbs. It is, of course, presumptuous to speak of a failure of imagination in a novelist as great as Tolstoy is; but we know that he depended on living models and actual events, and in *Resurrection* he had no model for Máslova beyond a recollection of the servant girl he himself had seduced when he was a youth. Tolstoy's imagination was not of the kind that adds to life in the sense of fusing something new and blinding with it; his imagination was a luminary which lit up and brought back the living detail of experience as the moon in midsummer will miraculously turn a dark landscape to the sparkle of its lost daytime life. What Tolstoy recovers is the motion of time in the events themselves, the continuous approach, young-eyed and innocent, towards the death he feared so much. In that all-searching light of his, life is seen with clarity, understood with awe and watched with compassion; for it moves upon a scene we shall soon leave and which is recreated with the desire of the animal to preserve the goodness of its brief moment.

And then, another point that is bound to strike us: what an advantage the prophet has over the preacher, the bad Christian over the good Christian, the Dostoevskian over the Tolstoyan when they come to writing religious novels. The preacher is forced to prove his point. Sinners *are* reformed, we all know; men and women *do* undergo conversions; they *can* be made better; they may even be none the worse for being made better; and not, as in Dostoevsky, all the better for being worse. But the life of no man or woman can be mapped so neatly into black and white: the value of a life, imaginatively, is in all of a life. What is interesting is that *Resurrection* is written on that socially Messianic impulse which informed nearly all the Russian novels of the 19th century; and that it stands at the beginning of the deterioration of the impulse towards precise ends. *Resurrection* may be said to be the first of the Soviet novels of immediate propaganda for visible objectives. When he was young Tolstoy had dreamed, characteristically, of a religion that was not otherworldly, but which would create heaven on earth, and it is not surprising that many of the Soviet novelists are Tolstoys watered down who have added nothing to his realism. How natural to choose him for a model. No subtler master of the didactic—if we leave allegorists like Bunyan or satirists like Swift aside—has ever written. His is close to the method of Swift, but Swift enlarged from the reign of island hatreds and the dryness of the 18th century.

For Tolstoy is one of the preachers, at least while he is preaching, who does really convert, where others build up in the audience an obstinate resistance. Tolstoy really does most cunningly persuade. We are glad that Nekhlúdov's life is changed when he sees his guilt; we recognise one by one all his feelings; we applaud his honesty, for we are, in some corner of our souls, honest too. Our Protestant heritage makes us glad that he acts. We are glad, too, that Máslova is recalcitrant, angry and bewildered at first; that she can exactly estimate, in her detached and feminine way, what there is of opaque self-exaltation left in him and what there is of transparent repentance. Her sense that repentance is unnecessary makes her real as woman (if not as a character, for she is a shadow) and when, at the crisis of her relationship with him in the prison, she resists what she regards as an attempt to rape her spiritually as she was raped physically, our deepest sense of justice is called out. "The old man", as Tolstoy touchingly said of another tale of his, "wrote well."

How has Tolstoy managed to persuade us while he writes? Not by any special light which came to him after his conversion; not because, except in a purely literary sense, he was imbued by the spirit of the Gospels. He persuades us, as all the epic writers do, by his native possession of the sense of simple inevitability, and he has this sense from his profound affinity with the peasants with whom, as a feudal nobleman, he was in natural communion. He believes, as a peasant might do, in a lost golden age when all was good. "If each man believes in the Spirit that is within him," says the saintly old tramp as he crosses the river with Nekhlúdov, "we shall all be united. Each man will be himself and all will be as one." Each man wakes up in the morning and sees the sky: Tolstoy's religion is like the primitive response to night and day. His simplicity is harsh and unjust enough where he is proud and scornful; and yet it moves us because it springs from a universal feeling that the simple is possible. But his simplicity is not all of a piece; it is not mere tenderness. It is cunning also. Gorki has recorded in his wonderful portrait of Tolstoy how the old man conveyed an impression of knowing all there is to know and of having made his mind up about everything; how he would suddenly bark out harsh, bitter, and coarse sayings and chuckle with malice, grinning like some animal before the horrors of life. He seemed, Gorki said, sometimes not like a human being but a stone; a piece of nature mindlessly contemplating itself and not wishing (we may suppose Gorki to mean) to escape from nature by adding to it in the sociable fashion of other men. What Tolstoy saw, in his egotism, his solitude, his strong animal passion, was the simple physical fact, and he puts this down as if, in the naivety of love and the satisfaction of ever-watching eyes, he were discovering it for the first time. So, for example, in his picture of the early love of Nekhlúdov and Máslova he sets down things so plain and so true that we are struck by their boldness:

> Katúsha, too, was under the same spell. And this was dominant whether they were together or away from one another. The mere knowledge that there was a Nekhlúdov and a Katúsha seemed to be a great joy to them.

In the wonderful scene of the Easter service it is the same: how serene and always limpidly in movement the tale is, as if life were a brook rippling away through the grave course of time itself:

> Mária Ivánovna's pastry-cook, a very old man with a shaking head, stopped Nekhlúdov and gave him the Easter kiss while his wife, an old woman whose silken kerchief did not hide the Adam's apple in her withered throat, drew a saffron-coloured egg from her pocket handkerchief and gave it to him. A stalwart young peasant in a new sleeveless coat with a green sash came up to him.
> "Christ is risen," he said, with smiling eyes, and as he drew nearer Nekhlúdov could perceive the peculiar, agreeably peasant odour; then tickling him with his curly beard, the youth kissed him squarely on the mouth with his firm fresh lips.

Again:

> He noticed, too, that Princess Sóphia Vassílyevna, even during the conversation, was all the while casting uneasy glances at the window, through which a slanting sunbeam was moving towards her, a betrayer which might shed too bright a light on her wrinkled face.
> "Please lower the curtain, Philip," she said, with a glance at the window hangings as the handsome footman entered the room in answer to the bell. "No I cannot agree with you, I shall always insist that he has a great deal of mysticism and poetry cannot exist without mysticism." Angrily one of her black eyes was following the

man's movements as he adjusted the curtain. "Mysticism without poetry is superstition, and poetry without mysticism is prose," she said, with a sad smile, her eyes still fixed on the footman and the curtains. "Philip, that's not the one I meant; it's the one in the large window," she exclaimed.

Tolstoy persuades because he is always bringing his next word to our lips, gently unveiling what we shall all recognise when we see it.

Persuades but, of course, does not convince. The philosophy of Tolstoy is atavistic; it is a retreat into the collective common mind of the peasant. In one way, though hating Marxism and keeping apart from revolutionary politics, he prescribes a similar ideal. His Puritanism is revolting; his egotism is monstrous. It is interesting that gluttony had been one of his vices; he had enjoyed his lusts with the ferocity of a Tartar. And in *Resurrection*, though Nekhlúdov is sympathetic throughout, we find the prison chapters dreary, the criminal histories as boring as a chaplain's memoirs when we compare them with the rich and intense portraits of Dostoevsky's *The House of the Dead*. Compare them: which writer has enlarged our knowledge of the human spirit? Not the preacher. The good things in *Resurrection* are the account of the early love of Nekhlúdov, the brilliant, ironical, immensely wily and experienced descriptions of fashionable life and the back ways of the law. We can smell the wine on the breath of those torpid judges; we catch the officials in the very act of improving their careers. And how charming—for Tolstoy was unable to resist the sense of a man's delight in women's beauty, wit and experience—are those civilised parties which we are asked, in vain, to regard as the hollow haunts of vanity and hypocrisy. It is this rounding against his own instinct and his own civilisation which is unbearable in Tolstoy, as all self-mutilation is, and which strike us as dishonest. Gluttonously he has swallowed pleasure and now there is no more. And yet, we cannot say that his Puritanism with its self-display, has the aridity, the meanness, the smugness, the bent for the hypocrisies of success or the lapses into sentimentality, the cult of the possible, which our kind of Puritanism has commonly had. At least Tolstoy preached the impossible.

22

The Art of Koestler

BETWEEN imaginative writing and journalism the distinction is easy to make; but in some periods the critic is not required to refine on it. In the 19th century the readers of Dickens or Dostoevsky could see the journalism of these writers at a glance, and could without difficulty snip an editorial on the Poor Law, or a feature article on the Russian soul and its need to occupy Constantinople, from the imaginative pages. The readers of great European journalists like Herzen, Engels and, in our own time, Trotsky, were in no danger of mistaking these writers for artists in an important sense, for great artists towered above them. Today the relation has changed. It is generally agreed that the last decade has been unpropitious for the imaginative writer and that the distinguished work of our years has been fragmentary and small in compass; and as the imaginative writer has receded, so the journalist has advanced. It is he who has towered and glowered, the obstreperous, overgrown child of events; and it becomes necessary once more to mark his difference from the creative writer. The task is delicate because the distinction may be thought invidious. It is not, for many imaginative writers have been journalists in the last decade and with every advantage to the range of their interests and their talent. The digestive process of journalism is coarser than that of art, and we have lived through a period when a coarse digestion became indispensable. The journalist has had the task of accommodating violence to the private stomach and of domesticating the religious, revolutionary and national wars in the private conscience. He has been the intermediary between our private and public selves and, in doing this office, has become a hybrid and representative figure, the vacillating and tortured Hamlet expressing our common disinclinations and our private guilt. For it is typical of the contemporary journalist that his case-history goes with him. Like Hamlet, he travels with his court of private disasters, his ghosts, his Ophelias, even his Rosencrantz and Guildenstern; and though we may often think the sight ridiculous, we must give him the credit for attempting the creation of a new kind of first person singular, a new hero, who can "take" the assaults of decivilisation, who has invented a certain style which enables him to face the spectacle of mass suffering and official medievalism, with passion, stoicism and humanity. To him the style is as important as the humanity; and eventually we may be sure that artists will collect his vestiges, as once they eagerly collected the sacred relics of Byronism.

To the journalism and the reporting of the higher kind the work of Arthur Koestler is a copious guide. He is not at the level of Malraux or Silone, for he lacks the hard self-control of the Frenchman, the brain and luminous sensibility of the Italian. Koestler's gift is bold and fresh, but it is theatrical. He is the declaiming and compelling actor. No one has known better than he when to drop what he is doing and rush to document the latest convulsion. In this fashion, he has run through the political infections of our generation; through Marxism, Leninism, anti-Stalinism; and practice has accompanied theory. He has known and documented the political prisons and torture houses. He has belonged to the class described in his book *The Scum of the Earth*, the human wreckage of the Left which Fascism scattered over Europe. How much in his writing is personal experience and how much is an intense imaginative identification with the people he describes, is not important; or rather, only the identification is important. It is passionate, because it is moral; it is complex because it is at once theatrical and aware of itself. There are other qualities: Koestler is more than a simple reporter. He is intellectually volatile; it is second nature for him to generalise about

THE ART OF KOESTLER

events; he is politically trained, and likes to be politically bespattered. It is the business of the journalist to interview everything and Koestler is able to interview philosophy, science, economics, history, and to come back with a notebook full of general ideas which are put to dramatic use. For the rest, the traits of the profession are emphasised in him by his lack of roots. He was born a displaced person; half-Hungarian, half-Jew, he was educated in Vienna, worked in Germany and Palestine, lived in France. He has been created to wander without mundane allegiances. His allegiances were always with the world of ideas or myth; and when these failed, to the world of random physical events. Guilt and self-pity have been the price. With some exceptions—Strindberg is one—imaginative writers appear to allay their neuroses in works of art; but the neuroses of the journalist are exacerbated by his special opportunities for seeing life.

Yet definitions like these do not bring Koestler into the intimate scope of the English critic. He is separated from us by the education and the politics of the Continent, by the vast difference between the large, stable middle-class in England and the small, precarious middle-class of Central Europe. He can easily dazzle us because we have no café conversation and no café writers. We have no skill in playing poker with ideas. We are not trained to pretend that things which are entirely different may (for the pleasure of effect) be assumed to be opposites. We have no eternal students. We have no intelligentsia. These differences have led Koestler himself to as complete and conventional misreading of English life as any that have been done by Continental writers. (See *The Yogi and the Commissar*.) We must assume that our judgment of him will suffer from similar difficulties of contact.

We come nearest to him in *Scum of the Earth*. This is partly because the book is a personal record of the events at the fall of France where, at last, English experience came close to the experience of the Continent. A second reason is that here Koestler has cleaned his slate and is putting down just what he saw and heard and, with emotion, is pulling down the curtain on a period. This report is alive; it is packed with human beings; it is resilient and almost buoyant. He is in his natural element, or rather in one of his natural elements: anarchy and disillusion. His eyes are skinned for every incident as, sombre and sardonic—but not with detachment—he notes down the fates of his friends. This book (and *The Gladiators*) contains his least opaque writing.

But we first heard of Koestler in *The Spanish Testament* and here a play is beginning, not coming to an end. We see the sullen sky over Vigo harbour glowing "under an evil spell." It is the Koestler spell. We are in for melodrama. "The constriction in the throat that affects a whole town, a whole population, like an epidemic"; as in the theatre, generalisations, simplifications. The characters wear the make-up of revolution. This writer does not appear to know Spanish history, but he knows current Marxism. He is briefed. He is in control, and can switch on and off when effects are needed. Sardonic anger, raw humour and the punctures of anthropological inquiry let the wind out of his hysterical passages at the right moment. All this is good journalism, but compared, say, with Brenan or Borkenau on Spain, it is slapdash. Koestler was a smatterer, and the only thing of value that emerged was personal: *The Dialogue with Death*. There have been finer, more sensitive, more humane and more objective accounts of life in Spanish prisons than Koestler's, for Koestler had to be the leading actor, and he writes with one wall of the prison down; but the attempt at a personal revelation is intellectually impressive, and precisely in the study of hysteria which elsewhere in his writing is his least attractive quality. In the end, when the curtain comes down in *The Spanish Testament* we are not entirely convinced or convicted. Perhaps because we have been over-convinced. The impression remains after other books by Koestler. Against ourselves must be put his strongest card;

he has had to combat the English unwillingness to face the appalling facts of medieval atrocity on the Continent.

Yet this may not be the explanation of our uneasiness. The source may be literary; Koestler has a voice, an urgent voice, vital, voluble and lively, above all never boring—a voice, but an arid and mechanical style. On the face of it this is an unkind criticism to make of a displaced writer who is not writing in his own tongue, who has to make shift to write our own and has mastered it. But we suspect that no language is an inconvenience to him; language is a machine; not even in his own language, we feel, has he any love of words or any sense of their precision and grace. Here is a passage from *The Yogi and the Commissar*, and I think the manner itself forbids belief in the argument, and leaves us with the sensation that Koestler himself would only half-believe in it if he could express it simply, for it is only half-true:

> The law of the novel-perspective prescribes that it is not enough for the author to create "real life", he must also locate its geometrical place in the co-ordinate system, the axes of which are represented by the dominating facts, ideas and tendencies of his time; he must fix its position in an N-dimensional space-time continuum. The real Sylvia spins around the centre of a narrow family-vortex of conditioning factors, whereas the author, in promoting her to novel life, places her in the centre of a vortex formed by the great trade winds, typhoons, depressions, and hurricanes of her time. Of course he need not describe or even mention them. But implicitly they must be there.

Koestler uses words as thought-saving gadgets from the ironmongery counter, and draws especially on the vocabulary of science and economics which is paralysed by patents. Like the Latin tag, they may appeal to the vanity; and the Central European mind appears to be susceptible to technical coagulations, but neither exactitude nor illumination issues from them. The love of jargon suggests the lack of an instinct or a sense, and suggests a deaf and arbitrary nature.

The deficiency is more damaging to Koestler's reporting than to his earliest novels. Shaky as some passages in *The Gladiators* are—it was his first "English" novel, and, presumably, a translation—they are pretty free of vices of style. The jargon of Marx, Freud, Einstein, would have been grotesque in a story of ancient Rome and the Spartacus revolt. We are captured at once in this novel by the sardonic vivacity of the author, the raciness of his reporting, his light mastery of the novelist's and historian's material, even by his boyish humour. We also feel a quality which is rare in the melodramas that come after: the sense of the human tragedy and a pity that is truly pitched and moving. That feeling for tragedy is never recovered, and in my opinion *The Gladiators* is his most impressive book. No personal hatred, no extraneous obsession with persecution or guilt, clutters the running of the narrative, or impedes the growth of the argument: for though the matter of the Trotsky-Stalin conflict is present in the chapter on "the law of detours" and is implicit in the main crisis of the book, Koestler has not yet projected himself into the Moscow trials. Success destroys: the revolutions that fail preserve their myth; and to Koestler faith and myth are everything. Another reason for Koestler's excellence in this book is that it has a settled subject, set in the remote past, and history has agreed on it. By gift a reporter, he is a hundred times better in recording what is given than in contriving imaginatively what is not; with him, controversy simply brings out the "old soldier" of the clinics.

The subject of *The Gladiators* is the rising of the slaves under Spartacus, their race to triumph; the tragic split with Crixus, and the final defeat. On the one hand the laxity and shamelessness, the experience and corruption of Rome are comically and diversely rendered with a ribaldry and a talker's scholarship that recall the early Aldous Huxley. These Roman portraits are plump and impudent medallions, cheerfully unclassical; they are the footnotes of Gibbon turned into agreeable and scabrous cartoons. On the other hand is the raw, rushing, high-voiced rebellion, tearing down the roads, laughing, shouting, guzzling, raping, killing. The wings of the traditional humane ideal raise riot above its own lusts; the brotherhood of the camp makes the spirit flesh. There is a pity for the mindless hopes and follies of simple people: this is the only book of Koestler's to show us the lowly material of revolution in the mass, the simple man who, even in his excess, does not wish to die, and whose last look, as he falls, is of surprise. (In the later books, the dying of the revolutionary leaders has lost all human quality; it has become a transaction of policy.) The masses in *The Gladiators* are incapable of salvation, and between the Gadarene downrush which Crixus will lead, and the slow, painful political course for which the mind of Spartacus is pathetically groping, they chose the former. He who cannot stand the screams of his own prisoners, is overwhelmed by the necessity of being a tyrant. He parts company with half his horde; "objectively" he ought to have killed them.

We feel the earth under our feet in this book, and whether or not it has the developed qualities of a novel is not important. In fact, it is a collection of brilliantly placed episodes, linked by a commentary; and growing characters are not required. (This is fortunate, because it turns out in his later work that Koestler has little power to create or sustain large characters.) All that is required in this book is that his pictures of people shall have instantaneous physical reality —Spartacus himself needs very little to fix him in our mind's eye—and that the atmosphere and the feeling, shall be actual like the news. The best of Koestler is in a passage like the following one on the fate of the Praetor; and the end of the passage indicates where Koestler goes wrong:

> On foot—for his horse had been left with the robbers— the bald-headed Praetor Clodius Glaber climbed down into the plain. He had been separated from his fleeing

soldiers, and walked through the night, alone. He strayed from the trodden path, stumbled over the crooked, stony edge of a vineyard, looked around. The vineyard, studded with pointed stakes, looked like a graveyard by the stars' light. It was very quiet; bandits and Vesuvius dimmed to unreality, Rome and Senate were blotted out; yet one more deed asked to be done. He opened his cloak, felt the place with his fingers, gently pressed the sword-point to it.

The deed asked to be done, but it was only now he understood its full meaning. Little by little the point must be driven home; little by little it must tear through the tissue, cut tendons and muscles, splinter the ribs. Not till then the lung is reached, tender, mucuous, thinly veined; it must be ripped asunder. Now a slimy shell, and now the heart itself, a bulbous bag of blood—its touch beyond imagination. Had ever a man accomplished this? Well he might, with a sudden thrust, perhaps. But once you knew of the process and every one of its stages, you would never be able to do it.

"Death" up to now a word like any other, seemed removed into unattainable distance. All the relatives of Death, such as Honour, Shame and Duty, exist for him only who has no ken of reality. For reality, mucuous, unspeakably delicate, with its mesh of thin veins, is not made to be torn to bits by some pointed object. And now Praetor Clodius Glaber knows that dying is unutterably stupid—more stupid still than life itself.

He realizes that his shoes are full of pebbles. He sits down on a stone and empties the shoes; he observes that the pebbly discomfort had been a responsible element of his despair. As compared to the ignominious defeat of his army, the sharp little pebbles—seven in all—admittedly shrink into ridiculous insignificance. But how can you sift the important from the unimportant if both speak to your senses with equal vehemence? His tongue and palate are still covered with the stale taste of interrupted sleep; a few forgotten grapes lurk between the vines. He plucks a few, looks around; only the stars are witnessing the curious sequence of his actions, and their sight is no rebuke to him.

He feels ashamed and yet he must admit that his actions

are in no way senseless; no amount of philosophy can alter the fact that grapes were made to be eaten. Besides, he has never before enjoyed grapes so much. He sips their juice together with the tears of an unexplained emotion. He smacks his lips with defiance and shame.

And night with the lights of its indifferent stars gave as a further knowledge unto Praetor Clodius Glaber: all pleasure, not only defined versions of it, and Life itself, are based on age-old, secret shamelessness.

Why can't these central Europeans learn when to stop? The myth of "age-old, secret, shamelessness"! Not *another* myth, we exclaim, not a new thesis, a new antithesis, a new synthesis!

The real core of Koestler's thought in *The Gladiators*—it is taken up again in a moving passage towards the end of a later book *Thieves in the Night*—is in the words of the Essene to Spartacus:

> "Prophecies are never worth anything," said the Essene. "I explained that before, but in the meantime you've been asleep. Prophecies do not count; he who receives them counts."
>
> Spartacus lay in thought, his eyes open.
>
> "He who receives them will see evil days," he said after a while.
>
> "Aye," said the Essene. "He'll have a pretty rotten time."
>
> "He who receives them," said Spartacus, "will have to run and run, on and on, until he foams at the mouth and until he has destroyed everything in his way with his great wrath. He'll run and run, and the Sign wont let go of him, and the demon of wrath will tear through his entrails."

Spartacus listens to the Essene through the night, until the sky lightens: "The Black shadows in his eye sockets had, as it were, evaporated . . . Spartacus looked again at the glowing East and at the mountain whose everyday shape gradually broke the spell of its nightly distortion."

Night, dawn, noon, the spell: the symbols are theatrical.

Spartacus fails, but now the dawn has come; we are moving towards the success at Noon, the darkness at Noon which is the corruption of success. This is an ancient and haunting Jewish theme. The Race, by numberless pronouncements of Jehovah, has been fated to be destroyed in success, to be searching for ever.

Darkness at Noon is a *tour de force*, a book terrifying and claustrophobic, an intellectual thriller. The efficiency, the speed, the smooth order of the narrative as it runs fast to its end, are extraordinary. Here is the story of a man arguing his way (or being argued) towards the confession of crimes he has not committed, an interpretation of the Moscow trials, a dramatised examination of the problem of ends and means. As a novelist, Koestler has a superb gift for the handling of argument in a living way; he knows when to break off, when to slip into the personal or the small incident, when to digress into the minor character, where to tighten the screw. Rubashov, the accused, makes the pace all through the story; he is an alert, intelligent man, a brain where Spartacus was passive. And occasionally, like a sudden fragment of sunlight in this grey and horrifying book, horrifying in its grim pistol-barrel logic, glimmers of human illumination occur in Rubashov. They are moving. But when all praise is given, *Darkness at Noon* remains a melodrama. Rubashov and Gletkin are a sad pair of Jesuits consumed and dulled as human beings by their casuistry. The Communists have taken over the doctrine of original sin from the Roman Catholic Church, and have tacked the Calvinist doctrine of Predestination on to it; but they have dispelled the visionary and emotional quality of these dogmas, with the dull acrimony of the makers of company by-laws. An irredeemable dreariness surrounds the lives of Rubashov and Gletkin. They are not "great"; they are merely committee men or chess players.

The book is not tragedy. Yet to be destroyed by your own Church or by your own beliefs ought to be tragedy. It is

THE ART OF KOESTLER

surely tragic for the young to destroy the old. There were (if Koestler had not been so gifted in the art of making a case) tragic springs in Rubashov's history. Somewhere in the tale, Ivanov (one of the Inquisitors who is drugging himself with drink) remarks that the murders of Raskolnikov were trivial because they served, or failed to serve, private ends; had they served the ends of the collective morality, they would have been significant. But in *Darkness at Noon* the official killing of Rubashov to serve the collective end fails to reach this high standard. It is a police act, not a tragedy, the end of a case. Koestler could reply that the casuistry of Gletkin & Co. has destroyed the concept of tragedy on the collective plane; but the casuistry is, after all, Koestler's. Rubashov, who has betrayed so many people in the name of "objectivity", has destroyed himself in advance, and is simply getting what is coming to him. By inference, the same will happen to Gletkin. The two rascals are agreed. Wolf, as the Tsarist officer says, eats wolf. Great ideas are in conflict, but in this book they are not embodied in great men.

We have to turn to the greatest of all novels about the revolutionary, Dostoevsky's *The Possessed*, to see that *Darkness at Noon* is a powerful book, but not an imaginative work of the highest kind. It has the intensity of obsession, the interest of surgery, but no largeness. It is a document, pulled up by the roots from a native soil. The revolutionaries of *The Possessed* are living people with biographies, and they are set among other living people. Russia breathes in Dostoevsky's novel, its landscape, its towns, its climate, its history, and grants them the pardon of time and place. For it is evident, from our post-war contacts with them, that the Russians are as Dostoevsky drew them; a people living by wont in a natural atmosphere of suspicion and mistrust, and consumed by fantasies. *The Possessed* is soaked in its own people, grows out of Russian soil. It is felt.

Compared with *The Possessed*, *Darkness at Noon* grows out of nowhere. It is Central European allegory. Yet even the Party is not the same in all countries, and the problem of ends and means is decided not by moralists, but by temperament, feeling, tradition. The objection to *Darkness at Noon* is not that it has overstated its case, but that it has stated only a case; the book understates its field of human, psychological and historical reference. Koestler's own mind is like a prison, with its logical corridors, its dazzling but monotonous lighting, the ingenious disposition of its control towers, its traverses and walls. And there are also the judas slots through which we are led to observe the sudden, shocking, physical revelation; those cells where the dingy human being stands in his day dream; and, outside, the courtyard where the man circles, dragging his shame in his scraping feet. No selfless emotion, no love above all, can be felt there, but only the self-love and self-hatred of the prisoner. And Koestler, who occupies this prison, is like some new and enterprising prison governor, humane enough, but more and more attached to the place and infected with the growing belief that the guilty are ourselves, the free, the people outside. This is a position he shares with the Communist intellectuals of his generation. Their habit of hypnotising and magnetising a subject by the incantations of repetitive argument, so that it becomes rigid, is his. *Darkness at Noon* might be called a major act of literary hypnosis. And the argument is so successful and complete that we begin ceasing to believe in its human application the moment we put the book down.

After *Darkness at Noon* there is a decline. The tight organisation of Koestler's gifts goes slack. Disillusion brought his power to a climax; and since then he has descended to nihilism. *Arrival and Departure* is an attack upon belief itself, due to an enterprising encounter with psycho-analysis:

> If one wanted to explain why Peter had behaved as he did, one had to discard from the beginning his so-called convictions and ethical beliefs. They were mere pretexts of the mind, phantoms of a more intimate reality. It did not matter whether he was a hero of the Proletariat or a

martyr of the Catholic Church; the real clue was this suspect craving for martyrdom.

More accurately, this book is Koestler's attack upon himself as a member of the small middle-class intelligentsia of the Continent, and it ends by justifying isolation. The Cause has been thrown over and humanity goes with it. Koestler appears to have had a theatrical view of faith; it was a vision, not a bond. By a really crass misreading of Freud the neuroses of the revolutionaries are made to cancel the traditions of humanism, indeed any strivings of the mind. The civilised, the believing and creating mind is dismissed. Peter solves his conflicts by refusing to recognise one side of them, and after he has exploded his beliefs goes off to fight nevertheless because "reasons do not matter." Intellectually a poor book, it has all the old skill in story-telling, the old lack of acceptable characters; an incapacity to describe love —love equals lust, etc.—but a terrifying power to describe torture. The effect is overpowering. One could do with the old framework of good and evil to hold this picture in, and the framework existed if Koestler had cared to recognise it. The despised liberal English and Americans of the ordinary kind were impelled to fight and destroy the nation which committed these atrocities. Koestler's atrocities appear to have been taken out of the moral scheme and to have become pornographic. He is like Ivanov in *Darkness at Noon*, who said that ever since the invention of the steam engine, there has been no normality, only war. A remark that is deeply untrue. There is always normality. *Arrival and Departure* shows those vices of style—the use of jargon—which have marked his essays, and the psycho-analysis is too schematic for words.

With *Thieves in the Night* Koestler returns to something nearer the mood of *The Gladiators*, and his ambivalent attitude to violence—and to ends and means—is almost decided. He has come full circle, i.e. he is *very nearly* prepared to justify violence; or rather he has quite decided to throw out justification. He is among the people whom he really envies and admires, the violent people, the people with grenades in their lorries. This is an old legacy from Communism; one can see it in Malraux also. If anything, Koestler is more depressed by the Zionists' capacity as colonists than by their readiness for killing; practical capacity has no Byronism. We have the suspicion that the Neanderthalers of *Darkness at Noon* are being reproduced in the Promised Land. Can it be that the inhabitants of Utopias are always dull and muttonish:

> I have watched them ever since they arrived—these stumpy, dumpy girls with their rather coarse features, big buttocks and heavy breasts, physically precocious, mentally retarded, over-ripe and immature at the same time; and these raw arse-slapping youngsters, callow, dumb and heavy, with their aggressive laughter and unmodulated voices, without traditions, manners, form, style. . . .
>
> Their parents were the most cosmopolitan race of the earth—they are provincial and chauvinistic. Their parents were sensitive bundles of nerves with awkward bodies—*their* nerves are whipcords and their bodies those of a horde of Hebrew Tarzans roaming in the hills of Galilee. Their parents were intense, intent, overstrung, over-spiced—they are tasteless, spiceless, unleavened and tough. Their parents were notoriously polyglot—they have been brought up in one language which had been hibernating for twenty centuries before being brought artificially back to life. . . .

But the Joseph of *Thieves in the Night* has found what Peter of *Arrival and Departure* had defined as a psychological aberration: a Cause. More than a Cause: something that none of the Koestler characters has ever had—the lack is their fatal weakness in debate, a nutritional deficiency of Marxist teaching—a country. It is the embryo country, the almost theoretical country of Zionism, but still a country. In his youth, Koestler had lived for a time in the Jewish communities of Palestine, but had, for some reason, tired of them and left; now, once violence has arisen, his personal interest and his alert journalist eye for the topical story have been stirred. The truth is, of course, that he is cosmopolitan and European; that is his real virtue politically; he sees the interaction and unity of European events, and this rational attitude is clearly in conflict with his new Faith, and so much so that scepticism, detachment, the yearning not to be so committed is the impression that still survives the rifle shots and the Hallelujahs. Such a conflict makes an excellent basis for Koestler's best vein: his talk, and this book has some readable passages.

> Joseph looked round the terrace and sighed. The khamsin lay on people's faces like a spasm. The women were plump, heavy-chested, badly and expensively dressed. The men sat with sloping shoulders and hollow chests, thinking of their ulcers. Each couple looked as if they were carrying on a quarrel under cover of the *Merry Widow*.
> "I can't blame the gentiles if they dislike us," he said.
> "That proves you are a patriot," said Matthews. "Since the days of your prophets, self-hatred has been the Jewish form of patriotism."
> Joseph wiped his face. The khamsin was telling on him. He felt sick of it all: Judaism, Hebraism, the whole cramped effort to make something revive which had been dead for two thousand years.
> "It is all very well for you to talk as a benevolent outsider," he said. "The fact is, we are a sick race. Tradition, form, style, have all gone overboard. We are a people with a history but no background. . . . Look around you, and you'll see the heritage of the ghetto. It is there in the wheedling lilt of the women's voices, and in the way the men hold themselves, with that frozen shrug about their shoulders."
> "I guess that shrug was their only defence. Otherwise the whole race would have gone crackers."

The possibility that the terrorists are really Fascist or copying Fascist methods raises the old bugbear about ends and means, and these discussions are boring.

The central figure, narrator and diarist of this report is now, for the first time, English, an English half-Jew. A naïve snobbery is disclosed here; he belongs to that romantic idol of the Continent, the English country gentry. It is the Disraeli touch. When this character goes to Palestine, he has a low social opinion of those members of the British ruling class who do not come out of the top drawer. One lady—imagine it—has an official position and yet is only the wife of a sergeant! The only real "lady" is an agreeable sketch, but women have always to be punished in Koestler's novels, and she is made to go through a boring official dinner when afflicted by her periods. Koestler's attitude to sex has always been neurotic—least in *The Gladiators*—and, in one of his articles, he threatens to raise the question of the menarche, no doubt as a new myth in the space-time continuum.

Bedevilled by his journalistic habit of treating differences as opposites—it makes a brighter page—Koestler can only draw the Jewish colonists with ironical sympathy and vigour, by covering the Arabs and the English with ridicule. As we ourselves—see *Passage to India*, George Orwell, etc.—have a robust tradition of satire at the expense of our own people, Koestler's looks thin and conventional; the attack on the Arabs, since it is rarely done in English, is fresher, but historically silly. All the same, the bias of the book works to its advantage as a piece of reporting, but only in the first half, that is, say, up to the rape of the girl Dina. The narrative is brisk and dramatic, the picture of the colony is in full colour, the description of its way of living tolerant and moving. We see an Old Testament world; but debated of course, and enlivened by Koestler's short, snorting, schoolboy humour. After the rape—and rape or lust without love is a special interest of Koestler's; down to fundamentals; strip the pretences, debunk, be honest, away from liberal and *petit bourgeois* prevarications in the bedroom—after the

THE ART OF KOESTLER

rape, suspiciously enough, the novel disintegrates, wanders around, and Koestler's doubts appear. The story ends in 1939, which is very lucky for the Anglo-Jewish hero who, in any case, is going to be violent, not with bombs after all, but with a wireless station.

One new quality appears in *Thieves in the Night*; an interest in landscape. The descriptions of Galilee are imaginative. Koestler's talent has always been for the hard, surprising, physical image that stamps a person, a crowd, a place on the mind; and now he is extending this poetic interest to places. It brings an amenity up to now uncommon in his work. We welcome it for in his intense and strung up work there have been no points of rest; the vice of the "dynamic" conception of life is that it does not record the consolations of inertia, and never contemplates a beautiful thing. His attempts consciously to inject beauty have ended in the sentimental.

Thieves in the Night is an improvement on *Arrival and Departure*, but it represents the coarsening and mechanisation of a talent. One looks back upon his novels. What is the final impression? They are not novels; they are reports, documentaries, briefs, clinical statements, animated cartoons of a pilgrim's regress from revolution. They are material, formative material: their opponents, as well as their disciples, are formed by them. The effect is hypnotic. It is a paradox that these lively and fast moving books, at a second glance, have no motion at all, Koestler has fixed them, made them static; it is he with his "case" who is on the move; the story and the people do not move of themselves. Our eye is following *him* and not them. The result is that, underlying the superficial excitement, a bored sensation of unbelief is built up—why read about people who merely illustrate an argument and are foils for the author? Quickly the people recede before the inevitable half-truths of a magnetising talker with a good conceit of himself; and while he rarely makes a dull remark, he also rarely makes one that common experience does not flatly contradict. And yet the confidence with which Koestler grasps important themes makes the continued privacy of the English novel look eccentric. It commonly has been eccentric, but at any rate, except for Orwell we have no novelist of the social or public conscience who has Koestler's scope or force—no journalist or reporter either. It is the price we pay for our lack of interest in general ideas for their own sake: empiricism is not dramatic. General ideas become, however, an infatuation; for example, it may be that the Soviet runs a police State, forced labour camps, etc., because Russia has always had these things, and not because of a recent ethical lapse. It may be that Koestler has imposed a Central European efficiency upon the Russian scene in *Darkness at Noon*. Perhaps the English novelist is wise to avoid general ideas and to stick to life as it is presented to himself, and to leave what he doesn't know to the newspapers and the Blue books. For the novels of Koestler are skeletal. They are like the steel frameworks of modern buildings before the bricks go in; and up there, shaking all over with the vibration of the thing, is Koestler furiously concentrating on his pneumatic riveter. A guilty figure: he can't get over an old wish that it was a machine gun and the principle is maddeningly similar. So guilty does he feel that presently he stops work, harangues the crowd below, and the building is never completed. It remains, a stimulus, an incitement to others, a theatrical outline against the sky.

23

Tristram Shandy

A LITTLE of Sterne goes a long way—as long as nearly 200 years, for his flavour never dies in the English novel. It is true we cannot live on tears, fancy cakes and curry. But, take him out of the English tradition; point out that George Eliot, D. H. Lawrence, Conrad—the assembled moral genius of the English novel—ignore him; explain that he is not Henry James; despise him because he created "characters", a form of dramatic person out of fashion for a generation or more—and still his insinuating touch of nature comes through. He is obvious in figures as different as Thackeray and Firbank; and *Ulysses* is sometimes thought of as the *Tristram Shandy* of our century. We see the releasing hand of Sterne in those instances where the English comic genius leaves the usual moral territory of satire or the physical world of knockabout, and finds a third region which is neither pure intellect, pure fantasy nor pure imagination and which is indeed an evasion of all three. To call this the eccentric strain explains nothing; it is well known that the English are eccentric. Sterne—it is better to say—is mad, using the word as we commonly do in England to avoid facing and judging people who themselves are engaged in not facing what they are really up to. Eccentricity is, in fact, practical madness. It is resorted to, Henry Adams said in his severe and shrewd New England way, by those who are up to something shameful or stupid or muddleheaded. And, in England, most of us are.

It is possible that the comedy, half artifice and half nature, which we extract from our "madness" is fundamentally stupid; there is an excessive and stupid streak in Ben Jonson where this comedy abounds. All the same we have sometimes raised stupidity to the level of a fine art.

The "madness" of Sterne, the hostile critic might say, is a practical device for foisting upon the reader a brilliant but shameless egotism, an inexhaustible selfishness and a clever smirking insincerity. Compare his shamelessness with Boswell's: the Scotsman is wanton, transparent and artless, haunted by fear of the Presbyterian devil, whereas we can be sure the devil himself was afraid that the half-Irish Sterne would drag him into bad company. Boswell calculated nothing or, at any rate, nothing right, except his money. Sterne calculated eloquently. Constantly he reckoned up how much he was going to feel before he felt it; even calculated his words so subtly that he made a point of not ending half his sentences and preferred an innuendo to a fact. He relied on the reader's imagination. I notice that in the sympathetic and unprejudiced inquiry that Mr. Peter Quennell made into Sterne's character in *Four Portraits*—and this contains the most illuminating study of Sterne that I know of—there is the suggestion that he was the first to use the word "sentiment" in our imaginative literature and to found the modern meaning of the sentimental. I do not know whether this is so, but it ought to be. For Sterne was a sentimentalist, because his imagination was morbidly quick to impose the idea of a thing, its image-provoking words and its *ambiance* long before the feeling was evoked. He could talk his heart into beating. He could talk tears into his eyes. Or so we feel as we read him; never sure whether this sociable, good-natured, too impressionable man is sincere or not.

One can see Sterne's temperament at work in the account of the beginnings of the Widow Wadman's love of Uncle Toby. The widow's passion was not born until she had seen him among her things in her own house:

> There is nothing in it out of doors and in broad daylight, where a woman has a power, physically speaking, of viewing a man in more lights than one—but here, for her soul, she can see him in no light without mixing something of her own goods and chattels along with him—till

by reiterated acts of such combinations he gets foisted into her inventory——

This may be a universal truth about love, but down to the last *double entendre*—and, above all, because of it—the fancy encases the feeling as it did in the parallel circumstances of Sterne's courtship of his wife. His passion warmed when she let her lodgings to him in her absence.

"One solitary plate," he wrote,

> one knife, one fork, one glass! I gave a thousand pensive penetrating looks at the chair thou hadst so often graced, in those quiet and sentimental repasts—then laid down my knife and fork, and took out my handkerchief, and clapped it across my face, and wept like a child.

Obviously one who felt so strongly for a chair could live very well alone in the comforts of his own imagination.

Alone: it is that word which rises at last to the mind after it has been dragged for miles at the heels of the bolting, gasping fancies and verbosities of *Tristram Shandy*. The gregarious, egotistical Sterne is alone; garrulously, festively and finally alone. If there is one thing he likes better—again, in literature as in life—than the accident of meeting, it is the agreement to part. One can put this down, at a guess, to his severance from his detested mother. In *Tristram Shandy* it is notable and important that all the characters are solitaries. Mr. Shandy and his wife, Dr. Slop, Uncle Toby and the Corporal live shut up in the madhouse of their own imaginations, oysters itching voluptuously upon the pearl within. Mr. Shandy silences his brother with his philosophical systems and his cross-references, never sees a fact but he recedes from it into abstraction, and is determined that the palaverings of the search for Truth shall have one end only: that he gets his own way in his own home. The blameless Uncle Toby sits in his innocence, conducting his imaginary campaigns, short of speech and blinking at the world. Mrs. Shandy hurriedly agrees with her husband; nobody knows what is on *her* mind. Dr. Slop is shut up in the horror of his pendulous belly and Corporal Trim does what he's told, loves his master, but lives by his memories of his poor brother Tom in Lisbon. Habit rather than communication keeps them all happily together. They are bound by ennui, grey days and indolence. But, read the dialogue: it is a collection of monologues. True, Uncle Toby and the Corporal have occasional awkward interchanges, but the general impression is that no one answers serious questions and that they know one another far too well to listen. In family life there is nothing to do about the hard core of the human ego, but to accept it. The indecencies and the double meanings of Sterne, if anything, intensify the solitude; they provoke private reflection and erect barriers of silent lecherous satisfaction. How can the Widow discover where Uncle Toby was wounded, when he can only answer: "In the siege of Namur." Sterne displays the egotist's universe: life is a personal dream.

Those who deny Sterne talent of the highest order and think of him as outside our tradition, must strip away half our tradition and character first. Sterne's discovery of the soliloquising man, the life lived in fantasy, is the source of what is called the "great character" in the English novel, a kind which only Russian fiction, with its own feeling for "madness" in the 19th century, has enjoyed. *Tristram Shandy* is the inspiration of the solitaries of Dickens, the idea-ridden people in Peacock and many others in our literature; they are not literary theories but comic abstractions from a faculty of life. It must be admitted that Mr. Shandy and Uncle Toby are both very stupid men; they are funny because Sterne is so much cleverer than either. He plays tunes on them. They are also bores—always the richest game for the comic instinct. If we compare them with other great bores, like Bouvard and Pécuchet, the Shandys have the advantage of not riding their hobby-horses to any purpose. They prove nothing either to us or to themselves, but illus-

TRISTRAM SHANDY

trate rather the vegetable inertia of the fanciful life and display the inhabiting of one's temperament as the most sensible thing to be engaged in. Every dog to his basket. Even in the torpor of their domesticity, the imagination can beguile.

The bother was that Sterne was a bore himself, as boring in his way as Mr. Shandy is. That Irish loquacity which he got from his mother and his early years in Tipperary had deluded him. He has that terrible, professional, non-stop streak of the Irish. One feels, sometimes, that one has been cornered by some brilliant Irish drunk, one whose mind is incurably suggestible. Although we have a hypnotised picture of Uncle Toby's dubious fortifications they take on, in our minds after an hour or two, the heavy appearance of those surly battlements one sees during the migraine. *Tristram Shandy* must be the most put-down book in English literature. One can respond, of course, to the elaborate cunning of its counter-point; there is method in the anarchy. But the book is a collection of fragments in which every fragment sticks: Mr. Shandy fallen geometrically with grief in his bed; Uncle Toby dazed by the fire; the pipe stem snapping as the child is born upstairs; the ludicrous discussion about the landboat, with its foreshadowing of Peacock; Bridget putting Mrs. Wadman to bed; Mr. and Mrs. Shandy on the "bed of justice" with the inevitable chamber pot sticking out from under the vallance while they talk of putting young Tristram into breeches; the pretty picture of Brother Tom going into his sausage shop in Lisbon where there was a Negress driving off fleas with a feather.

Sterne has a genius for mosaic; for being any self he has decided to be; for living in the effervescence of his nature. The sentimentalist is a cynic, naturally:

> Love, you see, is not so much a Sentiment as a Situation, into which a man enters, as my brother Toby would do, in a *corps*—no matter whether he loves the service or no—being once in it, he acts as he did. . . .

Many have wondered at the feverish receptivity of his eye and some have seen the dread of death—for he was a consumptive—in his determination to look at each event through a microscope as if enlarging it would slow the course of time. That Sterne's sensibility to the passage of time was unusual is certain; he seemed to see each minute as it passed, and to be eager to hold it with a word. But others—of whom Mr. Quennell is one—see in his minuteness the training of the painter. Every sight, every thought was a physical model. There can be no doubt that he broke into the stream of consciousness and was the first to splash about there—in rather shallow water; there can also be no doubt that he was never going to commit himself to anything deeper. It was enough that one thing led to another and that the sensibility was ready for the change. It was Sterne's wife, a woman heavily committed to housework and a bad temper, who, for a time, went out of her mind.

24

The Roots of Detection

WHAT is the lineage of the detective story? It begins, presumably, with the first detective: Vidocq. After that important invention, Hoffmann's *Mlle de Scudéri* seems to be next in the succession and here the moral and technical basis are properly laid down. We are on the side of virtue and justice against evil conspiracy and plausible accusation, and the latter have to be exposed step by step. Poe's *The Murders of the Rue Morgue* grew out of *Mlle de Scudéri*, but in Poe the stress is on the horror of crime and evil, rather than on detection. I have never read the Frenchman, Gaboriau, to whom Wilkie Collins is said to owe a debt, but Wilkie Collins is, at any rate, the first properly uniformed and impressive detective novelist in English literature. The pure conundrum, intricate, sufficient to itself and an exercise of the faculties, has at last been extracted from the double meanings, the symbolism, allegories, crimes and hauntings of the Germanic or the Gothic tales, by the pragmatic English genius. When young Franklin Blake in *The Moonstone* is finally shown to have taken the moonstone without knowing it, the explanation is that he has been doped with laudanum, and not that he has a second self, or a higher and lower nature; he is allowed no more than an accessible and godfearing Unconscious. In short, Wilkie Collins is as British as they are made.

Two new editions of the *Tales From Hoffmann* and *The Moonstone* have been published. Tenuously united, at some point, in the roots of their art, the two authors are suggestive in their fundamental divergence. The Hoffmann which retains many of Gavarni's excellent illustrations, is well-edited and contains *The Golden Pot* (which Carlyle translated), *The Sandman, The Deed of Entail, The Story of Krespel* and *Mlle de Scudéri*. I will begin by quoting from Mr. J. M. Cohen's acute analysis of Hoffmann which has explained to me why (when it comes to the test) I prefer Hoffmann's kind of tale, a book like Hogg's *Confessions of a Justified Sinner*, or (with reservations) *Jekyll and Hyde* to nearly all works of detective fiction. "There are for Hoffmann three realms", says Mr. Cohen, "a comfortable Philistia—comically drawn in *The Golden Pot*—a borderland of dangers and hidden significances, and a third region of spiritual power and serenity." In Collins and his descendants there is Philistia alone: the detective novel is the art-for-art's sake of our yawning Philistinism, the classic example of a specialised form of art removed from contact with the life it pretends to build on. It is an abstract reduced to the level of harmless puzzle and pastime. It provides a pleasant way of not-reading, sharpening the instruments of the intelligence, but giving us nothing to use them on. We could go on—if we were attacking detective fiction—to say, as people used to in the old Marxist days, that it exemplified the spirit of self-regarding isolation in middle-class culture, and that, in its way, it was as precious as Pater. Or, in its defence, that it represents a core of private sanity, a tenacious belief in the effectiveness of intelligence and reason, which still survives in us despite the conditions of our age.

Hoffmann's world, on the contrary, is the underworld or overworld of Romance, the world of Good and Evil, not of Right and Wrong. We shall meet the flesh and the devil, wickedness and virtue, imagination and the world. A tale like *The Gold Pot* is a charmed allegory of the life of the artist. Those who find German fantasy repugnant, who groan before its archaic paraphernalia and see in its magic, its alchemy, its visions, its hypnotic dreams and trances, its ghosts and its diabolism, all the disordered tedium of the literary antique shop, will find Hoffmann more engaging, more concrete, and cleverer than he seems at first sight. He is a wonderful story-teller, his humour is gracious, he is circumstantial and his invention is always witty. In *The Gold*

THE ROOTS OF DETECTION

Pot, for example, where the artist takes to drink, he is represented not as a drunkard but as a little creature imprisoned in a bottle. *The Entail* is a vivid and satisfying *nouvelle* and the management of the two sleep-walking scenes is the work of a master of ingenuity. And if his world is Romance, then it defines what Romance ought to be: not extravagance, but life reflected perfectly in a mirror or a lake, true in detail, but mysteriously ideal. Mr. Cohen says:

> The most important events in Hoffmann's life were fantasies; his early love of Cora Hatt and his later love for Julia More had no basis in reality—the ladies were not as he imagined them; on the other hand the Napoleonic wars, which he affected to disregard, were the very real background to a great deal of his life. Dream and reality had changed places for him.

(And here Hoffmann became the forerunner of those characteristic modern Romances: the imaginative case-histories of Rilke and Kafka.)

But greater authority was given to his dream visions by the decay of religious myth in the age immediately preceding his. Robbed of the immediacy of miracle stories, which had been part of Christianity's millennial heritage, the 18th century was forced to look for evidence of the supernatural elsewhere, in order to satisfy man's instinctive belief in events not subject to material law. Following Swedenborg's lead, they looked to mesmerism, spiritualism and psychic phenomena, for the proof of God's existence; the artist's frenzy and the madman's alike provided evidence of possession by forces superior to man's; dreams rendered everyone familiar with a world outside the closed kingdom of cause and effect.

And, I suppose, the late survival of medieval life and of folklore in Germany, must be partly due to the destructive effect of the Hundred Years War, on culture. War and revolution *do* give a meaning to life, but the heart and the sensibility feel that meaning to be of a low order and even spurious. Hoffmann is a sweet dessert wine, but he has that extra clear-headedness in a restricted field which is often noticeable in the fuddled; he was a startlingly complete artist, though in miniature. He had grasped the lesson of folklore; that the extraordinary, the unheard of, must be made minutely, physically real, and the pleasure he gives is that of exactitude and recognition.

Like Hoffmann, Collins, of the divergent branch of Romance, was a lawyer. Collins takes a practical view of the cranky new material and makes a fine art of not seeing beyond the end of his nose. How thoroughly, exhaustively and yet memorably one has the whole story of the moonstone at one's finger-tips. I find it hard to remember nearly all plots, but I can remember every detail of *The Moonstone*, though the plot must be one of the most elaborate in literature. The explanation lies in his skill and his perfect balance. He never goes too far, and is very particular; he also understands the reader's anxiety to follow, whereas Dickens in *Edwin Drood* had no mercy and counted every confusion in the reader's mind as a victory. As Hoffmann was at heart, Collins is a rational man. There is, of course, no fantasy or mystery-mongering in Collins. The Hindus in *The Moonstone* use a boy medium, but (to our relief) Collins knows all about mediums. He uses the character of an opium addict, but not —we thank heaven, again—for exploring opium dreams, but as one of the perfectly working pistons of the plot-machine. Delirium comes in and we approach the alarms of free-association and psycho-analysis but Collins is interested only in the *utility* of the mysterious. The doctor's free associations are there—to be taken down in shorthand. There are many high moments in the book, but the best is fittingly at the climax: the scene where Franklin Blake, drugged once more with laudanum, re-enacts his part in taking the moonstone from Miss Rachel's cabinet; and here Collins displays his mastery of one of the great principles of story-telling,

THE ROOTS OF DETECTION

which is to appear to do the same thing twice, but on the second occasion to make a significant alteration. The moment where Blake drops the stone which the onlookers expect him to hide is wonderful. The art of the story-teller lies, of course, in surprise; but the art of surprise must come from the continuous knowledge that the reader, in his anxiety, is always playing for safety. It is the story-teller's business to make the path of safety into a path of change and danger. There is a parallel scene in the sleep-walking scene in Hoffmann's *The Entail*. The first time the guilty servant walks in his sleep the observer realises that silence is essential. The second time he forgets to tell a second observer to be quiet. The man shouts and the tragedy comes down with a crash.

Sergeant Cuff, Collins's detective, has been much admired. He is well characterised, as all Collins's people are; he is something like a real detective—Holmes owes many details to him—and is never in danger of becoming a legend. His withdrawal from the middle of the tale which is beyond his professional competence, and the fact that he is wrong, are excellent moves. Only the suicide of Rosa Spearman jars, and here one suspects a superlatively clever writer is taking on too much stage-property. There is said to have been a film company which liked a scene from a moving stairway in all its films because the company owned a piece of moving stairway. Having exuberantly introduced some quicksands—a favourite Victorian property—into his tale, Collins had to use them. There are complaints, too, about the excessive characterisation of the narrators. This does, indeed, delay the narrative; but with one character, the pious, tract-distributing Miss Clack, Collins hit upon a wonderful type; and though he piles on her follies where the genius of Dickens would have cut them until she was a comic fantasy, Miss Clack is a startling break with the slightly sententious habit of the other narrators. Smugness was thought to be the defect of Collins's character, but it was the engaging smugness of the most fertile example of efficiency in the English novel. Never was there such a specialist. *The Moonstone* is the first and the last of the detective novels, and I would like to ask the addicts what more has really been added to the genre since his time.

25

The Poe Centenary

A HUNDRED years after his death what are we to make of Poe? He is a writer into whom large, inexact things may be read and from whom many things important to literature have been taken; a second-class writer, yet a fertilising exclaimer. The paradox is that his genius was merely probable and narrow and yet his influence was wide. Read those poems again which Baudelaire compared to crystals: it is a strange comparison for verses so slack in their simplicity, so mechanical in their devices. And yet we are haunted by overtones of an exceptional experience. It is no ordinary tomb on which Poe weeps; there is more than loss in those tears. There is guilt and dismay. Afterwards, the mourner will be haunted not by the dead but by himself. When we turn to stories like *The Pit and the Pendulum*, *The Murders of the Rue Morgue*, *Ligeia*, or *The Fall of the House of Usher*, the accent is self-assured, but we are not, after two wars, bounced or interested by the rhetoric of suffering and sadism. D. H. Lawrence found the material conventional, meretricious and vulgar. The voice of incantation appears to be disguising the experience, is slurred and constructs the conventional nightmare of the drug addict or the facile alcoholic:

> Not hear it;—yes, I hear it, and have heard it. Long—long—long—many minutes, many hours, many days, I have heard it—yet I dared not—oh, pity me, miserable wretch that I am!—I dared not, *dared* not speak. *We have put her living in the tomb!* Said I not that my senses were acute? I *now* tell you that I heard her first feeble movements in the hollow coffin. I heard them—many, many days ago—and yet I dared not—*I dared not speak*! And now—to-night—Ethelred—ha! ha!—the breaking of the her-

mit's door, and the death cry of the dragon, and the clangour of the shield!—say, rather the rending of her coffin, and the grating of the iron hinges of her prison, and her struggles within the coppered archway of the vault.

Efficient, silly and yet its harangue can overpower. It is theatrical and yet not pure theatre. If we set aside the skill of narration—and we ought not really to do so because part of Poe's gift to literature is his teaching and example of the conscious artist—there is more than the expert tale of mystery or horror; there is the sustained enacting in conditions amounting to claustrophobia, of a universal human pain. The redeeming thing is Poe's gift of generalising morbid experience.

Poe's parents (it is well known) were actors; and one is obliged to see him as an actor-writer. Perhaps his technical genius in creating new literary forms came from the application of the actor's temperament to a medium that was alien to it. He comes on to the stage, among his grotesque properties—the pit of the Inquisitor, the rotting ancestral mansion, the luxurious Disraelian palace or the jewelled valley—and with the first oratorical words and the first hypnotic gesture, he has created an atmosphere. An atmosphere, the hostile must say, that one could cut with a knife. We suspect the old trouper and there is no doubt that his prose comes out of the catalogue; he goes from one cliché of Romance to the next; the names of his characters, the Lady Madeleine, Ligeia, Berenice, Lenore, are shamelessly stagy; and like the notorious "Nevermore", are made for the parodist. But what grips the reader is that Poe is evidently not acting an *alien* part; the story is *his* story, this is his pain, enlarged and generalised as poetry is, and it can suck us into its whirlpool just as, irresistibly, the death ship of *The MS. Found in a Bottle* was drawn down into the ocean. Suffering and guilt are his subjects: to magnify is his method.

There is a point at which the magnifying glass makes the object too large, when the close-up loses nature; and that is

THE POE CENTENARY

the point of vulgarity in Poe. But I do not believe there is a story in this assiduously inventive writer which is not taken from his own state. He was the first writer of any importance in English to take, possibly from Hoffmann and Vidocq, the notion of the tale of detection. He must have been one of the first writers of scientific romance. These are remarkable inventions. It is not merely by lucky chance that he saw the interest of these forms of writing, for both his extraordinary flair for literary genre and the peculiarity of his temperament predisposed him to them. They seem, when we speculate upon it, to be the natural interest of his divided nature and the fruit of personal guilt which has been turned to literary advantage. We can see the clever mind of the expert neurotic observing its own sensibility and its terrifying private fantasies. The mysterious, he sees, can be chemically split; explanation can be, he perceives, as exciting, sensationally, as the mysterious thing. In the tales of the dying woman prematurely buried, in the story of Ligeia rising from the dead to poison and annihilate her rival, we can see Poe dreading the death of his Virginia, wishing for it and willingly incurring remorse and punishment. One understands what such themes could suggest to Baudelaire and Dostoevsky; moreover, the writings reflect a life that seems itself to be a direct expression of Poe's own theory of "the unity of effect." His character is, in a sense, to be read at a sitting; it was constructed, we feel, from the end first; it was a suicide, the deliberate seeking of a pre-conceived fate. For Poe is steeped in pride; allowing for D. H. Lawrence's manias, his criticism that Poe blasphemed against the Holy Ghost within him is a true one.

Poe the alcoholic, Poe the incestuous, Poe the unconscious homosexual, Poe the Irishman, the Southerner, the derelict, Poe isolated in American life and ruined by the *odeur de magazine*—these versions are familiar. They have their share of truth. In a quietly provocative introduction to *The Centenary Poe*, Mr. Montagu Slater reminds us of the part played by simple financial misery in Poe's life. He got

£2 for *The Raven*. It seems doubtful whether writing for magazines ruined him: he was a magazine-man. He was a brilliant lecturer. He was not a physical weakling: he had been a regimental sergeant-major and a fine swimmer. Mr. Slater goes on to a vague argument of the kind that might be useful if it could be fully documented—and I do not see how it can be—that art for art's sake began with Poe, and has remained dominant in Western literature ever since. He links the doctrine with solipsism and with Poe's own doctrine, expressed in characteristic tones of incantation in *Eureka*: that the soul is a particle of God that must return, annihilated, into His Oneness. Poe's famous proposal of the short poem, that long poems are merely short ones connected by prose, that works of art must be grasped at a sitting and that there must be unity of effect, is made to support Mr. Slater's argument. But to say that intensity and the love of beauty above all else have any special connection with art for art's sake is to force argument. Poe's doctrine of the instantaneous has, indeed, been realised, as Mr. Slater says, in many important forms of modern art; but that is far from meaning that copious works are more diverse, or that intense works are incapable of deep humanity. The personal voice and experience of Poe underlie his artificialities, and we now understand that what used to be called morbid experience is universal and has a direct bearing on spiritual life.

One great difference in kind between Poe and Sartre, Camus and Graham Greene, whom Mr. Slater regards as the latest if not the last of Poe's aesthetic line, is one of energy. In the sense that he carries within him the feeling of power which was felt in the early 19th century, Poe is electric: a positive neurotic, a wilful madman, an aggressive suicide. His terrors, his pains, his guilt, his punishment, his melancholy itself, are represented as inflations and energies of the soul. They are not presented as maladies to be cured and he does not wish to lose them. He feels, romantically, all the larger and more powerful because of them as if they were a gift and privilege. The Romantics felt all the greater for their cult of death and pain, whereas psychology has taught us to regard our sickness as mutilation or a misleading of our powers. Poe is perfectly able to live his derelict and isolated life regardless of the community. A loquacious and throbbing pride enables him to do so; his sorrow runs a pipeline to the eternal. The later writers lack this aggressiveness. Pain is inflicted upon them. They are ciphers of passivity—as, indeed, the ordinary man is among the political horrors and farces, the double-faced institutions of our time, where persecutors and persecuted change places with the nullity of papers in a file. Though they attempt to dignify themselves with the belief that they are drifting to annihilation in the One, the Nothing, the Historical, or the Nevermore, they bob up and down on their way over Niagara with the feebleness of corks. Long ago they lost their bottles. They do not die: they blackout. Destruction is taken out of their own hands. They just run into it absurdly. Poe on the contrary did not believe life was a fraud; he believed it was an orchestrated tragedy; he had the Romantic afflatus. Loss and death were inevitable; pain was an action felt or done. It is pure speculation but, if he could be reborn, one imagines him writing his stories not about the victims of the Inquisition, but about the great repressed subject of our day: the morbid psychology of the Inquisitor and torturer and their guilt; simply because that is now the dominant, positive and energetic aspect of contemporary pain. The Inquisitor has had his romantic wish for power: what has *he* paid for it?

It is usually said that Poe is an un-American and cosmopolitan writer, and Baudelaire declared that America was Poe's prison. But Poe was a natural prisoner. It seems to me he was very American and especially so of his time; intellectually aggressive and provincial, formed by journalism, a practical and exacting technician and critic—see his analyses of novels by Dickens and Hawthorne—as cranky in his way as Thoreau, Emerson and Hawthorne, for example, of rather wild personal independence in opinion. Above all, he is American in the capital hold that nostalgia has on his emotions. It is the melancholy, lonely dominant note in the feeling of American literature: from the Mark Twain of *Huckleberry Finn* to T. S. Eliot. It is indeed this feeling which encloses even the slack poems, that seem to us sentimental or merely pathetic; it is on a general and native longing, that he is able with all his power of rhetoric to play. The melody that runs through his writing, impure but sweeping and haunting, the loneliness of his incantations, themselves seem to be designed to deploy that simple feeling; and the dream world which is not really a dream world, owes its effect to the fear and the longing it is meant to convey. We feel that a nation of lonely people is projecting his fantastic palaces or is considering his unlikely dungeons; for in a new and rapidly successful country, part of the human personality is a casualty, and in that injury is the desire that cannot be realised.

26
Oliver Twist

OLIVER TWIST is the second novel of Charles Dickens. It was begun before *Pickwick* was finished when he was twenty-six and in the full conceit and harassing of sudden fame; and *Barnaby Rudge* was started before he got Nancy murdered and before Bill Sikes slipped by accident off the wall on Jacob's Island into his own noose. It is a novel speckled with good London observation, but the critics agree that the book which gave the word Bumbledom to the language is a gloomy and inferior work, stretched out on an incredible plot, blatant with false characters and false speech and wrecked by that stageyness which Dickens was never long to resist. The story is a film scenario full of tears and "ham", an efficacious splurge of Cockney self-pity. On the other hand, the reader must protest that all this is no drawback to his excitement. The popular thriller is generally based on the abstraction of sinister human wishes from the common reality of life; and, willingly suspending disbelief, we can eagerly accept Fagin, even Bill Sikes and Mr. Brownlow, even Nancy and Rose Maylie, as permitted fantasies. Is it because of the hypnotic fame of Dickens or because he is completely responsive to the popular taste for uninspected myth, that all his characters stay in the mind? Only the neurotic Monks and the creaking, sceptical Grimwig, have one false foot in the world of our experience.

A new edition of *Oliver Twist* has the advantage of a really brilliant, melancholy and subtle appreciation by Mr. Graham Greene, himself a thorough initiate in the art of writing thrillers. It is one of those uncommon prefaces that expertly test the technical merits of a book and enlarge its suggestion. Before turning to his main points, there are two obvious yet easily forgotten virtues in *Oliver Twist* which put what might have been a total failure on its feet. For there is no doubt that *Oliver Twist* "comes off." In the first place it is a literary novel, nourished by Dickens's early reading. The echoes from Monk Lewis, the touches from *Jonathan Wild* in the framing of the portraits of Mr. Bumble or the Artful Dodger, the preface which curiously boasts that at last we are to be given real criminals—except in the matter of bad language—and not romantic ones, are all touching and agreeable glances from a spuce young author towards his tradition. (And, as Mr. Greene shows, we certainly get real thieves' kitchens and the sour poverty of criminal life, the background but not the foreground.) In the second place, the book is given a kind of authority by the frank copying of Fielding's mock heroic and disquisitional moralising. By this Fielding displayed the assurance of his sensible morality, and it is true that Dickens debases the manner by turning it into something journalistic, sprightly and even facetious; nevertheless, the manner enabled him to assume a central place in the tale, from which he could exploit, without confusion, the variety of its moods.

It was Mr. Edmund Wilson who first saw the biographical importance of the melodramatic and criminal episodes in Dickens's work. They are for the most part the least successful as literature. They are commonly over-acted and, indeed, too much stress on these and the didactic side of Dickens, is likely to take us away from his greatness. It is all very well for modern critics to neglect the comic Dickens for there, as a writer, he was completely realised. On the other hand, the impurity of Dickens as a creator is an important fact; in his confusions and concealings, strange psychological shapes are disclosed. His relation was with the public which he bowed to and upon whose not always reputable feelings he played. Upon them, as upon an analyst, he enacted a transference. Mr. Graham Greene's main point is, in a sense, an extension of Mr. Edmund Wilson's into the field of religion. He suggests the religious cast of Dickens's imagination:

OLIVER TWIST

> How can we really believe that these inadequate ghosts of goodness [Mr. Brownlow and Rose Maylie] can triumph over Fagin, Monks and Sikes? And the answer is, of course, that they never could have triumphed without the elaborate machinery of the plot disclosed in the last pages. The world of Dickens is a world without God; and as a substitute for the power and the glory of the omnipotent and omniscient are a few sentimental references to heaven, angels, the sweet faces of the dead, and Oliver saying, "Heaven is a long way off, and they are too happy there to come down to the bedside of a poor boy!" In this Manichaean world we can believe in evil-doing but goodness melts into philanthropy and kindness. . . .

And Mr. Greene ends with this paragraph:

> . . . Is it too fantastic to imagine that in this novel, as in many of his later books, creeps in, unrecognised by the author, the eternal and alluring taint of the Manichee, with its simple and terrible explanation of our plight, how the world was made by Satan and not by God, lulling us with the music of despair?

That is too fantastic, of course, as a description even of Dickens's demonic imagination, of his unconscious as distinct from his conscious, orthodox religion. The terror of *Oliver Twist* is the acted terror inherited from literature and married to personal hysteria. The Manichee is good theatre. But the suggestion is an interesting one and if we follow its lead, we must be struck by the flashes of contact between *Oliver Twist* and the Manichaean myth. The child of light is lost in the world of darkness—the terrors of childhood are the primitive terrors of the dark—from which the far-away Elect will save him. When he is saved, the end of the world of darkness is brought about—Nancy is murdered, Sikes and Fagin are hanged. We might grope farther along the strange tunnels of the Manichaean allegory and discover there a suggestion upon which the Freudian analyst of the tale of ghosts or terror will immediately pounce. These tales are now held to be artistic transpositions of the fear of castration and when one turns (as an ignorant reviewer so often must) to the authority of the *Encyclopaedia Britannica*, one indeed finds that the thriller writers have pious if tainted progenitors in the 4th century. In their belief "primal man descends into the abyss and prevents the further increase of the generations of darkness by cutting off their roots." What is notable (one reflects) is that the enormous preoccupation of Victorian literature for murderous melodrama—and we remember the horrifying success of Dickens in his public readings of murderous scenes—goes with an extreme sexual prudery in literature. Murder—as the saying is—is "cleaner" than sex. We seem to see a violent age seeking a compensation for its losses.

Whether or not the imaginative world of *Oliver Twist* is without God in the Christian sense we must leave to the theologians; the interest of Mr. Greene's suggestion is the inevitable implication that the emissaries of light, the Elect, are the middle classes. It is Mr. Brownlow and Miss Maylie who come down, to the tune of the ineffable music of the Three Per Cents. Only by sitting at the throne of Grace could they face the abyss of darkness in which the industrial poor, the everlastingly guilty were damned and lived waiting for their doom. Only by making Rose Maylie an angel could the existence of Nancy be assimilated; only by making kindness old-fashioned and respectable, could Sikes be faced as a modern, sullen and temperamental brute. It does not follow, as Mr. Graham Greene suggests, that the evil represented is stronger than the good, in the imaginative effect; the balance between these cardboard unrealities is perfect and a thieves' kitchen always sounds more dramatic and "strong" than a drawing-room. And so, too, on a more reputable plane: against the half-dreamed figures of Monk and Fagin at the window that seemed like the imprint of a primitive memory, must be placed those other half-waking intimations Oliver had of some happiness in a far-away past never known. What we are convinced of, even though by the long arm of coincidence, is the long arm of humanity and justice.

Oliver Twist is a literary novel. Magnificent juvenilia is Mr. Graham Greene's just phrase. The plots of Dickens were to improve and one does not know whether to put down their tedious elaboration to Mr. Chesterton's belief that they were an attempt to set out "something less terrible than the truth." That looks like a Chestertonian attempt to put down something more eccentric than a fact. Perhaps Dickens in his exhibitionism wanted to put down something *more* terrible than the truth. Either explanation sharply applies to the disastrous passion for plot general to the Victorian novel. It is a fact that Dickens had the greatest difficulty in inventing probabilities and that may be related to the fantastic turn of his mind.

All the main strains of his genius are crudely foreshadowed in *Oliver Twist*. There is the wonderful clean snap of scene and episode; nearly everything is "realised". Mr. Greene has perceived one of those reflective passages, memory evoking or regarding its own act, which Proust admired, and there are occasional phrases—the absurd servant's face "pale and *polite* with fear"—or touches of detail that show the hand of the master. We recall things like the wisp of human hair on Sikes's club, that sizzled for a second when he threw it in the fire; the notices in the country village warning vagrants to keep out. Sikes's speech is ludicrous—'"Wolves tear your throats," muttered Sikes'—but his death is wonderful; one remembers the boy at the window taken by surprise when the hanged body drops and shuts off his view and how he pushes it aside. The crude London scenes have the rattle of the streets in them; it is a novel of street journeys.

Mr. Bumble's proposal of marriage and all the sour and tippling termagants which foretell Dickens's long gallery of patchy and disgruntled women, have the incalculable quality of nature. Dickens (and Forster supported him) believed Oliver to be real; and indeed he sometimes is. He is hardly the evacuee of our time; a hundred years had to pass before the happy English middle classes were to discover what a child from the industrial slums could be like. Oliver is simply "one of Lord Shaftesbury's little victims". But the misery and the fear of Oliver are very real, his leaning to virtue (now so unfashionable) profoundly convincing. Why should we complain if Vice is over-exposed and Virtue over-exalted; the convention has the authority of Hogarth, and belongs to the 18th century, the morality of pre-industrial England. Hence—we may be tempted to think—not the absence of God or the taint of the Manichee, but the author's lingering assumption that the belief in justice, the knowledge of retribution and of the passion of mercy are self-evident in human nature, and that a good dose of terror and a long tangled plot of ill-chance and malignance will bring them out. Dickens was not the first or the last novelist to find virtue more difficult to portray than the wish for it.

27

Meredith

"HE put a laurel on my head and then gave me a buffet in the stomach," Meredith said when he read Henley's appreciation of his work. And when we turn to what Henley really did say we find this: "Meredith is a sun that has broken out into innumerable spots.... He writes with the pen of a great artist in one hand and the razor of a spiritual suicide in the other." There is also the judgment of Henry James. "Poor old Meredith," Henry James is reported to have said. "He writes these mysterious nonsenses and heaven knows what they all mean." To which Meredith replied: "Poor old James. He sets down on paper these mysterious rumblings of his bowels—but who can be expected to understand them?" Later on, Henry James expanded his thoughts to Edith Wharton. The central weakness of Meredith's art was unconscious insincerity. He was a sentimental rhetorician "whose natural indolence or congenital insufficiency, or both, made him in life, as in art, shirk every climax, dodge around it and veil its absence in a fog of eloquence." But when Meredith died, James relented. He said, "He did the best things best."

The bother—it must seem to a contemporary eye—is that Meredith so *strained* after the best things. He lived off the hyperbolical. Even the worst, dullest, the flattest things had to be cooked in hyperbole. To our restricted stomachs he is high feeding. To read him is like living on a daily diet of lobster; a kind of brain fever follows it. Half-way through *The Egoist* or *Harry Richmond*, through *Evan Harrington*, *Beauchamp's Career* or *The Ordeal of Richard Feverel*, we have had a surfeit not of the matter but of the manner and the mayonnaise. We know we are confronted by the vitality of genius, but we are uncomfortably convinced that we are also faced by one of those calamities of genius, which the English 19th century occasionally provides. It is a calamity comparable with the disaster of Carlyle. What is the explanation? Is it that the eloquence of the Celts—the Welsh, the Irish and the Scots,—outruns what they have to say, and leaves behind it brilliant but broken and unfinished works of art? Is it that they are brilliant beginners only? It is, we must feel, the virtue of Meredith that every sentence *is* a new beginning; but his vice that almost no sentence is a continuation from what has already been said. He is a man fixed gyrating to the spot.

In a forbearing and rather idle life of Meredith, written a few years ago, Mr. Siegfried Sassoon made the sound point that Meredith was a young man's novelist. He brims with the earliest, sun-dazed sensations we have at the age of twenty, before experience has taught us that the senses and the heart itself, are our gaolers. He is bursting with the young man's pleasure in the exaggerated and fantastic, the bombastic and consequent. What back-slapping, what mysterious private jokes go on in his suburban walking tours! In youth our judgments are driven off the track by our natural energy and this part of Meredith we acquiesce in with some nostalgia. But, sooner or later, Romance collides with reality, what goes on inside the Meredithian figures seems to have only a perfunctory relation with what they do and then—perhaps because the pride of Meredith's imagination has been too strong for them—they become vulgar and ugly without Meredith being aware of the fact. The early love scene in *Richard Feverel*, to take an example, has been much admired, but the end of the affair is an over-furnished bathos, and sets the early lyricism in a new and dubious light. Richard had been just as much in love with the Thames Valley as with a young lady, and Meredith did not know it.

The lumpish inequalities of the Victorian novel have been put down to the fact that the Victorians so persistently wrote beyond their range and often seemed to have had little idea of what their true range was. They seem to have been—as I believe Lord David Cecil has written—sure of themselves only in what they knew from their childhood. After that their growing up was uncertain. It was their energy that drove them beyond their artistic means; and energy is indeed the fundamental subject of the 19th century, provoking questions that are never answered because, in the end, the Victorians considered energy was its own justification for it led inevitably to progress. The discovery of German idealism confirmed the cult of energy. Carlyle took from Germany that Gothic halo of the hero and put it —though intending the very opposite—on the head of the rosy, humdrum cult of effort in commerce and manufacture. In copying Carlyle's style and going to school with Carlyle's German masters, Meredith carried the new heroism on to the end of the century.

It is bad (one is inclined to say) when the Scots are educated in Germany; when the Welsh go there, and add their taste for local giants to the Teuton's infatuation with the leader-hero, the result is grotesque. Meredith brings the Victorian novel to a close with a panegyric of power and that, as Irving Babbit pointed out years ago, is the penultimate act of the Romantic movement. The last act we have seen, in our own time: its suicide and annihilation. Henley was perceptive when he made his remark about the razor of the spiritual suicide in Meredith's hand.

Energy is always Meredith's subject. It draws out his full powers in *The Egoist*. This brain-vexing novel has all Meredith's vices as a novelist but turns them into something like virtues. These virtues belong to the original English tradition of the 18th century which is built on the diffuse, the sense of theatre, on the comedy of moral types and a general reference of all moral issues to "the opinion of the world." Educated, well-bred, instructed and experienced people subscribe to a polite opinion, and what they lose thereby in private sensibility, they gain in the assurance of summary judgment. They are certainly unable to go to the lengths

Proust went to or to the edge of that abyss where behaviour ends and the soul is exposed and alone. But the 18th-century writers had considerable curiosity about human beings and Meredith has very little. He has taken the types. Would we recognise Colonel de Crayl or Mrs. Mountstuart if we met them? Only after a process of de-cerebration: two women are compared to yachts. Bursting with himself Meredith knows people only as they stimulate his vanity, only so far as they help him to cut a figure in uttering "the opinion of the world", and to dominate the brilliant dinner party. Meredith himself, transfigured and universalised into a general ogre as Sir Willoughby Patterne, is the only "character" in the book, but we know him also as the theatrical projection of a moral category. One of the really colossal acts of Meredith's energy as an egoist is performed at the end of this novel when, having exhausted the egoism of Sir Willoughby, Meredith turns in search of fresh prey and discovers Laetitia (of all people) to be an egoist too. No doubt she is in her way. So are we all egoists. But to generalise the theory like this makes character meaningless. If all the characters in the book are Meredith, they become nothing. By going on to the stage with his puppets, Thackeray at least gave them a minute but individual life; but Meredith goes on to the stage and drives the people off by acting all their parts for them.

The method kills an ordinary problem novel like *One of Our Conquerors* by sheer effusiveness and insensibility. The exhibitionist metaphors reduce a novel, which has a well-stated social theme, to the clownish:

> "We cry to women: Land Ho!" he shouts in the middle of a passably affecting scene in this book. "A land of palms after storms at sea; and at once they inundate as with a deluge of eye-water.
>
> "Half a minute, dear Victor, no longer," Nataby said, weeping, near on laughing over his look of wanton abandonment to despair at sight of her tears. "Don't remind me. I'm rather like Fenellan's laundress, the tearful

MEREDITH

woman whose professional apparatus was her soft heart and a cake of soap."

Or there is that awful, prolonged comparison of the clouds over London with Ruben's *Rape of the Sabine Women*.

But in *The Egoist*, and if we except the opening chapter, passages of exuberance are toned down. He continues the course set by *Jonathan Wild* and, even in the subject—self-love, isolated from all other human passions and set supremely among them—there is a typical 18th-century simplification. There are two over-riding qualities, it seems to me, that give this tiring novel, with its impossible dialogue, an important breadth and authority. The first is the total power of Meredith's own egoism and self-knowledge; egoism is his subject, unashamedly understood in maturity, and seen (since he could not be tragic about it) on the highest comic plane. The second quality lies in the constant implication that Sir Willoughby is more than himself, more even than a general moral analysis of egoism: he has the spread and weight of England behind him. His character is a portrait of the dominant English temper of the time; in the high noon of its self-confidence Sir Willoughby and the presumptuous, over-fed English scene play into each others' hands.

Meredith's capacity for putting England into his characters—once again at the opening of *One of Our Conquerors* or in *Beauchamp's Career*—enriches his novels with a temporal emotion. What other novelist, before Kipling, has so explicitly done this? Only another exotic—for there is something very exotic in the Welsh Meredith—the Jew, Disraeli. The rest of the English novelists always take England for granted.

The duality and depth of the main theme of *The Egoist* eclipse the tedium of its minor scenes. Sir Willoughby's egoism was more than conceit; it has the conscious zest of the man-hunt. He was quaintly incapable of jealousy of individuals—his enemy was the world, the mass which confounds us in a lump . . . the pleasure of the world is to bowl down our soldierly letter "I."

or again

Consider him indulgently: the Egoist is the Son of himself. He is likewise the Father. And the son loves the father, the father the son. . . . Are you, without much offending, sacrificed by them, it is on the altar of their mutual love, to filial piety or paternal tenderness.

Self-torture itself is indulged to feed this ravenous pride. In this book there is no doubt about it: Meredith had the razor in his hand.

We know why it was in his hand. Exuberance exhausts itself, the theatrical Celt is spent. And there are those three or four lines in *Richard Feverel*:

Well! All wisdom is mournful. Tis, therefore, coz, that the wise do love the Comic Muse. Their own high food would kill them. You shall find great poets, rare philosophers, night after night on the broad grin before a row of yellow lights and mouthing monks. Why? Because all's dark at home.

Horrible writing. It is the Stratford-on-Avon style, Romance decaying into the language of advertisement. Peacock's daughter had just left Meredith when he wrote these self-pitying words but "all was dark at home" in Meredith's life long before that and long after. His, we may surmise, was the darkness of loss and self-love. It is generally said that Meredith was a great snob and that he was ashamed of his humble origins "in trade", but once the natural period of snobbery in youth was passed, there is no evidence of unusual social snobbery in Meredith. He enjoyed his gifted

MEREDITH

and ridiculous ancestors. But snobbery as a form of romanticism does certainly pervade Meredith's novels, and that was passed down from father to son in his family. The Victorian novel derives half of its subject and most of its comedy from this social and spiritual delicacy. Book after book deals with it: if a man looks like a gentleman, dresses like a gentleman, how is it that he is still, quite patently, not one? This was a fundamental question in the Meredith family. They were handsome tailors who could easily make the clothes and the money and were gifted actors who could live the part they dressed for. In them, we feel that everything that has been said about "being in trade" [in the words of the 19th century], has been concentrated and has become even transcendental. They know all the victories, all the defeats, and are ripe with the comedy of their own situation; they are acting, with a self-knowledge that is both Romantic and comic, a role which the rest of England is taking with either mundane or godly seriousness. When, indeed, Meredith talks of England in his foreign and detached way, he is seeing a real England which the English are too solemnly involved in to see themselves. No other writer has so richly and so ironically conveyed the sheer pleasure the Victorians had in social position.

We can see how the fundamental question in the history of the Meredith family gave Meredith his subject. Old Mel of *Evan Harrington*, courtly, arch and amusing, had simply bounced into the county. His son, Meredith's father, who was crippled financially by the old man's sallies into the great world, was cured of the ambition but not of the preoccupation with it. When we get to Meredith himself the impulse has reached its platonic stage. An only child who had grown up without a mother, Meredith inhabited the solitude of clever boys and lived like a prince, secretly, in it. In him romantic snobbery reappeared in its highest incarnation, as the love of the rare and superb, as the belief in epithet and refusal of reality unless it was highly inflected.

And there is a terrifying will in Meredith's dreaming

childhood. It is interesting to compare his case with Hawthorne's. The proud solitude of Hawthorne in New England had the same preoccupation with the ancestor; but whereas Hawthorne really was, within the prim New England limits, a kind of aristocrat, Meredith was not. He had to be his own ancestors and the success of his family had made him an optimist. How vastly he would have been improved as a novelist if, like Hawthorne, he had felt the worm in the bud; but, not being an aristocrat, he had no worm in the bud; he blossomed wilfully, fully, and was too sanguine. We are alarmed by this precocious Hampshire child who, seeing his own superiority as an intellect, briskly takes his education into his own hands and goes off to school in Germany without consulting his elders, alone. His will, though it is the will of a spoiled, handsome boy, is astonishing. The disciple of Darwin—with Hardy he is the only English novelist to make use of Darwin's ideas aesthetically—was seeing to it that the excellent shall survive.

And that is what Meredith's snobbery is: the will to excellence. Of all the Victorian novelists he presents the subject with most profundity. He knows snobbery at all levels and he knows the price that has to be paid for it: coldness of heart, egoism, artificiality, self-sufficiency and meanness are the price to be made for the richly imagined role. The accomplished snob must be impenetrable. Evan Harrington is openly warned of this. The young snob, the secret prince and dreamer, who is lost in the glitter of his vision of honour and his own talent, runs the danger of becoming an actor for life and, in any crisis, his lost sense of reality will make him evasive, lonely, perhaps cowardly and without trust in life. There will be wounds—the defection of Meredith's wife—which will never be forgiven. And insincerity, an emotional over-dressing will haunt every rhapsodic sense of the better and enchanted thing.

The best things in Meredith lie in his general perceptions of character, for he has the great novelist's gift of generalisation. By that he moves with a brilliance that catches the breath and excites the mind. The social utterances in *Beauchamp's Career* are resounding in their comedy and penetration. And then he excels in plain comedy and the purveying of minor characters. They abound, a little crudely —but the crudity is very English—in that novel. There is Mr. Tripehallow letting Beauchamp "twig"—there is a good deal of vulgar "twigging" in Meredith—that he has heard all about his French mistress:

> "You young nobs capering over our heads—I nail you down to your morals. Politics secondary. A-dew, as the dying spirit remarked to weeping friend."

There is the interchange between bland Mr. Oggler, who runs adverbs in pairs, a forerunner of the disciples of the success-religions of our time, with his "honestly and sincerely."

> "I really and truly don't know what it is not to know happiness."
> "Then you don't know God," said Carpendike, like a voice from a cave.

Then the candidate's sordid friends at the election:

> "I repeat, my dear sir, the infant candidate delights in his honesty, like the babe in its nakedness, the beautiful virgin in her innocence. So he does: but he discovers it's time for him to wear clothes in a contested election. And what's that but to preserve the outlines pretty correctly, whilst he doesn't shock and horrify the optics. A dash of conventionalism makes the whole civilised world kin."

And there are the epigrams:

> "He is no true Radical. He is a philosopher—one of the flirts and butterflies of politics."

For in his unique fiction of overfed England, Meredith did not restrict his comedy to personal relationships. These, indeed, were incomplete to him, unless what he would call the comedy of the ideologies, were fixed round them like a frame. His people were hatted in what they believed.

Mr. Sassoon believes that the three-volume novel was the ruin of Meredith. That convention may have led a careless technician to throw his plots together and rely on brilliant presentability to fill the gaps. But we cannot have the virtues of a writer without his vices: the fact is that Meredith's virtues are all in his personal mobility, his aplomb and his presumption. His stories do not progress; they are waltzed with violence from line to line, and chapter to chapter. The unremitting footwork of Meredith may give us the first chapters of *Richard Feverel*, may take us to that comical scene in the solicitor's office where young Ripton is caught reading a book about Woman under his desk. Or to the wonderful set portrait of Adrian "the wise youth" who "caused himself to be required by people who could serve him"; to the death of Old Mel, the unveiling of Sir Willoughby, or to one of those artificial scenes—excellent devices and a development from Fielding—like the temptation of Sir Austin. The staginess of Meredith is in the 18th-century tradition and is an effective method of linking the main action by witty discursions before the curtain. But the same method perverts narrative. It is a kind of snobbery raised to the *n*th, that hopes to pass off a plain sight of gambling at the table as everything except what it is:

> He compared the creatures dabbling over the board to summer flies on butcher's meat, periodically scared by a cloth. More in the abstract they were snatching at a snapdragon bowl. It struck him that the gamblers had thronged in on an invitation to drink the round of seed time and harvest in a gulp. Again they were desperate gleaners, hopping, skipping, bleeding, amid a whiz of

scythe blades, for small wisps of booty. Nor was it long before the presidency of an ancient hoary Goat-Satan might be perceived, with skew-eyes and mouth, nursing a hoof on a tree.

A snobbery, or poetry curdled and gone wrong. There is too much labour in that passage for good poetry; there is too much exhibitionism in it for it to be tolerable prose.

"All is dark at home": the comic writers are injured poets. Meredith is our most foreign novelist, and in some ways this foreignness brings him near to us today. He is pagan, too. He has the aptitude for a provoking generalisation. He has reacted to science. He has a gambling intellect. He saw, better than his more sensible contemporaries, some of the outlines of our world. No doubt, the poetic approach can be called a new form of the Old Victorian humbug, but it enabled him to sharpen his psychological eye: Richard Feverel's seduction after the champagne dinner is a vulgar piece of writing but at least it is true to life in the essentials. (What distresses us is that Meredith does not know when he is vulgar.) The notion that Sir Austin Feverel's System was a means of unconscious revenge is as rare a perception as anything in Henry James. And *Modern Love* is not only one of the finest sonnet sequences of the language: it is also a recognisable, an unabashed and almost contemporary *Huis Clos*. Meredith appears, in England, at the first break of the intellectual with society, and that in itself brings him closer to us. Just as Thackeray held that he was born several generations too late, perhaps Meredith's difficulty was that he was born at least two generations too soon, and so, like Thackeray, he ends by satisfying nobody. That air of experience is specious because it is heartless: that thumping sense of the world is too thumping: he has gone to the intellect and its pride to seal off the wounds of life, as a young man will before he learns that the brain will do nothing for us. That last sight of Meredith, so often reported, of an old man with a loud voice shut off by deafness from his friends, muttering his fantastications, bitter and still straining for more brilliance in a final defiance of reality, is a parting allegory.

28

Poor Gissing

ABOUT Gissing I once heard H. G. Wells throw off this remark some years ago: "Poor Gissing," he said, "he thought there was a difference between a woman and a lady. There is no difference, as we all know." On second thoughts we know nothing of the kind. Thinking for the third time and reading again that drastic yet moving cartoon of Gissing's life which Wells drew in his *Autobiography*, we suspect that in his life and in his work, Gissing was not a deluded romantic but a man born out of his time. It was an accident—though a very likely one—that the literature of social conscience should bounce along the ebullient, flashing and practical course laid down by the optimism of Shaw and Wells; the still expanding economy of England guaranteed that those members of the lower middle class who had impatience, clear-headedness and energy could get out of it; but the story might have been different if England had not continued to get richer. The social conscience might have been pessimistic. The stress might have been placed on the spiritual casualties of the class struggle, as it was in Gissing, and not on the material hopes.

When Gissing's novel *A Life's Morning* was published again a few years ago, it contained a thoughtful introduction by William Plomer. Some words of his seem to hint at the observation I have just made. He says:

> It is hardly to be wondered at that Mr. Wells, who was a good friend to Gissing, thought him "horribly miseducated" while Gissing thought Mr. Wells (so Mr. Wells says) "absolutely illiterate." It was not that Gissing looked forward and Mr. Wells looked backward; it was that when Gissing looked forward and Mr. Wells looked backward neither liked what he saw. What worried Mr. Wells

was that Gissing was "not scientific" and had had a classical education.

When Wells wrote of those members of the lower middle class who had the gift of creating good luck, who could invent a fire, and fight for their lives like Mr. Polly, Gissing wrote of the trapped, who were too weak, who too often felt (as he said with bitter penetration) the final impulse of self-pitying egoism "towards the fierce plunge into ruin." To these the struggle presented itself as an attempt to grasp with failing hands the spiritual content of life.

To this point the contemporary social reformer has belatedly arrived, after a generation of successful revolution. The crises of the unclassed, the poor women, shop girls, teachers, dressmakers and governesses of Gissing's novels are always spiritual as well as economic: "It was her terrible misfortune" (Mr. Plomer quotes from *Demos*) "to have feelings too refined for the position in which fate had placed her." We feel for Emma Vine but we also smile expectantly at this judgment on her; Emma is a stock comic character who has been made serious. Gissing, who had the sensibility and tastes of a cultivated man, himself tired eventually of creatures so stolid, so maimed and so frustrated in the fulfilment of either their own or his ideal. Emma is one more Victorian "lady" who forgets she is a woman; one more victim of the comedy of gentility. All the same, we take the point because it is, for all the unconscious comedy, a real point. The heroines of George Eliot had similar aspirations; and thrived on them because they were better off. That class-ache was and is profoundly true to the inner English life.

Among the more spirited and sociable figures of the late Victorian novelists Gissing is the one who brings the accusing, self-consuming face of failure, the lordly silence of the lonely man. His failure is the source of his persistent fame; he is one of those novelists who are neither discarded nor made immortal, but whose reputation drags its heavy-footed way in a kind of perpetual purgatory. His lack of humour, his lack of fantasy—that essence of the English novel—leave him worrying unattended on the pavement of his anxieties and his scholar's dreams. Take books of his at random: *Thyrza, Eve's Ransom, Denzil Quarrier, Odd Women, The Unclassed*—they are well, but stiffly written, without individuality, but as Mr. Plomer says, in the sound conventional prose of the scholar; their psychological passages are acutely argued but the words never fly, never leave the ground. The dialogue is stilted, though the reported speech of the slums is alive. Their plots groan. Their characters (if we except Dickensian shapes like the Irish schoolmaster in Tootle's Academy in *The Unclassed*) are weighed down by self-pity or moan under an excess of good intention, and only when we break through this encasement do we find how real they are. There is—how right Wells was in this respect—a fundamental sentimentality and more than a touch of conceit and pretence. Gissing was a novelist in error, for he lacked the gift of melting life and pouring it into the mould of artifice. Life and artifice stand side by side in his novels like some ill-assorted couple.

If these very grave criticisms are true why do we read Gissing? The answer is that at certain points in nearly all his novels, he speaks seriously about matters which no other novelist has taken so seriously. Instructed by his reading of the French and Russian novelists he is bleakly aware of the situation of his time. Snobbery, priggishness have been subjects for wit and gregarious laughter to the other English novelists. Injustice has aroused passion, but these novelists end by coming round to the sociable view. Gissing conserves the lonely, the private personal opinion. He is a thinking person thinking for himself; and his contribution as a novelist—as Virginia Woolf suggested—is the thinking of ordinary people who so far had not been credited with thought. No more than the French or Russians is Gissing afraid of prigs and dreamers. He sets out to find them; he can be relied upon to discover them in the seamstresses of *The Unclassed*, in a villain like the manufacturer in *A Life's Morning*, a character who comes to life when the desire for refinement stings him like a gadfly. Or in that tired clerk Mr. Hood who had all his life desired to see Holborn Viaduct—a comic character, there, and how austerely refused! This discovery that in all character there sits a mind, and that the mind of the dullest is not dull because, at its very lowest, it will at least reflect the social dilemma into which it was born, is arresting.

Where the discovery is most fruitful is in Gissing's portraits of women. Women were known to have feelings. They were known to be shrewd. But who supposed them to have thoughts beyond themselves! The fact is that Gissing realised women were ladies, and now that the modern novel since D. H. Lawrence has presented them as sexual combatants and aggressors, it is refreshing to discover again their thoughts about their social condition. This is one of the best points in Mr. Plomer's valuable and sympathetic introduction: and I would go further and say that no English novelist of the realistic kind has drawn women so variously and so intimately. In this sense Gissing's feminist novel, *Odd Women*, is one of his most interesting. It is a picture of loneliness in urban life. Once one has broken the back of the first chapter or two, one's impatience with Gissing's old-fashioned methods of narrative goes. Life shows its teeth. The lonely rooms of London, the lonely pedestrians, the real population, one is inclined to say, of this seedy and disconsolate place take possession. We see the three daughters of an improvident doctor thrown on the world, untrained, almost penniless, hardly educated and terrified of losing caste. They are contrasted with a fierce and vivacious young feminist, Rhoda Nunn. Gissing analyses the fanatical Rhoda Nunn and he prepares for her the most delicate psychological drama. (One understands, after this portrait, the admiration Henry James had for Gissing's work.) He finds for Rhoda Nunn a man of the world whom she converts to her feminism, and having done so, she is made to realise that vanity not love has impelled them. Her brain has deceived her; she is obliged to behave unjustly and irrationally like any "silly" woman; and wrecking her own happiness, returns to loneliness and feminism again. She has passed through the strict spiritual test to which Gissing put all his women—for that, he felt, is what the minds of so many women fear and desire—and is left matured by the test but, of course, unhappy. Gissing despised happiness. He had the masochistic imagination of the adolescent.

In life and in literature Gissing's method was severely to criticise women in order to be gratified all the more by the discovery of their graces. This led, of course, to being overgratified and to self-deception in life, but it led to balance in literature where he could be ironical and urbane. This is Mrs. Rossall of *A Life's Morning*:

> This lady had just completed her thirty-second year; her girls were in their tenth. She was comely and knew it, but a constitutional indolence had preserved her from becoming a woman of fashion, and had nurtured in her a reflective mood, which, if it led to no marked originality of thought, at all events contributed to an appearance of culture. At the time of her husband's death, she was at the point where graceful inactivity so often degenerates into slovenliness. Mrs. Rossall's home-keeping tendencies and the growing childhood of her twins tended to persuade her that her youth was gone; even the new spring fashions stirred her to but languid interest, and her music, in which she had some attainments, was all but laid aside. With widowhood began a new phase of her life. Her mourning was unaffected; it led her to pietism; she spent her days in religious observance, and her nights in the study of the gravest literature. She would have entered the Roman Church but for her brother's interposition. The end of this third year of discipline was bringing about another change, perhaps less obvious to herself than to those who marked her course with interest, as several

people did. Her reading became less ascetic, she passed to George Herbert and the "Christian Year" and by way of the decoration of altars proceeded to thought for her personal adornment.

The attempt to revive Gissing is desirable, for we are less likely to be depressed by his novels and to misjudge him than his contemporaries were. By a long detour through the wilderness of literary reputation he arrives at our door. But this revival will confirm, I am afraid, his substantial failure as a novelist. The shadow of Ryecroftism (as Mr. Plomer says) is often dank upon his work; in short he lacks the quality of self-disregard which is essential to novelists. It has been complained justly that his novels have the very amateur fault of being without focus or central plot. Precisely: Ryecroft's shadow takes its place. That unshaped ego is blobbed over his tales. But Gissing is a store-house for novelists. One of his books, the study of Dickens, is a translucent piece of criticism. For the rest, he foreshadows a type which has become commoner: the uprooted intellectual of a later generation, cut off by education from his own class and by economic and social conditions from any other place in society. From this point of view Gissing's novels are less dated than those of the early Wells; despite our wars and our large social changes, the forgotten neighbourhoods of large English cities are still packed with Gissing characters, even though the material conditions of their lives may have improved. Their essential spiritual problem, the problem of industrial society, remains untouched:

> Natural men, revolting against the softness and sweetness of civilisation; men all over the world; hardly knowing what they want and what they don't want; and here comes one who speaks for them—speaks with a vengeance. . . . The brute savagery of it! The very lingo—how appropriate it is! . . . Mankind won't stand it much longer, this encroachment of the human spirit. . . . We may reasonably hope, old man, to see our boys blown into

small bits by the explosive that hasn't got its name yet.

Those words, spoken by a Gissing character in *The Whirlpool* and discussing the newly published *Barrack-Room Ballads*, still stand.

29

An Emigré

THE daily evil of the emigré is his isolation. He has lost the main ground of the moral life: that we do not live until we live in others. The temptations that face him are embittering to any man capable of reflection: he can live in the past; he can become an uprooted dilettante; he can cultivate, in the words of Heyst in Joseph Conrad's *Victory*, that "form of contempt called pity" which comes easily to the isolated man; he can regard anarchy as the ruling spirit in the world. Crime may come nearer to his fingers and, with less obstruction, to his imagination than it does to rooted people. In a world like our own, the solicitations of the police, the secret agent, the revolutionary, the traitor, are very likely under one guise or another, to come his way. No doubt these extreme enticements are evaded by most emigrés, who alleviate the sense of persecution by living in the past and keep their nostalgias and their rancours indoors; but, mild or extreme, they unite to force upon the isolated man his main addiction. He becomes pre-eminently a conscience.

Isolation and conscience are the dominant motifs in the novels of Joseph Conrad and, two of them especially, *The Secret Agent* and *Under Western Eyes*, become more and more suggestive to the contemporary reader. They attract because they are free from that sudden fogginess, that enlarged bad temper which Conrad called Destiny, and from the melodrama or rhetoric, which play tricks with the lighting and climate of many of his ambitious works. They have the compactness, the efficiency of that peculiarly modern form of writing, the thriller with a bitter moral flavour. And they put a central modern question to ourselves—what is our attitude to treachery and other moral consequences of a belief in revolution?

AN EMIGRÉ

Conrad's terms are out of date, of course, though not as seriously as might be thought. Anarchists do not throw bombs in London; in Russia, the tyrant is not assassinated. But the essentials of European history have not changed since the Eighties of last century; what was talked about has simply come true. The revolutionary thug who has the fine art of bursting Razumov's ear drums in *Under Western Eyes* is an anthropoid forerunner of thousands who have gone one better than that in the police states. Conrad is a reactionary; for him the old despotism and the new Utopianism are complementary forms of moral anarchy. Their end is cynicism, more despotism, more destruction and to that opinion some have now reluctantly come. But Conrad was a fixed reactionary; he had never tried to tack across the revolutionary tide; he hated the Russian revolution as a Pole who was already a generation away from the hatred of his time; his hatred was glued into the past. The positive contribution of his political views is that they double the precision of our dilemmas of conscience by presenting them in reverse. The weakness—let us get it over at once. Conrad's judgment is true and untrue, but what he said of Heyst in *Victory* points out the weakness:

> The young man learned to reflect, which is a destructive process, a reckoning of the cost. It is not the clear-sighted who lead the world. Great achievements are accomplished in a blessed warm mental fog.

Conrad is an exile. He is not committed except to pessimism. He is, for private and public reasons, tortured by the danger of becoming a moral dilettante. Because he is so excruciatingly aware of all the half shades of that case, he has his authority.

Razumov in *Under Western Eyes* is a sympathetic character. He is the recurring "lonely" being in Conrad's novels. Another Conradian theme, perhaps Slavonic and certainly Romantic: he has a "double" in Haldin, the student assassin.

"In times of mental and political unrest," the Razumovs of the world keep

> an instinctive hold on normal, practical everyday life. He was aware of the emotional tension of his time; he even responded to it in an indefinite way. But his main concern was with his work, his studies and with his own future.

Not a prig, not a careerist, not dull; he is intelligent and sensitive. His worse fault is a bad temper which comes from one of Stendhal's definitions of misfortune: "Not having the evils of his age"—if we can use the word "age" in a double sense. The irrational driving force in him comes from insecurity and loneliness; he is a bastard. Just when Razumov's good resolutions are ripe, Haldin the terrorist hides in his room and by the very contact, dooms Razumov to eternal political suspicion. There follows a scene in which Conrad's highest dramatic gifts as a novelist are brought, uncorrupted, into play: the picture of the student's room, Razumov's despairing journey through the snow at night to the inn to fetch the cab driver who will enable the exalted assassin to escape, Razumov's discovery that the man is dead drunk; and then the journey back in which, having failed, Razumov revolts against his unjust situation and his own quietism, changes his mind and betrays Haldin to the police. The scene is a very long one and also exposes Conrad's weakness—the creaking sentence, the rumble of stage scenery and some staginess of dialogue.

Conrad wrote *Under Western Eyes* perhaps to bring a harder Western focus upon a theme of Dostoevsky. There is an evident Polish contempt for the lack of fixed positions in the Russian mind; or, at any rate, an ironical wonder at its readiness for cynicism. With brilliant ingenuity he caps scene after scene with its opposite. The exalted assassin is plainly sensitive about the "greatness" of his action. Razumov has acted from a sense of right and discovers even *that* will not be its own reward; exile alone is possible. Guilt (as

AN EMIGRÉ

always in Conrad) marks the drifter. Yet even exile is poisoned, though not by remorse; it is poisoned because the authorities can now force Razumov to become a spy on the revolutionaries as the price of concealing his act. Razumov is obliged to take on the mind of a guilty man when, by his morality, he is virtuous; in doing so, and by contact with Haldin's young sister in Geneva, he comes to see the innocent and honourable illusions that precede conversion to revolutionary action. The inevitable Russian confession follows, not because Razumov has changed his mind, but because he longs for moral freedom.

What is contemporary in this book is the response to seediness, treachery, slackness and corruption. This response is the direct product of the last words of Heyst in *Victory*:

> Woe to the man whose heart has not learned while young to hope, to love—and to put his trust in life.

Conrad himself found a strong if not lasting interest in the order and discipline of life at sea, and his scorn is softened in *Under Western Eyes* by the attempt of one kind of Slav to understand another. In *The Secret Agent* there is no such emotional entanglement; his scorn, unrestrained, now becomes almost overpoweringly rich and pungent and his irony leaves nothing standing.

The masters of Conrad's day were Meredith and Stevenson and Conrad's book about the lazy agent-provocateur who gets his feeble-minded brother-in-law killed by mistake, shows the strong influence of these writers. *The Secret Agent* is a thriller, a very artificial form of writing which realism rarely redeems from its fundamental fantasy. No thriller can be believed and even when meaning and psychological ingredients are put into it, its people and events cannot really bear the weight. *The Secret Agent* begins with the incredible character of Vladimir, the absurd, highly-stylised intellectual plotter, and the artifice is at odds with the truly real and powerful elements in the book: the descriptions of

London, the portraits of those perfect if intellectually diagnosed Londoners, Mrs. Verloc, her mother and Steve. Outside of this warm, human centre Conrad is dangerously exhibitionist. Here conscience has its sardonic comedies and he seems superbly to be showing off his obsession with the dirtiness, the shabbiness of foolish or dishonoured minds:

> His descent into the street was like the descent into a slimy aquarium from which the water has been run off.

A detail like that—and Conrad is a master of image—describes a London street and defines the book. Verloc's birth control shop takes one down and down to the grubbiness of London's back streets and the pathetic vulgarities of cheap civilisation.

Conrad's genius was for picturesque discussion rather than for narrative—he was tortured, one is told, by the difficulties of invention—and what always impresses is his rummaging about, back and forth, in the lives of his characters. Verloc, the agent, is wonderful in his laziness, his dull humour, his amorousness, his commonplaceness and his injured vanity. It was a master stroke to make this destroyer respectable and to pounce upon the isolation—once more, the Conrad theme—in which this foolish member of the French letter trade lived. Towards the end, when the idiot Steve has been killed through Verloc's irresponsibility, it is wonderful that Verloc quite unblinkingly expects the tragedy to make no difference to his relations with his wife. After all, she has got *him*! The murder is not well done. It is, in fact, too cleverly done, with an eye for all the effects and shows Conrad at his most self-conscious. The crime is in keeping with the contrived tone of the book, the general unsavoury sapience; but the author's irony is too much with us. Mrs. Verloc is as wonderful as the husband she kills. She is a simple, reserved woman, governed by the desire for security, living on two or three strong and usually concealed feelings. Her words, in the London way, rarely reveal what

AN EMIGRÉ

these are; in fact the way in which she talks off the beat of her feelings the whole time is well-observed. But when she discovers that her husband is a monster, that he is a worse monster because he does not realise it or does not see why *that* should upset his domestic bliss; when she realises he is a moral idiot and that his reply to grief is "Let her have her cry. I'll go to bed with her, that'll put her right," a terrifying woman rises up with a carving knife in her hand. Afterwards, it is perfect that she relapses into the simple resource of a feminine guile, so pathetically vain, that a crude crook can do her down as easy as winking.

Head, the police superintendent, is another sound portrait. His Assistant Commissioner belongs to the dubious higher moral reaches which thriller writers have a perennial fancy for: contact with crime and the police sows in them the desire to have everything taped: God comes to Scotland Yard. The Assistant Commissioner, one notices, has the now professional "sense of loneliness, of evil freedom", but this is, at the last moment, made real to us by one of those sardonic afterthoughts by which Conrad saves himself from sentimentality. The Assistant Commissioner, we are told, finds "the sense of loneliness and evil freedom *rather pleasant*". This is indeed why he is an Assistant Commissioner: he is a hunter. (It is always, in Conrad, the small additional comment, that puts on the rounding and convincing touch.)

Conrad, the exile, the isolated man, was the master of any atmosphere. That gift comes at once to the sensibility of the emigré. Like the French novelists, like Meredith and Henry James, he moves in narrative from idea to idea, to the change in moral climate rather than from event to event. The first part of *Under Western Eyes* comes beautifully to a close on Councillor Milukin's short inquiry when Razumov says he is going to retire: "Where to?" Obviously there is nowhere. Conrad's novels are marked by such crucial sentences, which change a whole view of life, and his dramas are the dramas of the change of view. Conrad, the dilettante, takes the soul or the conscience, and tries them now in this position, now that; a new Good means a new guilt. Heyst in *Victory* knows the reason: the son of a brilliant man who has seen through all human values, Heyst is a born exile in a world that shocks. His aim must be to avoid committal. But like the Captain in *The Secret Sharer* who has the runaway hidden in his cabin, Conrad also has the committed "double" in his life. This dichotomy provides the drama and the rich substance of his books.

30
The Octopus

IT was like a visit to the theatre or the waxworks. One walked into the Langham Hotel out of the London daylight and was shown, at last, into a large, darkened apartment twinkling with candles. Heavy black velvet curtains were drawn over the windows; masses of exotic flowers were banked against them and, enthroned in an enormous bed in the midst of all this, sat the genius: a small, ugly, dank-eyed woman with her hair down her back, scratching away fast with a quill pen on large sheets of violet-tinted paper and throwing each sheet on to the floor when it was done with. A large dog guarded the morning's work from the visitor's touch. One had gone to have one's head bitten off either by Ouida or her dog.

Ouida would be under thirty at this time, a woman with her father's excessive nose and a rude grating voice. Already conceit, indeed megalomania, had settled on a theatrical character. She is not the first novelist to have delusions of grandeur—Scott had his Abbotsford, Balzac had coronets put on his luggage—for when one is dealing in fantasy, it is not unnatural to help oneself. In the secret room of Ouida's life, where the shames of her childhood in Bury St. Edmunds were hidden, there must have been a shrewd, hard, frightened being which stiffened its chin and told her that she had earned the right to folly and exorbitance. She had become the most famous novelist then living in the world when she was hardly out of her teens; she had slaved as only the best-sellers can; she had raised her unhappy mother from poverty to wealth; she had proved that the "realities" so meanly admired in a gossiping provincial town were despicable. She was original. The day-dreams of an adolescent girl had been imposed successfully upon herself; they were triumphantly imposed upon the world. How was it done? At the end of her life when she lay dead of neglect in a wretched Italian tenement, her maid reverently placed two of her mistress's quill pens on the table at the foot of the bed. The quill which had flamed over the violet paper in the gloom of the Langham, which had tossed ahead of the sprawling cavalry charge of Ouida's prose, had once more proved itself mightier than the reviewer's bitter pen.

Firbank, as Miss Bigland, a new biographer, and other critics have pointed out, had read his Ouida. The day-dreams of Bury St. Edmunds where her plausible French father came to fill her head with nature lessons, tall stories of international plots and the dazzling intrigues of European courts, were the day-dreams of the whole of middle-class England and America. Liberal democracy was bored with its routine. The aristocracy and idle rich with their Turkish tobacco and their tremendous sins—how these haunted the heads of Victorian wives and their hard-working husbands. It did not matter that Ouida was ignorant of the fashionable world; all the better could she describe what the fashionable *ought* to look and sound like. The fashionable world itself, so childishly romantic and sentimental underneath its brisk airs and its levity, rather wished it like that, too. Her novels were the fantasies of the outsider, of those who have to keep their station in life, of those who, obeying all the rules and calculating all the main chances, keep one corner in their minds for visions of an insouciant and gorgeous race which performs such non-interest-bearing acts as wrecking a career "to save a woman's name from the breath of slander", and lives with heroic and insolvent melancholy in recklessly furnished rooms. "Beauty", the guardsman,

> had the drawing-room floor of a house in Kensington Gore, well-furnished and further crowded with crowds of things of his own, from Persian carpets bought on his travels to the last new rifle sent home only the day before. . . .
> A setter, a retriever and a couple of Skyes

THE OCTOPUS

(Ouida was always crowded with crowds of dogs)—

> were on the hearthrug (veritable tiger skin). Breakfast in dainty Sèvres silver stood on one table sending up an aroma of coffee, omelettes and devils; the morning papers lay on the floor, a smoking cap was hung on a Parian Venus; a parrot, who apparently considered himself master of the place, was perched irreverently on a bronze Milton, and pipes, whips, pistols and cards were thrown down on a Louis Quinze couch, that Louise de Kérouaille or Sophie Arnould might have graced. From the inner room came the rapid clash of small-swords, while "Touché, touché, touché! Riposte! Holà!" was shouted, in a silvery voice, from a man who, lying back in a rocking chair in the bay window of the front room, was looking on at a bout with the foils that was taking place beyond the folding doors.

Snobbery is often a form of romanticism; it is the chastity of the perfectionist. But on Ouida's level romance is not romance until it is snobbish; and not, we may say, as we look back upon the Victorian novel, on her level alone. One of the better rumours about Ouida's novels was that they were the secret work of the not very nice George Eliot; and do not George Eliot's heroines unfailingly go up in the world as they become more refined by moral struggle? Are there not pages of Tennyson that look like Debrett put into verse? And are there not, indeed, modern novels in which souls are brought humbly to the Faith by the glamorous sight of an earl on his deathbed? The material luxury of Ouida's early novels, with their crammed marble halls and their general air of being expensive bazaars of history, is the expression of an expansive society becoming every year richer on colonies and luxurious colonial wars. And is it far-fetched to see in the hysterical dialogue of her books something of the repressed emotional violence of Victorian society? Why else this taste for melodrama and the smell of sulphur:

"Your lips were mine," she cried, laughing still in that mocking mirth, "their kisses must poison hers. Your hand slew him! its touch must pollute hers. Oh, lover, who lived on my smile! Did you not know the dead love would rise and curse the new?"

There can be no doubt when one has read Miss Bigland's account of Ouida's painful and ludicrous love affair with the Marchese della Stufa in Florence, that she herself felt in phrases of this operatic violence. And underlying it is her curious, rather seductive melancholy, the fervid not unintelligent Byronism which her French father must have brought over to Bury St. Edmunds from the Continent. [What happened to him? "Only the Emperor knows."] It was a sadness all the more romantic for being decked out with shrugs, floods of ungrammatical French and Bohemian cynicism; and it was also the inevitable undertone of the day-dreamer's life as, exhausted, she wakes up from her drug.

Miss Bigland's new life of Ouida is fuller than the memoirs already in existence. There are still many mysteries, but it is a just book and cannot help being entertaining. It is marred, however, by a prose that is stiffened with clichés which are a good deal duller than Ouida's. What takes one's breath in nearly every detail of Ouida's life is her boldness, her huge guzzling confidence in her powers, her ability to impose her life, as if she herself were a work of the imagination and not a human being. One is aware of a gusher. There is an appalling vitality which is undistracted by self-criticism or unstayed by the existence of any other person. She plays up shamelessly to the men. She had, for the purposes of her work, an extraordinary speed of assimilation, a greed for more facts to be turned into more dreams. Her so-called immorality—Miss Bigland has no difficulty in showing that Ouida was a prudish woman whose sensual desires had been sweepingly sublimated—enabled her to break conventions and, for example, to give dinners "for

THE OCTOPUS

Guardsmen only" which were very useful in supplying her with local colour as well as giving her the best kind of publicity: the scandalous. A word or two about the Foreign Legion, a skirmish, an Arab café, and men who wish "to forget", would soon be transfigured by her reckless imagination. She saw the thoroughbreds crushing the skulls of the enemy; she threw in an abduction. Her tragedy (some thought) was that she was a *grande amoureuse* who was too ugly to find a lover. One suspects that her only "lover" had been that elusive refugee, her father. Though she may be said to have been continually in love all her life with one man after another, there are no signs that her love was anything more than a terrifying and possessive hallucination and often known to herself alone; if disclosed, it drove every man to horrified flight. He had seen the octopus and it wore white satin.

Ouida was an actress who never settled to her role. Now she was a foreign aristocrat, now the great political figure, now the humanitarian defending the virtuous poor against the wicked rich, now the cynic as wilful as her one remarkable creation, the Cigarette of *Under Two Flags*; now the misunderstood artist, who will not sell her soul to a public of hucksters. They were the leading roles of an internal drama.

Her financial recklessness, which ultimately ruined her, was another egotistical refusal to face reality. One need not go into her endless quarrels with her friends, her appalling rudeness, her idiotic law suits which made her a byword. And yet, as many intelligent and sensitive people thought, the impossible woman had some talent. Her conversation was often worth hearing. The kind of tragic dignity of the battered dreamer attends her end. A total independence of human kind—they imposed reality—was her desire. Her unassuaged personal emotions were unloaded upon her swarms of dogs; for them she fought her friends, quarrelled with the Italian authorities and indeed, in the end, starved and neglected herself.

BOOKS IN GENERAL

There are some apologists for the novels of Ouida. She is said to have been an influence, though it is surely unkind to see it extending to Lawrence, as Miss Bigland does. We must agree, however, that she raises an early peacock wail of passion in the Victorian novel. *Pascarel* (which is admired) seems to me watery and unreadable stuff. The studies of the lives of the Italian poor are more interesting; they indicate a break with the earlier English preoccupation with Italy and, indeed, Ouida with a social conscience is a sentimental but bold writer. As Miss Bigland justly says, the reviewers who brought academic guns to bear on her fiction were themselves a little ridiculous in their solemnity. I have read only two or three of her novels and of these I prefer the unredeemed like *Under Two Flags* and *Strathmore* to the more respectable ones; the cigars, the passionate riding crops, the Rhenish of her country houses, the shooting women of her Algerian camps and the overproof Cognac of her Parisian Avernus, to the trite Italian works of her reformed period. I confess I have not read *In Maremma* which is praised for its landscape. Shockingly repetitive as she was, wild in her skiddings across drawing-rooms and deserts, she was not without shrewdness. She had an eye for raffish character. One responds to the tidal wave of her awful vitality, the terrific swamping of her prose. One would have given anything to go to her parties in Florence. Mr. E. M. Forster has told us that it is the novelist's duty to "bounce" us. Ouida does that with all her might; so hard, indeed, that her novels bounce high out of sight into that luscious upper air—somewhere between Mayfair and the moon—where the super ego practises its incredible scales and beats its frightful bosom. In its way, her stuff is more honest than the worst of Disraeli or Bulwer Lytton from which it derives; and more genial than the Barclay and Corelli for whom she prepared the way.

31
Firbank

FUN in English literature is as regular as muffins; the honest bell rings in the sad fog of the London Sunday and we stir ingenuously between one indigestion and the next, in our drowsy chairs. Poke the fire, bring in the tea, and soon, if we cannot be gay, we shall be cheery. But folly is rare. High-voiced, light-headed, dangerous and abashing, it flocks in its own mad air, just beyond the reach of our hands. Congreve, Peacock have it now and then, Hood has a little, Lear, Lewis Carroll, Wilde and Beerbohm play with this brilliant and tragic froth. It is for the few writers with missing hearts, whose clown eyes and enlarged ears live for themselves alone; the comfort and normality of fun are alien to it. Like wit, folly is the child of the collision, the smash-up; its laugh is heard just as the last pane of glass goes out of the window and the first groans are heard. Something fatally damaged has to be feverishly replaced; an intolerable vacuum must be filled; a gag must plug the awful abeyance. We feel this at the ballet, the most lyrical and cruel of the arts; maimed in the power of speech and ordinary sense, human beings are transposed into impulse and movement, to what can go on without heart, to the cold poetry of self-parody.

To the ballet the reader's eye strays when he is reading the wild satires and fairy tales of Ronald Firbank—*Valmouth, The Flower Beneath the Foot, Prancing Nigger, The Eccentricities of Cardinal Pirelli, The Artificial Princess*. They are antics in a void left by life, elegies on burst bubbles. They celebrate the unworldliness of the rich, the childishness of aristocracy, the ubiquity of priests, the vim of the sensual life, the venom and the languor of taste and pleasure. They commemorate the comi-tragedy of the superlatives and fashions in which the heart thrills and dies a hundred times a day. There are anecdotes in Sir Osbert Sitwell's very funny, very touching and very acute portrait of Ronald Firbank, in the introduction to these novels; in one, it is said that Firbank once sold a Welsh cemetery. In another there is a tremendous purchase of orchids. In another he eats a single pea for lunch. Between the laughter of the macabre and the tears of extravagance, his hair-raising talent wanders, an unattached faculty in a world of its own. In their inexplicable way aesthetes like Firbank—but there have been none, of course, *like* him, for none has his wailing, brain-splitting, peacock laugh—transpose the smash-up of their time more clearly than many a writer whose earnest ear is to the ground. And it is a simple fact that technically Firbank cleared dead wood out of the English novel, in one or two convulsive laughs; laid down the pattern for contemporary dialogue twenty or thirty years ago and discovered the fact of hysterical private humour—the jokes the mind makes and does not communicate. If narrative and speech have speeded up, if we can swing out of one episode into another, without an awful grinding of literary gears, if we can safely let characters speak for themselves and then fail to keep up a conversation, if we can create an emotion by describing something else, it is in part due to Firbank's frantic driving.

Let us grant that Firbank's baroque paradises, his jazz-band kingdoms, his over-heated and flower-stuffed conservatories would have been intolerable if he had been a larger writer, and had not the skids and evasions of startling economy by nature. *Valmouth* is very pretty, but the beautiful note of weariness which has been carefully sounded becomes wearisome itself. The Negress and masseuse is, in action, a boring symbol of a virile culture and has the strictly limited speciality of a homosexual joke. Firbank is an on-and-off writer. One inhales him and it is important not to take too much at a time. Even so, he is tricky; for as one turns the page for the next hilarious breath, the story is over and one is caught with an empty nose. It is not easy to say what the novels are about, though we shall remember surgical sentences and wounding paragraphs by heart. *Prancing Nigger*, the most felt of his books, and one which was originally intended as a kind of documentary study on the unhappy condition of Haiti, can be defined, perhaps, more closely than the rest. Mr. Mouth, the evangelical Negro, and his simple pushing wife with a passion for society, are clearly going to their ruin, unaware that urban, industrialised Haiti is going to wring their hearts out of them; and there is in this book a rumble of indignation which replaces the stylish horror he lets fall in his satires on fashion and chic. A not very happy moral note is in this tale, and there is a rather gummy sentence or two about the evils of rootlessness, which are heavy on the tongue of a dandy; one cannot go in for both the stylish and the moral. But *Prancing Nigger* is made by its warmth and its lyrical pathos; and although Firbank may have made his Negroes sing hymns like

> *Time like an ever-rolling stream*
> *Bears all its sons away*

for the lark of it, the sentiment was close to his own sensibility to the transient in life. Time is his subject. He is a poet of the surface of life and the writers who can feather a surface are rare. The comedy is in the inconsequence; the poetry in the evanescence; the tragedy in the chill of loneliness and desolation which will suddenly strike in a random word. The element common to all these novels is melancholy: a girl's heart is broken, another's soon will be, fidelity is cut short by a shark and time cheats all these farded ladies who have spent their afternoons pleasantly cheating themselves and others. One follows these untrustworthy Royal Families and randy Princesses from the throne to the barouche, from the assignation to the confessional, through terraces and nunneries, embassies and balconies, lavatories and coronations, simply out of malice, to see egos as lethargic as *foie gras* ("Whenever I go out," the King complained, "I get an impression of raised hats"). Dissociation —we may guess—was the private smash of Firbank's stricken personality. His comic genius rises from the fatality of rarely seeing life steadily and never seeing it whole. It is in bits.

His art is to make stained glass out of the unlikely bits. The famous jokes come from that: "How one's face unbends in a garden." At a death bed: "Her spirit soars: her thoughts are in the Champs-Elysées." Of a woman putting her long head out of a box at the opera: "She ought to hatch."

The search for the *mot juste*, disclosed to him the wild territories of the *mot injuste*. A man's kiss has an "unsavoury aroma of tobacco and charcuterie." "Poor Princess! Has anyone the right to look so dying." Or

> Nevertheless some late sirens were only arriving. Conspicuous among these was Catherine (the ideal-questing, God-groping, and insouciant), Countess of Constantine, the aristocratic heroine of the capital, looking half-charmed to be naked and live. Possessing but indifferent powers of conversation—at Tertulias and dinners she seldom shone—it was yet she who had coined that felicitous phrase: *Some men's eyes are sweet to rest in.*

But the word is not always unjust. The satirist of the mannequins turns into the poet, and this line on a broken heart might have come from the affecting Murasaki (perhaps it did: Firbank was a talented collector):

> Such love-blank, and aching void! Like some desolate and empty cave, filled with clouds, so her heart.

The "new" slang: "love-blank"; the dead cliché: "aching void" are not accidents in that sentence. Firbank (one imagines) had the gift of shutting his eyes and testing society with his ears, so that the dead patter which was its soul, and the breathlessness which was its life, came over minutely, in crotchets and quavers and absurd chords to him like the whine of a tired dance band two floors below. He must have been the first disinterested, clinical listener to the lunacy of conversation, one of the first to notice the date of its sentences, and to telescope the rest.

It is pleasant to have five Firbank novels in one volume, but by the end one has had a surfeit. *The Eccentricities of Cardinal Pirelli* has a cloying and faded corruption and naughtiness. In general, the brilliant indecencies of Firbank (so wonderfully timed and without the tedium of lascivious lingering) are best when he is not being naughty about the nuns and priests. This kind of joke is wearying, a sort of Catholic convert smut which Firbank (who was a convert) did not escape. The best religious jokes are those in which the religious orders are treated as if they were so many *couturières*. The sisters of the Flaming Hood are always welcome. For myself, *The Flower Beneath the Foot*, with its wild account of an African visit to a European court, is the most successful of the satires. It is a sharp salad; and it contains the superb death-bed scene of the mad Archduchess. At the bedside the Princess is already writing the telegrams announcing the coming death:

> "Poor Lizzie has ceased articulating," she did not think she could improve on that and indeed had written it several times in her most temperamental hand, when the Archduchess had started suddenly cackling about Vienna.
> "Sssh Lizzee—I never can write when people talk"— *Ultra* feminine, she disliked that another—even *in extremis* should absorb all the limelight.

That must be the highest point reached by Firbank's ecstatic love-hate of the elements of excess and rapacity in female character.

It is a surprise that so much of Firbank has survived from the Twenties, but as he is totally unreal and Fashion is eternal, he is dateless, though one can see that his freakishness may be despised and its décor become a bore. There is a force of feeling, scattered in his works, which recalls the ambiguous emotions we meet in John Betjeman's poems, and which gives his absurd world a vitality and determination of its own. His absolute originality, as well as his technical brilliance, seem to make his survival as a minor treasure inevitable. A virtuoso, he is the natural victim of mode; flimsier than Carroll, he does not create a memorable character except, possibly, Mr. Mouth. Firbank's survival will be, one would say, like his work, on and off. It is the strength of detail that counts in writers like this; the taste—if that can outlast a generation—for a certain tone of voice, breathless, snobbish, frightening and full of malice. Unlike Max Beerbohm he is the incumbent of a fundamental literary innocence. In life, a hermit almost speechless, helplessly gesticulating, a bizarre and feather-headed traveller unable to communicate, Firbank would be found sitting among the silliest illustrated papers, "getting ideas" from them, and seeing life—by some alarming but beneficent deprivation—flat and without perspective. Of our contemporary satirists he alone has the traditional quality of total artifice.

32
W. W. Jacobs

THE scarcity of comic writing in the last thirty years or so is often remarked. It has vanished (some will say) with our happiness. It has gone with sanity and civilisation. The comic writer, who is above all a man of sense, has no place in our world. Certainly the attack on Zoschenko in Russia has indicated how unsympathetic official cultures are to the comic writer; and as far back as 1910 we had seen our own Wells abandon the cheerful greenery and sly alleys of comedy for the straight asphalt paths of propaganda. The apostasy seems inevitable when we consider the two wars. The break-up of the small patterns of living, the levelling of local life and its absorption into larger patterns, have turned characters into citizens. Mr. Polly and Kipps can break out of their cages now; they need submit no more to the local pressure that cramped their style and made them comical. For it is the pressure of set circumstances that helps to form and encrust the comic character and the only pressure one can see nowadays in our fluid society is of the kind that comes from inside a character rather than from his environment. I am thinking of the weight of personal mania; the English comic characters of our generation—the characters of Waugh, Wyndham Lewis, Firbank—are noticeably mad. They are without attachments, but like human snails they carry a house of private madness on their backs. How different the new comic is from the fixed characters of our tradition may be seen by going back to the last of the old school, to the stories and novels of W. W. Jacobs.

Jacobs had the fortune to grasp a small, fixed world at its moment of ripeness and decline, a time always propitious to the artist. A Thames-side clerk, Jacobs knew the wharves where the small coasting ships and land-hugging barge fleets tied up on their rounds between London and the wizened, rosy little towns of the Essex estuaries. This was a fading traffic: the cement, the flour, the bricks, the road flints, were more and more being diverted to the railway; the small mills and shippers were being devoured by the larger firms; the little towns with their raucous taverns and fighting inhabitants had already quietened; and unemployable and unspeakable old men sat on the posts of the empty quays, refining upon their memories of a past, spicy in its double dealing, prone to horseplay and cheered by the marital misfortunes of others:

> "Love?" said the nightwatchman, as he watched in an abstracted fashion the efforts of a skipper to reach a brother skipper on a passing barge with a boathook. "Don't talk to me about love, because I have suffered enough through it. There ought to be teetotallers for love the same as wot there is for drink, and they ought to wear a piece of ribbon to show it, the same as teetotallers do. ... Sailormen give way to it most; they see so little o' wimmen that they naturally have a high opinion of 'em. Wait till they become nightwatchmen, and having to be at 'ome all day, see the other side of 'em. If people only started life as nightwatchmen there wouldn't be one arf the falling in love that there is now."

To these rosy and high-tempered seaports whose lattice windows flashed with the light of the silver estuary mud, no stranger ever came, unless it was a gentleman-painter who disgusted the patriots by painting only the ruins; the yachtsmen, holidaymakers and estate agents of a later day had not yet appeared, to dissolve the nightwatchmen in free drinks and to develop in the young an even more ferocious financial cunning than their fathers had. In other words, Jacobs found a world unstained by change, its inhabitants contentedly absorbed in the eternal human problem of how to get the better of one another, a fruit mellow and ready to

W. W. JACOBS

fall into the comic artist's hands. The coachmen of Dickens, the landowners of the Russians, the booby squires of Sheridan and Fielding had been in their time precisely at this point of ripeness. The talent of Jacobs is a small one, when he is compared with the masters, but like theirs, his types are not chosen until they are already dated; like theirs his humour is fantastic and artificial. No notions of realism or social purpose, as Mr. Henry Reed rightly says in an introduction to *Dialstone Lane*, cross his mind: he writes, so to say, from the ivory fo'c'sle. He recognises that in his nightwatchmen, his decisive widows, his sailormen, he is dealing with an advanced and sophisticated culture which has become firmly barnacled on the coarse surface of common life; and that the elegance, the speed, the riposte and the intricate plotting of something like Restoration comedy, can alone do justice to his highly-developed people. Any page of his many short stories will illustrate this; indeed, only in his macabre stories, like *The Monkey's Paw*, or, as Mr. Reed points out, in the ambitious *Master of Craft*, will one find anything like realism. I take this from *Dialstone Lane*:

"I've got her," said Mrs. Chalk triumphantly.

"Oh!" said Mr. Chalk.

"She didn't want to come at first," said Mrs. Chalk. "She'd half promised to go to Mrs. Morris. Mrs. Morris had heard of her through Harris the grocer and he only knew she was out of a place by accident. He . . ."

Her words fell on deaf ears. Mr. Chalk, gazing through the window, heard, without comprehending, a long account of the capture of a housemaid which, slightly altered as to name and place, would have passed muster as an exciting contest between a skilled angler and a particularly sulky salmon.

Mrs. Chalk, noticing his inattention at last, pulled up sharply.

"You're not listening!" she cried.

"Yes, I am; go on, my dear," said Mr. Chalk.

"What did I say she left her last place for, then?" demanded the lady. Mr. Chalk started. He had been conscious of his wife's voice and that was all. "You said you were not surprised at her leaving," he replied slowly, "the only wonder to you was that a decent girl should have stayed there so long."

Mrs. Chalk started and bit her lip. "Yes," she said slowly. "Go on. Anything else?"

"You said the house wanted cleaning from top to bottom," said the painstaking Mr. Chalk.

"Go on," said his wife in a smothered voice. "What else did I say?"

"Said you pitied the husband," continued Mr. Chalk thoughtfully.

I have quoted only the overture to the gruelling hazards of Mr. Chalk's relations with his wife; Jacobs has something like Fielding's gift, which came from the stage, for capping situation with situation, for never letting sleeping dogs lie. Two things will strike us about that passage: first, the lack of conventional facetiousness. Facetiousness gets shriller and lighter; humour sinks deeper and deeper into its ribald and wicked boots. The other point is that the extreme elaboration of Jacobs's wit, the relentlessness of his innuendo, are applied to the traditional subjects of the English music-hall: the mother-in-law, the knowing widow, the fulminating wife and the henpecked husband, the man who can't pass a pub. Fighting, black eyes, man-handling, horseplay, stealing of people's clothes, assuming disguises, changing names, spreading lying rumours, the persecution of one man by his mates for a lark, are the common coin. A man in love is fair game. Bad language is never given verbatim, but it is never let pass. (The old jokes about swearing are given a new polish. Mr. Henry Reed quotes this jewel: "The langwidge 'e see fit to use was a'most as much as I could answer." Only Mark Twain's Mississippi boatmen could equal that.) The laziness of the working-man is another stock joke which, in spite of political pressure, has not yet died; indeed only the false teeth joke is missing. The feminine side of the mixture is conventional music-hall too. There is no sex. There is no hint of illicit love. With this goes a low opinion of married love. Young girls are pretty, tidy, heartless and always deceptively grave. They flirt. They terrorise with their caprices like any Millamant. They outwit everyone. It is their brief moment. Presently they will become mothers of ten squalling kids; and their husbands will be beating them; or they will become strong-willed monsters, the scolds of the kitchen, the touchy and jealous Grundys of the parlour.

Material of this kind dates when it is used realistically and it would be simple to show that Jacobs draws the working-class and the lower middle-class as they were before even the Nineties; and treats them as comics for reasons that are, unconsciously, political. It is certain that Polly and Kipps, for example, are greater characters than the Nightwatchman or thick-headed knockabouts like Ginger Dick, simply because Wells relates them to something larger than themselves. That is to attribute no artistic falsity to Jacobs's characters; they are merely limited and within those limits they are perfect. Jacobs's general impression of the poor is sound; the psychology of sailors, shopkeepers and so on is exact. And one important aspect of working-class character, or at any rate of male character when very ordinary men are thrown together, is strongly brought out and justifies his intricate plots from Nature; I refer to the observation that the rapid, oblique leg-pulling talk, with its lies and bland assertions which no one believes, is part of the fine male art of cutting a figure and keeping your end up. The plots in Jacobs are the breath of the fantasticating life of men. They are superior to the plots of a writer like O. Henry. They spring naturally from the wits of the characters as trickery comes naturally to cardsharpers; they seem to pour off the tongue.

The flavour and the skill of Jacobs are of course all in the handling of the talk. At first sight the talk looks like something merely funny in itself; but Jacobs had the art of adding the obstacle of character to narrative:

> "Come here," said the mate sternly.
> The boy came towards him.
> "What were you saying about the skipper?" demanded the other.
> "I said it wasn't cargo he was after," said Henry.
> "Oh, a lot you know about it!" said the mate.
> Henry scratched his leg but said nothing.
> "A lot you know about it!" repeated the mate in rather a disappointed tone. Henry scratched the other leg.
> "Don't let me hear you talking about your superior officer's affairs again," said the mate sharply. "Mind that!"
> "No sir," said the boy humbly. "It ain't my business, of course."
> "What ain't your business?" said the mate carelessly.
> "His," said Henry.

There is no doubt that Jacobs is one of the supreme craftsmen of the short story. It is extraordinary that he should have brought such pellucid economy to material that was, on the face of it, stuff for schoolboys, or the Halls; but in doing so, he transformed it. The comic spirit was perhaps his thwarted poetry. He knew his limits. The only carelessness or rather the only indifference in his work appears in his novels. Of these *A Master of Craft* suggests a partial attempt at the Mean Street realism of the period; and a desire to go beyond his range; it contains a lady-killing skipper—instead of the usual skipper-killing lady—and he is, for Jacobs, an ugly character. Jacobs shows his wounds a little in this book; but, for some reason, he slips back into his shell. I think we may be glad he decided to remain in the ivory fo'c'sle. The artificial, the almost pastoral Jacobs of *Dialstone Lane* is more satisfying. The spring sunlight of pure malice and self-possessed sentiment gleams on this story about three gullible townsmen who dream of going to

W. W. JACOBS

sea; and the story has two immortally awful wives in it: the oppressed and the oppressor. But it is a major error in the plot that the dream voyage actually takes place. Jacobs would never have been so slapdash in a short story.

33

The Hill-Billies

THE vogue of Faulkner in France at the present time is easily understandable. Writing after 1918 about a society which had not recovered from the Civil War and which was to be marked by the demoralisation of the period of Prohibition and the gangsters, Faulkner anticipated some of the circumstances of the lawless life which rose in France under the Occupation and in the Resistance. Society was paddling in general crime, publicly selling the law at every street corner, and the college boy and his girl in *Sanctuary* were vicious replicas of the adolescents who had first appeared in Gide, and who, in the last war, moved beyond civilised judgment. The only comment possible came from the Negroes—the verse occurs in *Sartoris*:

> *Sinner riz frum de moaner's bench,*
> *Sinner jump to de penance bench;*
> *When de preacher ax 'im whut de reason why,*
> *Say, "Preacher got de women, jes' de same ez I."*
> *Oh, Lawd, oh Lawd.*
> *Dat's whut de matter with de church to-day*

And the women had got the moonshine whisky.

Faulkner's obscure and rankling genius began to work at the point when, failing to find a place from which to make a judgment, he set to writing about people from the whirlpool inside them, floating along with experience as it came out. His confusing, difficult, punch-drunk novels are in fact elaborately patterned and, as time has gone by, they have become (I think, ingeniously) didactic; but they fill the demand made by some Existentialists for a novel without a centre and which works outwards from the narrator in all

THE HILL-BILLIES

directions at once. They exploit "the absurd", the cruel meaninglessness of existence and they hope, by making every instant of any character's consciousness a life and death matter, to collect at the end a small alluvial deposit of humanism.

Faulkner is an affected but seminal writer for those who are in situations similar to his. In England, because the situation does not exist or because our overwhelmingly strong social instinct can still fairly successfully cover-up and deal with disintegration at the same time, Faulkner's vogue has passed. He was admired for his devices and as a romantic and exotic; he seemed to have opened rhetorical or poetic avenues into popular life and speech and to have caught a kind of Elizabethan dramatic spirit. In the end, Southern misery and his mannerisms palled. We had heard enough of hill-billies for a lifetime and he seemed to be an obsessed provincial stewing too long in his own juice.

Soldiers' Pay, is Faulkner's earliest work in prose. Reading it again, one sees immediately, it is much fresher than the later, ruminating and didactic Faulkner. It has the lyrical hardness, the mark of experiment, the crispness of design which were to be found in *Light in August* and *The Sound and the Fury*, and is written before Faulkner became so deedily engrossed in his own complexity. He belongs to the period of difficult writing, obliquity, the self-propagating image that grows like a brilliant fungus all over his prose. And when this Southern dandyishness is given up, he is apt to convey the agony of the South in an agonising prose which appears to be chewed like tobacco and occasionally squirted out, instead of being written. The total effect is, however, hypnotic. After being trained for a generation since Joyce on difficult, associative writing, we ought not to be set back, and I can only suppose the English reader lacks the necessary links with the Southern Negro and poor white cultures. But there *is* more than that to the difficulty of Faulkner: it is not that he is allusive or perpetually putting fresh obstacles in the way of his vision, but that he gives all his allusions and

BOOKS IN GENERAL

obstacles the same value. I will quote a long passage from a late book, *Intruder in the Dust*, which describes the capture of a fugitive who has jumped into a river. In isolation it is excellent—but, remember, a whole book has been written in this eye-blinding, mind-stunning incantation:

> ... he saw the old man jump feet first off the bank and with no splash, no disturbance of any sort, continue right on not through the bland surface but past it as if he had jumped not into anything but past the edge of a cliff or a window-sill and then stopping, half-disappeared as suddenly with no shock or jolt; just fixed and immobile as if his legs had been cut off at the loins by one swing of a scythe, leaving his trunk sitting upright on the bland, depthless milklike sand.
>
> "All right, boys," old Gowrie cried, brisk and carrying: "Here he is. I'm standing on him."
>
> And one twin got the rope bridle from the mule and the leather one and the saddle girth from the mare, and using the shovels like axes the Negroes hacked willow branches while the rest of them dragged up other brush and poles and whatever else they could reach or find or free and now both twins and the two Negroes, their empty shoes sitting on the bank, were down in the sand too and steadily there came down from the hills the ceaseless strong murmur of the pines but no other sound yet although he strained his ears listening in both directions along the road, not for the dignity of death because death has no dignity, but at least for the decorum of it: some little at least of that decorum which should be every man's helpless right until the carrion he leaves can be hidden from the ridicule and the shame, the body coming out now feet first, gallowsed up and out of the inscrutable suck to the heave of the crude tackle then free of the sand with a faint smacking plop like the sound of lips perhaps in sleep and in the bland surface nothing: a faint wimple wrinkled already fading then gone like the end of a faint secret fading smile, and then on the bank now while they stood about and over it and he was listening harder than ever now with something of the murderer's own frantic

urgency both ways along the road though there was still nothing....

Faulkner clutches at every sight and suggestion with the avidity of suspicion and even mania, and all manias create monotony. This is true even of the mania for domestic realism in Defoe. But in that passage Faulkner is simultaneously conveying the effect of the event on a boy's mind —for the story is seen through the eyes of a boy. Faulkner's ambition is visually poetic and he is attempting the instantaneous delivery of a total experience. In all his novels, he is trying to give each instant of experience in depth, to put not only physical life as it is seen directly on the page, but all the historical and imaginative allusions of a culture at the same time. And to the eye alone. If the reader is stunned by the slow deliberate blow, that is precisely the effect Faulkner is seeking, for we do, in fact, live stunned and stupefied by the totality of our experience and our present position in our own life story is simply the little clearing we have cut and the devious fading path we have left behind us, in the jungle. Order, or at any rate pattern, is that which comes *afterwards* to this romantic novelist who begins in the middle of the mind. He is a man outside the imposed, clarifying authority of some established system of values. We do not really know the beginning of Faulkner's stories until we have reached the end, till we have worked our way out of the jungle.

Faulkner's method of story-telling requires no justification: it has the conundrum quality of a pattern, and intricate patterns are as interesting as elaborate plots. He is a superb creator of episode—the opening train scene in *Soldiers' Pay*, the comic brothel scenes in *Sanctuary*, the account of the raid on the Federal breakfast table in the opening chapters of *Sartoris*—and when he creates passing character, the awful politician Snopes for example, the ink bites. But the true justification of the method is that it creates the South in depth as, I think, no other part of

America has been created by a novelist since the time of *Huckleberry Finn*. American novelists have composed reports, records, chronicles of other regions, but the impression is of life in some passing, cynical, littered encampment; Faulkner, on the other hand, seems to be engaged in a compulsive task, as if he had undertaken awkwardly the building of a culture out of its ruins, as a one-man mission. And perhaps, because of its social tragedy, its knowledge of ruin and decadence, the guilt felt because of its crimes against the Negro, the South is America's richest artistic soil.

Faulkner has the ubiquity of the reporter who knows the corruption of a town or a region inside out. He has also the moodiness of the man of letters. His capacity to catch mood is apparent in *Soldiers' Pay* when he placed a dying, speechless, returned soldier in the midst of his story and played the reviving post-war world of 1918 around him, as it moved into jazz and bootlegging. His lyrical power in that book is mannered, but his mannerisms represent a passionate attempt to burn the scene into our senses for ever. He is excellent at crowded scenes; in social life, in dances, court house gatherings, riots, train journeys, Saturday night streets, where a sinister action winds separately in and out among the wanderings of people. He is a novelist of journeys. He is no great hand, indeed he is painfully stiff, in describing the inner life of sensitive people; and he is too concerned with the visual scene for the crucial business of creating large characters. Even his distinctive people are minor figures, and this suggests sterility of imagination. But he is remarkable in grasping the essential fragment, the live coal which keeps a life going, so that we are aware of living among the unconscious motives of people and of knowing how they will act. His men are rarely friends, his women nearly always enemies except for idealised creatures like Mrs. Powers in *Soldiers' Pay*. He is especially good at shallow young women, whom he hates and exposes, but whose points and vanity attract him. His weakest characters are the rhetorical cynics whose Shakespearian tone adds a vague oratorical fog to the tale; but this strange mixture of artifice and realism is his native mixture. In all his people, except the figures of pure evil like Popeye, he is sifting until he comes down to the infinitesimal deposit of humanity. His brutality is frightening because it is sardonic and always has a theatrical twist—one thinks of the man, running with a petrol can at a lynching, who gets himself blown up by mistake.

Faulkner's sense of human pain and the damage done to people, their blank cruelties and the disguised suffering which they have accepted as part of the furniture of life, comes from a maturity rare in American novels; and he has shown here the power to grow out of the bitterness and cynicism and bragging sentimentalities which Hemingway never advanced from. In the didactic novels of his later period there is no uplift. He inculcates the rudiments of humanity, by cunning and the correcting of observation. If the boy in *Intruder in the Dust* is likely to side with the accused Negro, it is because he has learned to test his experience and to listen to his sensibility. He will always remember what the smell of the Negro really is after being wrapped in the old Negress's quilt in her cabin: it is the smell of poverty.

I do not know whether these merits could have made Faulkner a great novelist, but they make him a source. Rancorous and obsessive, he has carried his quarrel with his region very wide, like some preacher chased out of town. And, what subjects—the English novelist will sigh—he has to hand. What advantages a lawless society brings to the writer.

34
The Eye-Man

ART was the religion of the Twenties; originality was its attempt to invent rituals. It was a time of calculated disorientation, of the impertinent even perverse occupation of new sites, a time of disconnection and energy in the arts. What would a total reconsideration of everything, from the word upwards, reveal? The result—as we glance back over the works of the period—was a good deal of physical glitter and exhibition and some pomposity; but, now time has ebbed away, some of the carefully constructed ruins of the time remain impressive—in their strange way, like paralysed and abandoned machines, the works of Wyndham Lewis most curious of all. They do not rust or decay, no ivy grows about them, they cannot be used and have never been assimilated into the landscape; old block-busting guns and tanks skewed on the abandoned field, they stand still, fantastic without their thunder. Their interest lies in their massive detail, for their purpose has become academic; we wonder why such rage was worked up in *The Apes of God*, why such electric flashes were sent out by *The Childermass*; until it dawns on us that these peculiar objects were machines for destructive laughter, whose target was really less interesting or, at any rate, harder to pinpoint than the glorious noise they made.

I do not mean that Mr. Wyndham Lewis's thought-war was useless; apart from anything else it was provocative, and its attempt to recondition classicism was interesting, though it led to political folly. But every artist understands himself. Mr. Wyndham Lewis wrote of his character Tarr that the "curse of humour was on him, anchoring him at one end of the see-saw whose movement and contradiction was life", and that he was "a sort of quixotic dreamer of inverse illu-

THE EYE-MAN

sions" who, unlike Quixote, "instead of having conceived the world as more chivalrous and marvellous than it was, had conceived it as emptied of all dignity, sense and generosity." It is the laughter that has remained and the curse has been removed from it. After twenty or thirty years *Tarr* is still an exposure of sentimental German romanticism—and ought to have warned Mr. Lewis and ourselves of the silly nastiness of Fascism—but it has become a considerable comic novel, a masterpiece of the period. It hangs round the company of Nashe, the Butler of *Hudibras*, the professional butchery of Smollett. Though it intellectualises in the cosmopolitan manner of the period, and does its best to look like a foreign book—and I suppose it might be called a piece of Welsh exhibitionism—it is restrained by the fundamental good sense, the lack of final intellectual cruelty, in our tradition.

The new note in *Tarr* was the notion of human relationships as mere fodder for a new master-race, the artists, those distorted Martians, all eye and brain and the will to power. This brought back the physical grotesque to our comic writing. *Tarr* is theatrical in the Celtic way; it is the savage comedy of small things made large—hence the proper comparison with Swift. But when one critic in the Twenties called the portrait of Otto Kreisler "almost Dostoevskian" there was an unconscious exactness about the description, for we are reminded of the comic Dostoevsky in his short, Westernised, civilised and expatriate phase, when he wrote *The Eternal Husband*. In a sense, Mr. Wyndham Lewis has always been an expatriate and that condition enormously stimulates the brain at the expense of feeling; yet perhaps the tendency to continual over-stimulus in his writing was only a new version of the Welsh obsession with fantastic verbal image and the behaviour of giants. We can even imagine a thesis on his debt to Meredith. The common dangerous Germanic ingredients are obvious.

The early success of *Tarr* was partly due to its shrewd penetration of the German character at the right moment, after the first world war. The raw, beastly, foolish, mad and simple cry-baby Otto Kreisler, the eternal hysterical student, is almost a tragic character. Lack of feeling on the author's part, Mr. Wyndham Lewis's high suggestibility, hold Kreisler back from the tragic apotheosis: he is ludicrous, detestable, pathetic. He comes, interestingly enough, very close to the character of the husband in Dostoevsky's Western novel. The memory of the second world war revives the accidental interest of *Tarr*, but Otto Kreisler and Montparnasse are so far away by now, that they begin to have the picturesque, sentimental charm of an old-fashioned Bohemianism, rather than a disturbing psychological point. I would not undervalue the nostalgic quality *Tarr* has acquired in the course of a generation; but what strikes one still is that its originality in description, episode and attitude to character, is more than innovation. It is an enlargement of the novelist's means; a new territory has been subdued: the *terrasse*.

Mr. Wyndham Lewis's originality lies in his use of a non-literary eye, the eye of the painter. He does not judge by experience, association, feeling or cogitation, before he has first considered all the physical implications of what he has physically seen. An eye, promoted in this way to an uncommon, even perverse position of power, becomes inevitably sardonic, expert in false, freakish, intuitive juxtapositions. It is almost certain to be brutally funny; it will sometimes hit upon important general truths. And so we get his gift for fresh generalisation:

"Well then, well then, Alan Hobson—you scarecrow of an advanced fool farm——"

"What is that?"

"You voice-culture practitioner——"

"I? My voice? But that's absurd! If my speech . . ."

Hobson was up in arms about his voice although it was not his.

Tarr needed a grimacing, tumultuous mask for the face he had to cover. He had compared his clowning with

THE EYE-MAN

Hobson's pierrotesque vanity; but Hobson, he considered, was a crowd. You could not say he was an individual, he was in fact a set. He sat there, a cultivated audience, with the aplomb and absence of self-consciousness of numbers. . . .

A distinguished absence of personality was Hobson's most personal characteristic.

The descriptions can be more precise, the more they are picturesque. Kreisler is shaving:

> His face, wearing, it is true, like a uniform the frowning fixity of the Prussian warrior, had a neglected look. The true Bismarckian Prussian would seek every day, by little acts of boorishness to keep fresh this trenchant attitude; like the German student with his weekly routine of duels which regimen is to keep courage simmering in times of peace. . . .

A dancer:

> A rather congested, flushed and bespectacled young woman, her features set in a spasm of duty. It was a hungry sex in charge of a flustered automaton.

And, in action, the figures become as grotesque as clowns in a circus, enlarged by the coarse fancy of a child's eye:

> She crossed her legs. The cold grape-bloom mauve silk stockings ended in a dark slash each against her two snowy stallion thighs which they bisected, visible, one above the other, in naked expanses of tempting undercut, issuing from a dead-white foam of central lace worthy of the Can-Can exhibitionists of the tourist resorts of Paris-by-night.
>
> Tarr grinned with brisk appreciation of the big full-fledged baby's coquetry pointing the swinish moral under the rose and mock-modesty below stairs, and he blinked and blinked as if partly dazzled, his mohammedan eye did not refuse the conventional bait.

The descriptions of people, of places and scenes are often surpassed for gritty vividness in *The Childermass* and *The Apes of God*; but in those books they are so piled on in the monotony of a morbid glitter that they eventually kill their effect. *The Apes of God* can be read for one or two fine broad scenes of libel—the dinner party with the Finnish poet bawling his French verse—and for its general blood bath in the literary society of the Twenties. Its fatal limitation is triviality of subject: it was topical to attack the cult of art, but there is a whiff of provinciality about the odd man out. Exciting sentence by sentence, image by image, it is all too much page by page. The note of sanity is excellent, but sanity that protests too much becomes itself a kind of madness. In *The Childermass*, a brilliant idea stands still and stuttering. The fact is that the influence of Joyce, the determination to be *avant garde*, was ruinous to Wyndham Lewis as he went on. To blow up Bloomsbury was an excellent idea: to sit out the long persecution mania of a cold war was too much.

But *Tarr* is a perfectly shaped and classical work. The characters are tried by the traditional and always rewarding test of their love affairs; and these are subjected to the scornful criticising of the brain. Like some repressed and arrogant savage, the brain is brought forward to make fun of the sogginess of human sentiment. Tarr does not apologise for being a two-girl man; he does not moralise, he does not torture himself, he is not even cynical. Human beings are enjoyed as the dangerous animals who are determined—whatever fairy tales they may tell themselves or others—to have their cake and eat it. They are dangerous because they dream, and dreams create an inflated physical world. Human nature is disgraceful; the only thing to be said for it is that it may produce a little, a very little, Art.

Mr. Wyndham Lewis's genius lies in his strange capacity for reducing mind to matter: "her lips were long hard bubbles . . . grown forward with ape-like intensity, they refused no emotion noisy egress if it got so far." Women for Kreisler

THE EYE-MAN

are "vast dumping grounds for sorrow and affliction", huge pawnshops in which he deposits himself in exchange for "the gold of the human heart or any other gold that happened to be lying about." Anything in life which becomes unmanageable—*i.e.*, his failure as an artist—becomes converted into love. The pleasure of *Tarr* is that it wallows in the nature of the physical world: the butcher's shop provides many an analogy, not always coarse, indeed often comically delicate. The body is not respected; it is frequently insulted, especially if it is female, but the happiest love is where the laughter is loudest; on the other hand, it is recognised that we need a relief from the happiest love. We need—or at any rate Tarr in his sardonic way, and Kreisler in his suicidal way, need—something different from what we had before. The tail (when we become his character, the eye men) is invariably wagging the dog. There lies the virtue and the strain of his hard-hearted genius; he carries the burden of his laughter which has tipped the scale against life. But in Kreisler cadging, scrounging, loving, fighting, crawling back, breaking up parties and ending in murder and suicide, he has created a permanent character. (The fact is he created Hitler.) It is a strange experience to put down a masterpiece in which one has had the impression of not only knowing the characters but of giving them a pinch all over to see if they were ready for the comic pot of life on earth.

BIBLIOGRAPHY

The following books are dealt with in this collection of essays. Other works consulted are mentioned in the text.

THE LIFE OF BENVENUTO CELLINI. (Third edition of John Addington Symond's *Life*.) Introduction by John Pope-Hennessy. Phaidon Press.

THE BETROTHED. (I Promessi Sposi.) By Alessandro Manzoni. Translated with an introduction by Archibald Colquhoun. Dent.

THE HOUSE BY THE MEDLAR TREE. (I Malavoglia.) By Giovanni Verga. Translated by Eric Mosbacher. Weidenfeld & Nicolson.

AS A MAN GROWS OLDER. (Senilità.) By Italo Svevo. Translated by Beryl de Zoete. Introduction by Stanislaus Joyce. Essay by Edouard Roditi. Putnam.

CONFESSIONS OF ZENO. (La Coscienza di Zeno.) By Italo Svevo. Translated by Beryl de Zoete. Essay by Renato Poggioli. Putnam.

THE SPENDTHRIFTS. (La de Bringas.) By Benito Pérez Galdós. Translated by Gamel Woolsey. Introduction by Gerald Brenan. Weidenfeld & Nicolson.

THE ESSENTIAL T. E. LAWRENCE. Edited by David Garnett. Cape.

THE NOTEBOOKS OF HENRY JAMES. Edited by F. O. Matthiessen and Kenneth B. Murdock. Oxford.

SAMUEL BUTLER'S NOTEBOOKS. Selections edited by Geoffrey Keynes and Brian Hill. Cape.

PRAETERITA. By John Ruskin. Introduction by Sir Kenneth Clark. Hart-Davis.

THOMAS CARLYLE. By Julian Symons. Gollancz.

NECESSARY EVIL. The Life of Jane Welsh Carlyle. By Lawrence and Elisabeth Hanson. Constable.

BOOKS IN GENERAL

THE LETTERS OF JANE WELSH CARLYLE. A selection by Trudy Bliss. Gollancz.

BOSWELL'S LONDON JOURNAL. 1762–1763. Edited by Frederick A. Pottle. Heinemann.

JOURNAL TO STELLA. By Jonathan Swift. Edited by Harold Williams. Clarendon Press.

SWIFT. A Study. By Bernard Acworth. Eyre & Spottiswoode.

TRAVELS THROUGH FRANCE AND ITALY. By Tobias Smollett. Introduction by Osbert Sitwell. Lehmann.

TOBIAS SMOLLETT. By Lewis Mansfield Knapp. Princeton.

MAUPASSANT. By Francis Steegmuller. Collins.

A WOMAN'S LIFE. (Une Vie.) By Guy de Maupassant. Introduction by Alan Hodge. Translated by Antonia White. Hamilton.

SAPPHO. By Alphone Daudet. Translated by Eithne Wilkins. Introduction by Alan Hodge. Hamilton.

THE MASTERPIECE. (L'Œuvre.) By Emile Zola. Translated with an introduction by Thomas Walton. Paul Elek.

THE DRAM-SHOP. (L'Assommoir.) Translated by Gerard Hopkins. Introduction by Alan Hodge. Hamilton.

THE GREEN HUNTSMAN. (Lucien Leuwen. Vol. 1.) By Stendhal. Translated with a preface by H. L. R. Edwards. Lehmann.

THE TELEGRAPH. (Lucien Leuwen. Vol. 2.) By Stendhal. Translated by H. L. R. Edwards. Lehmann.

THE JOURNALS OF ANDRÉ GIDE. Translated with an introduction and notes by Justin O'Brien. Secker & Warburg.

BIBLIOGRAPHY

OEDIPE. Thesée. (Oedipus. Theseus.) By André Gide. Translated with an introduction by John Russell. Secker & Warburg.

LES FAUX-MONNAYEURS. (The Coiners.) By André Gide. Translated by Dorothy Bussy. Cassell.

ANDRÉ GIDE. By George D. Painter. Arthur Barker.

ANDRÉ GIDE. By Leon Pierre-Quint. Translated by Dorothy M. Richardson. Cape.

THE FRIEND OF THE FAMILY. Nyetochka Nyezvanov. By Fyodor Dostoevsky. Translated by Constance Garnett. Heinemann.

RESURRECTION. By Leo Tolstoy. Translated by Vera Traill. Hamilton.

THE YOGI AND THE COMMISSAR. By Arthur Koestler. Cape.

THE GLADIATORS. By Arthur Koestler. Macmillan.

THE SPANISH TESTAMENT. By Arthur Koestler. Cape.

DARKNESS AT NOON. By Arthur Koestler. Cape.

THIEVES IN THE NIGHT. By Arthur Koestler. Cape.

SCUM OF THE EARTH. By Arthur Koestler. Cape.

TRISTRAM SHANDY. By Laurence Sterne. Edited with an introduction by Douglas Grant. Hart-Davis.

THE MOONSTONE. By Wilkie Collins. Chatto & Windus. Folio-Society.—Cassell.

TALES FROM HOFFMANN. Edited by J. M. Cohen. The Bodley Head.

THE CENTENARY POE. Edited with an introduction by Montagu Slater. The Bodley Head.

OLIVER TWIST. By Charles Dickens. Introduction by Graham Greene. Hamilton.

MEREDITH. By Siegfried Sassoon. Constable.

BOOKS IN GENERAL

A LIFE'S MORNING. By George Gissing. Introduction by William Plomer. Home and Van Thal.

THE SECRET AGENT. By Joseph Conrad. Dent.

UNDER WESTERN EYES. By Joseph Conrad. Dent.

VICTORY. By Joseph Conrad. Dent.

OUIDA. By Eileen Bigland. Jarrolds.

FIVE NOVELS. By Ronald Firbank. Introduction by Osbert Sitwell. Duckworth.

DIALSTONE LANE. By W. W. Jacobs. Introduction by Henry Reed. Eyre & Spottiswoode.

SOLDIERS' PAY. By William Faulkner. Chatto & Windus.

INTRUDER IN THE DUST. By William Faulkner. Chatto & Windus.

TARR. By Wyndham Lewis. Methuen.

Printed in Great Britain by
Butler & Tanner Ltd.,
Frome and London

53 - 5645 [53-11421] A. Powell

Soc. Science
5.00

BOOKS IN GENERAL

By the Same Author

*

Novels
MR. BELUNCLE
DEAD MAN LEADING
NOTHING LIKE LEATHER

Short Stories
YOU MAKE YOUR OWN LIFE
IT MAY NEVER HAPPEN

Literary Criticism
IN MY GOOD BOOKS
THE LIVING NOVEL

Chatto & Windus

*

MARCHING SPAIN
CLARE DRUMMER
THE SPANISH VIRGIN

Benn

*

SHIRLEY SANZ
Gollancz